STRATEGY AND BUSINESS PROCESS MANAGEMENT

Techniques for Improving Execution, Adaptability, and Consistency

CARL F. LEHMANN

Foreword by Dale Kutnick

CRC Press
Taylor & Francis Group
Boca Raton   London   New York

CRC Press is an imprint of the
Taylor & Francis Group, an **Informa** business
AN AUERBACH BOOK

CRC Press
Taylor & Francis Group
6000 Broken Sound Parkway NW, Suite 300
Boca Raton, FL 33487-2742

© 2012 by Taylor & Francis Group, LLC
CRC Press is an imprint of Taylor & Francis Group, an Informa business

No claim to original U.S. Government works

Version Date: 20120127

International Standard Book Number: 978-1-4398-9023-3 (Hardback)

Library of Congress Cataloging-in-Publication Data

Lehmann, Carl F.
  Strategy and business process management : techniques for improving execution, adaptability, and consistency / Carl F. Lehmann.
     p. cm.
  Includes bibliographical references and index.
  ISBN 978-1-4398-9023-3 (hardback)
  1. Strategic planning. 2. Management. 3. Business logistics. I. Title.

HD30.28.L448 2012
658.4′01--dc23   2012000509

Visit the Taylor & Francis Web site at
http://www.taylorandfrancis.com

and the CRC Press Web site at
http://www.crcpress.com

I dedicate this book to my mother Jane for teaching me empathy and respect, to my father Carl for teaching me common sense and perseverance, and to my wife Cathy and daughters Kerri and Julia for their steadfast love and support without which this book would not have been possible.

Contents

SECTION I Best Practices Used
in Strategic Planning

SECTION II   Execution—Best Practice
Use of Strategic Resources

Foreword

For centuries, process improvements have driven the progress of civilization from increased food yields and plant hybridization, to energy development/deployment, to building shelters and transportation, healthcare, new business/consumer products and services, and so on. In our modern era, improved processes have transformed how businesses create and distribute goods, exploit information, and manage and deploy capital. For much of this time, the secrets of processes were shared by word of mouth among families, friends, and guilds. The printing press enabled wider distribution, expanded by copiers, and most recently via digital media.

For the past 40 years, the secrets of many of the most "core" business processes have been codified in application software, which enables them to be industrialized and enhanced through further automation. Such processes have typically been stabilized and reasonably well documented, so that numerous enterprises (for the price of a software program and a computing environment) can enjoy the benefits of their methodologies. This software includes customer relationship management (CRM), enterprise resource management (ERP, which also supports a variety of financial and accounting, inventory management, as well as human resource and other modules), supply chain management (SCM), and others. Whether bought as a package or developed internally, these software applications have become part of the critical core functions used to support enterprises.

But making these industrialized processes widely available has also meant that they are increasingly commoditized, and companies can no longer differentiate themselves by simply executing them. So business leaders must invent, adapt, or otherwise procure new processes that enable them to transform their enterprises so they can be more efficient and effective, and better address product/service development and distribution, as well as customer acquisition, engagement, and management, plus all of the processes that support them. They must also be more agile in partnering with other enterprises that will supply critical components to their final product or service offerings. This externalization trend is forcing more "combinatorial innovation," assembling business components (which include processes) in new and different ways (e.g., think Apple's original iPod components that were assembled from many producers, and integrated by Apple engineers). These are the processes that will drive competitive differentiation and innovation. Business process management (BPM) will become increasingly critical in enabling enterprises to accurately document, track, manage, permute, and evolve these processes, especially as they cross company boundaries.

Concomitantly, *digitalization* (IT-enabled transformation of business processes) across all industries is accelerating, and driving more rapid transformation, increased complexity, and more competition. It is forcing enterprises to be more agile and to adapt approaches from other industries and disciplines, and to mix and match processes and components more quickly. Indeed, the speed and creative destruction affecting entire industries that have been digitalized (and often marginalized) during the past 10 years have been breathtaking (e.g., media, advertising, music, financial services, retailing, and others). During the next 10 years it will further penetrate service industries, farming, healthcare/medicine, pharmaceuticals, and all others. And, thus, the importance of recognizing, understanding, and responding to change agents (customer expectations, competitive rivals, outsourcing, new technologies for products and services, etc.) is escalating rapidly. BPM discipline can help manage these and other myriad changes occurring in the business environment that are fomenting even more turbulence, including the following:

- Regulatory requirements, especially around financial reporting and the processes that support it
- Process/procedure patents, although a gray area, lawsuits are escalating, especially in genetics, user interfaces, service approaches, and the like
- More documentation, for reporting, including e-discovery, litigation support
- More M&A and divestiture activities
- More rapid updates to existing processes

In the Prologue to this book, Carl cites an example of a CEO whose business hasn't done anything wrong, per se, but has been outmaneuvered by competition that has become more efficient, changed the rules, or changed the game. During the past 15 years, we have repeatedly witnessed this phenomenon: although Sony "owned" the portable music player business, and was continuously improving its devices around the Walkman brand, Apple snatched it with a totally different approach—a simpler device and a digital music store that enabled immediate gratification. Amazon changed the way people acquire and consume books; Starbucks changed the way people consume and experience coffee; Walmart transformed the way suppliers manage the inventory in its stores; Google evolved the way people search for information, and the way advertisers target potential buyers; FedEx offered new ways to move and track goods and packages; and Facebook has changed the way people socialize and share their personal information.

These companies departed from existing approaches or significantly modified them, and often left the previous competition struggling in their wake, unless they too evolved. As a result of these (and numerous other) transformative examples, coupled with the demographic and political changes and the inexorable digitalization noted above that are becoming pervasive throughout society, enterprises are moving more aggressively to manage their processes better as a portfolio of assets. As part of a portfolio, they can be combined in new ways, more easily evolved or further optimized, traded with other enterprises, monetized, and so on. Again, business process management (BPM) underlies this effort, which is why IT vendors including IBM, SAP, Oracle, Software AG, and others are acquiring BPM providers, or incorporating BPM tools into their software offerings.

Many works have been published on business process topics (including management, re-engineering, innovation, et al.), and pundits have for years spoken about the impending rise of BPM. Yet BPM has only slowly been adopted by enterprises, often due to its use of arcane vernacular. That is changing, concomitant with market demands. This book helps the reader by simplifying an otherwise complex BPM learning curve. It accomplishes this by dissecting a logical sequence of proven techniques and best practices across different disciplines and industries, and applying them to rapidly evolving business strategies and performance metrics. There are numerous examples and checklists that drive home salient messages. The book further synthesizes its findings into a decision framework and tools that can help practitioners to plan better and consistently execute business strategy. It should thus be valuable not only in proselytizing the BPM concept, but as a reference guide for those embarking on the BPM journey.

Dale Kutnick
Senior Vice President of Gartner Executive Programs

Preface

ABOUT THIS BOOK

Running a business often requires leaders and management teams to do things better and faster with fewer resources and at lower cost. Some organizations always seem to adapt and flourish at this and others struggle. Why?

Those that succeed do so because they always look at how they do things and continuously ask, "How can we run our business better?"

They answer the question by first learning the best practices of other highly successful organizations. Next, they look inward, studying how they currently do things. They then take what they've learned and experiment with changes, testing new ways to work smarter, better, and faster at lower cost using the resources at hand.

But doing this requires research, knowledge, planning, and tools. Proficiency and skills must be garnered from several disciplines that include:

- Crafting and adapting a competitive and defensible business strategy
- Translating business strategy into action
- Empowering and motivating the workforce
- Designing effective and efficient business processes
- Implementing information technology for cost-effective execution
- Aligning resources such as people, processes, and technology to consistently execute business strategy

Execution requires mastery of several skills including:

- Insightful leadership capable of orchestrating a multidisciplinary management team
- Tireless project, program, and portfolio management discipline to improve results continuously on time and under budget
- Skilled business analysts capable of getting to the heart of business problems and crafting innovative solutions and process designs

- Insightful technical expertise capable of uniquely applying information technology to ensure proper execution and results
- Meticulous methods to measure and manage execution and performance and make proper adjustments when necessary to remain on course

Such proficiencies and skills are beginning to coalesce into a new framework. Business process management (BPM) is emerging as a managerial discipline that is focused on execution, adaptability, and consistency. Its definition and interpretation will vary depending upon with whom you speak. However, simply stated, BPM is the art and science of how you do things and how you can do them better. How well you buy, make, move, and sell products and services determines success and profitability. Business processes determine how things get done. BPM brings order and discipline, treating business skills and processes as assets that create and deliver customer and shareholder value and enable competitive advantage.

Indeed, BPM is emerging as a managerial discipline, but it is not new. Anyone who is part of or runs a business does it every day. If you make and sell products or deliver services, you are performing and managing business processes. But, how well you execute, how quickly you can adapt to change, and how consistent your results are may be disappointing. What is new is how industry leaders practice BPM.

Successful practitioners of BPM optimize process performance while remaining sufficiently adaptive when challenges, change, or opportunities arise. They use BPM to structure and align their business processes workforce and information technology enabling them to consistently execute and achieve the strategic objectives, performance measures, and the results they seek.

But when business and IT professionals begin to research how to initiate BPM practices within their organization, they can quickly get overwhelmed. Many struggle with where to begin. Most simply don't know how many processes they use to run their businesses. Others prematurely conclude that they don't have the time or resources to pursue or sustain a BPM effort. Those who press on sometimes presume BPM to be part and parcel of various total quality management (TQM) methodologies including Lean, ISO 9000, Six Sigma, and others, all highly effective in business process improvement. However, they often focus too narrowly, addressing only a few of the skills necessary to master execution. The broader set of BPM knowledge is available; it's just scattered across many sources.

For example, if you were to begin reading about BPM you would discover that various authors approach the topic from different perspectives.

- Books approaching BPM from a strategic perspective are highly effective in explaining how to craft a competitive business strategy and somewhat effective in explaining how to properly structure organizational behavior to support it. However, they rarely discuss techniques to improve process design and analysis and only superficially address how IT architecture and capabilities are affected.
- Books approaching BPM from an organizational perspective are highly effective in that regard, and somewhat effective in explaining how best to formulate strategy. However, they too inadequately address process design and analysis and often fail to discuss how IT architecture and capabilities must support workforce behavior.
- Books approaching BPM from a process perspective are highly effective in explaining process structure and analysis in fine-grain detail; and somewhat effective in explaining how IT architecture must be crafted for execution. Typically, they only give passing mention to how strategy drives process design and redesign (especially redesign), and rarely address the implications of workforce behavior to support its proper execution.
- Finally, books approaching BPM from an IT perspective can go into extraordinary architectural and technical detail, and are usually effective in addressing process design and structure. A few will address workforce behavior but not sufficiently enough to drive execution properly. And, most overlook business strategy entirely because they are too engrossed with the technology.

Even after such study the reader must then assemble what was learned from each perspective into a useful managerial framework for analysis and implementation.

Few management teams and BPM practitioners have the time or resources to do this. Realizing these challenges, this book seeks to reduce the effort, complexity, and cost of learning all that is necessary to continuously improve business process performance and results. The approach to do so is twofold.

First, simplify and flatten the learning curve by researching the proven techniques and best practices from across all relevant bodies of knowledge needed to improve business performance.

Then, synthesize the findings into a comprehensive framework to help management teams and BPM practitioners become proficient in the best practices used by industry leaders to craft business strategy and align resources for consistent execution.

This book reveals what highly successful practitioners of BPM have learned in order to research and develop their own comprehensive framework. Most notably, they have crafted distinctive practices for structuring and deploying their resources to deliver unique customer value while keeping competitors at bay, but only after great effort. After years of successful results these efforts have become the best practices of industry leaders. Learning them will help readers approach BPM with the same mindset and rigor that successful practitioners use to keep focused and sustain the drive toward achievement. To create this awareness the book presents and analyzes the knowledge, foresight, and techniques industry leaders use to

- Formulate business strategy by
  - Analyzing competition
  - Focusing operations
  - Managing performance
  - Adapting to change
- Organize people and empower and motivate them to successfully execute strategy
  - Through workforce collaboration
  - Using collaborative objectives
- Reveal performance measures and controls to help achieve strategic objectives
  - Through process modeling and analysis
  - By managing events, exceptions, commitments, and resolution efforts
- Structure information technology to ensure strategic achievement
  - Through information acquisition, assessment, and dissemination
  - Using a process-centric systems approach
  - By practicing information technology portfolio management
- Align strategy, people, processes, and technology
  - By learning how to ask and answer the right questions using a derivative analysis technique

The book discusses and analyzes each of these best practices in succession, revealing important relationships that are often overlooked in many process and quality improvement programs, and rarely explained in other such books on the topic. Understanding these relationships and how to influence them for competitive advantage will provide the foresight necessary for you to begin aligning resources with strategy. Then by asking and answering the right questions, the qualities needed for your organization's resources to support its specific strategy will be derived. Derivative analysis is introduced in this book as a technique to identify and modify the unique elements of organizational behavior, business process design, and information technology needed for execution and strategic achievement.

WHO SHOULD READ THIS

You should read this book if you are a business or technology professional who is responsible for running a business, business unit, or organization (private, public, nonprofit, government agency) and held accountable for business performance and results, or if you are new to a position or organization and need to get up to speed quickly and take control of its operations.

Business professionals include owners, executives, VPs, directors, business unit managers, line managers, group leaders, and consultants. Technology professionals include IT executives, leaders, managers, project managers, analysts, designers, programmers, and consultants.

HOW THIS BOOK IS STRUCTURED

The book is structured in four sections. In the Prologue: The Management Team Is Summoned, a high-level perspective of the challenges businesses typically face is presented to set the stage for lessons that are taught in the book. It highlights business pain points that demand solutions, challenges with which many leaders and managers can empathize.

Section I: Best Practices Used in Strategic Planning provides summary reviews of the top best-selling authors on business strategy. They include

- *Competitive Strategy: Techniques for Analyzing Industries and Competitors* by Michael E. Porter
- *The Discipline of Market Leaders: Choose Your Customers, Narrow Your Focus, Dominate Your Market* by Michael Treacy and Fred Wiersema
- *The Balanced Scorecard: Translating Strategy into Action* by Robert S. Kaplan and David P. Norton
- *Adaptive Enterprise: Creating and Leading Sense-and-Respond Organizations* by Stephan H. Haeckel

The key messages from each are distilled to reveal the essential proven and reliable best practices used by leading Fortune 2000 companies to analyze and formulate highly competitive business strategy. Collectively, they create an unparalleled strategic planning framework, providing organizations with the insight and techniques necessary to accomplish the following:

- Command competitive knowledge
- Define strategy and focus investment to high-priority areas
- Measure performance from multiple perspectives
- Quickly respond to change or customer need

Section II: Execution—Best Practice Use of Strategic Resources builds upon the findings in Section I, discussing how industry leaders prepare their strategic resources—people, business processes, and information technology—for execution by

- Empowering and motivating the workforce using workforce collaboration and collaborative objectives
- Modeling and analyzing business processes to include human accountability and enabling techniques to measure, control, and manage the necessary performance outcomes
- Adapting information technology needed for workforce collaboration, performance measurement, and outcomes management as called for by business strategy and business process designs

Section III: How to Align Strategy and Resources to Improve Execution, Adaptability, and Consistency pulls together all that was discussed in Sections I and II, describing and demonstrating how to use derivative analysis as a technique to align business strategy, people, processes, and technology. Derivative analysis reveals the proper links among strategy, measurement systems, business processes, workforce behavior, and the information systems necessary to achieve strategic objectives. Discontinuity becomes obvious, blazing a clear path to properly structure resources to support desired outcomes.

The Epilogue: The Management Team Reconvenes wraps up what the management team learned and what is required of them to overcome and avoid the pain points presented in the book's Prologue from reoccurring.

Section IV: Summary Conclusion highlights the critical lessons learned and includes Summary Pages you can use to recall the guidance offered in each section of the book.

Overall, the best practices and lessons learned from this book represent proven and reliable techniques used by leading companies and organizations. Learning them will help you think as do successful BPM practitioners, shaping the mindset needed to guide your decisions and stay focused as you structure your business strategy and manage your processes to improve execution, adaptability, and consistency.

Introduction

We face a new era in process thinking, one that will be distinguished by operationally resilient processes, not just standardized and efficient processes. Operational excellence should no longer simply be measured by inward-looking, efficiency-oriented metrics. Instead, key tenets of BPM emphasize process visibility, accountability, and adaptability in order to continuously optimize results and compete in a globally diverse business environment.

To meet these challenges enterprises need to improve their ability to anticipate and respond to shifting market and customer demands. Businesses want their operations to become more resilient, especially given the frequency of disruptive events in a global economy. Yet, despite "business agility" being the mantra of BPM for the last 10 years, few organizations have actually achieved this goal. Although leaders in BPM are delivering more frequent changes to their processes and have fostered a culture of continuous process improvement, their processes are still not designed for change. Implementing change continues to be difficult, often requiring in-depth technical skills. More typically, IT delivery cycles rather than the pace of business still control process adaptability.

There are many reasons for this lack of achievement. One factor is that few organizations have identified those processes that truly need to become more agile. Few business leaders have asked themselves questions such as

- What are the signals in our work that would indicate operational change might be needed? And how can we monitor the environment for those signals?
- What events (internally and externally triggered) would drive us to change how work is done?
- What aspects of work specifically need to change and how often?
- Who should decide that change is appropriate and what specific change is needed?

- How can we communicate the desired change and ensure that it is implemented?
- How can we know if the change achieves the desired outcome? And if it doesn't, can we undo the change easily?

Furthermore, most organizations continue to focus on small improvements to structured processes when the bigger opportunity for process differentiation is in knowledge-intensive work. Work performed by knowledge workers is largely unstructured; that is, knowledge work is nonroutine and not performed in a predictable and sequential fashion.

Knowledge work involves research, analysis, high levels of expertise and judgment, collaboration, risk assessment, and creativity, as well as investigative, negotiating, and communication skills and more. The characteristics of knowledge work have largely precluded it from the benefits of software automation for decades. This can't continue. Why? Because leading economies around the world depend on knowledge worker success. The world's leading economies are all services based, not agricultural and industrial based anymore. Services-based industries depend on harnessing knowledge. Therefore, organizations should start to apply process management techniques to better support and coordinate these more unstructured work domains.

Yet the exposure is high because knowledge work is inherently more complex and will challenge traditional process thinking. Applying BPM to knowledge-centric domains does not mean forcing structure and routine onto these areas. Instead, advanced BPM-enabling technologies such as explicit models, real-time data feeds, virtualization, social media, and statistical analysis can be incorporated to coordinate (not automate) resource interactions, prioritize work, and make the process and individual work efforts transparent. By incorporating modern BPM techniques (such as empowering those closest to the customer experience of the work) and technologies, businesses can become more responsive to shifting market demands. BPM is increasingly about fostering effective work habits, not just standardizing processes to increase efficiencies.

Implementing BPM is difficult. The main problems for any significant change are the human barriers: inertia and vested interests. And knowledge workers are among the most resistant to process improvement. They see it as diminishing their expertise and unique insight. However, even this attitude reflects long-held misperceptions of process improvement. Process improvement does not always mean making all work routine.

A lot of BPM effort is about managing the aggregate performance outcome of the end-to-end process, not just increasing controls over the individual activities and tasks. To achieve operational resilience, the culture and attitudes of the organization must also change. The shift in management practices for BPM will not come easily but can have far-reaching consequences.

BPM is a discipline of disciplines and a process itself, not an event or final destination. The adoption of BPM will strengthen competitive advantage in well-positioned companies. BPM-centric companies will enjoy increased alignment between operations and strategy, greater operational resilience, less-intrusive compliance, and, of course, increased efficiencies.

Janelle Hill
Vice President and distinguished analyst at Gartner

About the Author

Carl F. Lehmann is a business process management (BPM) specialist. He helps organizations improve execution, performance, and outcomes. His career spans nearly three decades during which he developed and brought high-tech products and services to market, and helped organizations use high-tech products and services to run their businesses.

Prior to founding BPMethods, Carl ran strategy, product management, marketing, and professional services for a business-to-business (B2B) integration services firm. There he developed technology and solutions that managed supply chain processes for over 350 large companies, and provided electronic commerce services to over 3,000 small and mid-sized suppliers.

As a research vice president and business analyst for top IT research firms Gartner and META Group, he advised Fortune 500 firms, and a range of small and mid-sized companies in how to use emerging technologies to improve business process performance and results.

He is published globally with four e-books and over 200 reports and articles on the best practices used in B2B integration, supply chain management, and customer relationship management across a broad range of industries including aerospace, banking, chemicals, consumer electronics, distribution, energy, manufacturing, mining, pharmaceuticals, and retail.

Carl began his career as a project manager for AT&T and a product manager for Digital Equipment Corporation (now Hewlett-Packard). He is a graduate of Boston University, School of Management with degrees in finance and international management.

Carl F. Lehmann
Principal Analyst
BPMethods, LLC
Boston, Massachusetts, USA
www.bpmethods.com
carl.lehmann@bpmethods.com

Section I

Best Practices Used in Strategic Planning

Business strategy is essentially the art and science of formulating plans to align resources, overcome challenges, and achieve stated objectives. Achievement is fundamentally measured using a simple formula

$$R - E = P$$

where R = revenue, E = expense, and P = profit. For most organizations, revenue must be greater than expense ($R > E$). In the case of nonprofit and government organizations, revenue and expense should be equal ($R = E$). When strategy dictates innovation, growth, or expansion, operating at a loss ($R < E$) is acceptable, but only during planned investment phases of a business life-cycle.

Of course, given the challenges stated in the introduction, business strategy and the measurement of success are not this simple. Organizations often report anemic profit, disappointing returns on assets and capital, or unplanned expenses causing them to operate at a loss.

Why do so many organizations struggle with poor performance? To answer this question, an organization must examine the answers to other fundamental strategic planning questions:

- Were my objectives realistic and achievable?
- Did I misunderstand or underestimate the challenges?
- Did I have enough of the right resources?
- Was my strategy correct given my resources, challenges, and objectives?

Answering these questions requires analysis of visceral business concepts, such as competition, execution, measurement, control, and adaptation to change. All have been studied relentlessly by business schools, think tanks, and leading enterprises since the Industrial Revolution. Dozens of approaches and theories have been published in hundreds of textbooks, and in thousands of essays and articles. But a few seminal works on business strategy that emerged in the 1980s and 1990s have matured and are practiced with great success by industry leaders in every field. Those that stand out are

- *Competitive Strategy: Techniques for Analyzing Industries and Competitors* and *Competitive Advantage: Creating and Sustaining Superior Performance* by Michael E. Porter
- *The Discipline of Market Leaders: Choose your Customers, Narrow Your Focus, Dominate Your Market* by Michael Treacy and Fred Wiersema
- *The Balanced Scorecard: Translating Strategy into Action* and *Strategy Maps: Converting Intangible Assets into Tangible Outcomes* by Robert S. Kaplan and David P. Norton
- *Adaptive Enterprise: Creating and Leading Sense-and-Respond Organizations* by Stephan H. Haeckel

Although conceived in the 1980s and 1990s, these works are increasingly relevant today. They represent timeless common-sense approaches to business strategy and management. They offer proven and reliable best practices forged by years of pragmatic deployment by leading Fortune 500 and Global 2000 companies. Experience, iteration, and evolution have made them practical techniques for use by all organizations, large and small. In architectural and engineering terms, they represent the "pillars and arches" upon which modern business strategy and execution are founded.

All include common-sense themes on how best to formulate strategy, measure performance, and align resources, which are explored in this book. Of greater interest and importance, however, and the reason why I chose these particular works, are the best practice concepts unique to each author.

- Porter teaches organizations how best to compete.
- Treacy and Wiersema teach organizations how best to focus operations.
- Kaplan and Norton teach organizations how best to manage performance.
- Haeckel teaches organizations how best to adapt to change.

The best practice lessons from each of these authors successively build upon the others, providing a comprehensive approach to analyze and formulate a highly competitive business strategy. Collectively, these lessons create an unparalleled strategic planning framework, providing organizations with the insight and techniques necessary to command competitive knowledge, define strategy, and focus investment on high-priority areas, measure performance from multiple perspectives, and quickly respond to change or customer need.

Understanding business strategy is important, but how does this help you improve business processes and run your business better? Our intention is to put strategy and execution in context. What you seek from a business perspective (your strategy) derives the resources you require and how to structure them for achievement (execution). Successful practitioners do not view them as mutually exclusive. They have a deep understanding of these contextual relationships and use this awareness to consistently execute and improve adaptable processes that support the organization's chosen business strategy.

Industry leaders begin a discussion on business strategy by first defining and analyzing the purpose of their organization and the environments in which they compete.

Prologue: The Management Team Is Summoned

THE CEO SPEAKS

The CEO asked me to remain seated and silent behind him for the moment as the management team entered the boardroom. They had all met me briefly before, one on one. There was no need for a cordial reacquaintance. He greeted each attendee with a dismissive wave urging them to their seats, setting a tone consistent with the severity of what he was about to say. When all were settled he took his seat and began.

Ladies and gentlemen,

Two years ago our company was at the top of its game. We had been increasing revenues at a compound average growth rate of 42% for five consecutive years. We doubled our profit margins. Earnings before interest, taxes, depreciation, and amortization were consistently above 35%. Customer satisfaction was at an all-time high pushing us into the number 1 or number 2 positions in all our markets. As a result the management team and workforce all shared in a handsome bonus and profit-sharing plan. Our shareholders could not have been happier.

Tomorrow I'll host a conference call with our major shareholders, investors, and Wall Street analysts telling them that for the second quarter in a row we will report a loss.

The seasoned executive then closed his eyes and exhaled as he bent his head, burying his chin in his chest. After a brief pause he looked up, rose from his chair, and leaned slightly forward to put both hands on the heavy mahogany conference table. He addressed the team in a resigned manner,

"What makes matters worse," he said, *"is that I cannot show positive guidance. I expect this news to cause our market cap to fall at least 20%. You know how our shareholders will react.*

So! Before I meet with them I want some answers.

Who can tell me what has changed? And please don't tell me it's the economy. He leaned farther forward, bridging the distance from the team exclaiming, *In the last two years three new competitors entered our markets and stole our customers. That doesn't happen because of the economy.*

Everyone at the conference table was frozen in an uncomfortable silence. None dared even move else they be called upon.

The CEO let the management team stew for a bit. Then, before anyone was able to respond he stood straight up, softened his demeanor, and changed his tone. He went into problem-solving mode. He wasn't interested in placing blame or concerned about lack of motivation. He needed to put in motion a plan for the organization to realize again, and maintain, its leadership role. In a professional and assuring voice he continued.

Ladies and gentlemen, I know why we faltered and why our customers abandoned us. I know what changed.

For the last two years we have been doing everything just as we had for the prior five years. Our business strategy, products, and services; the way we managed partners and suppliers; the way we treated customers; the way we measured performance; the way we went to market; and the way we solved what we thought were our real problems: all performed exactly the way we did them when we climbed to the top two years ago.

Nothing changed!

But everything changed. And that, ladies and gentlemen, is our problem; we didn't adapt to the change. Our customers, competitors, and the markets changed around us and we did nothing about it. Worse yet, we didn't even see it coming.

He took his seat, leaned forward panning all in the room from right to left and continued.

We are all responsible for what happened and will be held accountable for fixing it. The board has called a meeting with me this afternoon and is likely to be calling for some swift changes. Now let me assure you. You are the finest group of people I have had the pleasure of working with in my career.

He sat back in his chair.

Together we have done wonderful things. Each of you possesses a unique set of skills and talents that are indispensable to this firm and its customers. Our sales and services teams are top notch professionals. Our customers love working with them. Our product management teams can solve problems and innovate circles around competitors. Our marketing teams make us look great and get us a seat at any table we seek. Heck, our engineering and manufacturing teams could turn a bag of dirt into a time machine if we found a customer willing to pay for it.

The team chuckled, and thankfully, the tension in the air eased.

No, we don't need to change our people. We need to get back to basics. We need to take a fresh look at how we do things and figure out how we can do them better, consistently, while responding to change as it happens, so we keep these negative circumstances from reoccurring.

He rose from his chair.

That is why I introduced you to Mr. Lehmann and why I asked him to join us.

He turned back, looked me in the eye, and knowing no others could see, smiled and winked, affirming that I now had the undivided attention of a captive audience. Then he gestured for me to take his place at the head of the conference table.

* * *

What follows is a series of discussions I have with management teams on business strategy, process management, and techniques used by industry and thought leaders to improve execution, adaptability, and consistency. I set the stage for these discussions by calling out common business issues with which most management teams can empathize.

RUNNING A BUSINESS VERSUS
RUNNING A BUSINESS WELL

There are many ways to measure performance. The balance sheet, income statement, various operating ratios, key performance indicators, and market and customer research are all part of monthly, quarterly, and annual assessments. Most of the metrics used to run a business help determine whether it is operating to plan or veering off course. As a professional, when you sense that you're off course, you take action to get back on plan. But sometimes that is a bigger challenge than anticipated; and other times, even if you're on plan, it may not be the right one when unanticipated changes force you back to the planning table.

The difference between running a business, and running it well, lies in how well the organization knows its customers, how well it assesses competitors, how well it delivers differentiated value, and how quickly it brings an appropriate response to change. The vehicle used to make these assessments—strategic planning—also helps organize people, resources, and investments to achieve revenue, profitability, expense, and market share targets within a defined timeline, usually one year.

But change happens quickly and often without warning. The plans set in motion at the beginning of a planning horizon can easily go awry. Contingency planning is the typical reaction, but for many organizations it's an afterthought and often inadequate in its scope and resolve. What do you do when a new product introduction is unexpectedly delayed, when suppliers fail to deliver as promised, or when your biggest customer threatens to go to the competition?

Failing to achieve planned objectives or appropriately responding to dynamics as they occur can damage financial performance, customer satisfaction, brand value, or worse. Indeed, nearly every executive across all business disciplines believes that his or her most difficult challenges are staying on plan and properly reacting to uncertainty and change. Companies large and small need pragmatic methods to realign resources or make strategic adjustments as early as possible, certainly faster than the competition. Although this seems intuitive, it has been difficult for organizations to accomplish.

Many organizations are their own worst enemies. Conflicting objectives, poor communications, and overly competitive cultures often prevent them from rapidly disseminating information to the right people at the right time. Moreover, most business processes are too departmentalized and fail to consider the economic impact of process performance across the organization. For example, to enable a cost leadership strategy, a procurement department may redesign a supply chain process to lower inventory carrying costs by requiring some of its suppliers to drop-ship products directly to end-user customers. The new process may affect how supplier invoices are received and reconciled, in turn causing the finance department to delay supplier payments. Delayed payments may violate a contractual agreement negotiated by the strategic sourcing team that ties discount rates to on-time payments. The lost discounts increase overall costs negating the intended savings sought by the procurement department.

This is usually accompanied by disjointed information systems that fail to share relevant data on a timely basis from across an organization. Different people in an organization might access different applications that only execute parts of a business process, using different tools to report and analyze results. These are among the typical challenges organizations face when attempting to execute a business strategy.

USING BEST PRACTICES TO ALIGN STRATEGY AND RESOURCES

Highly successful practitioners of business process management have learned to overcome these challenges. They have crafted distinctive practices for structuring and deploying their resources that deliver unique customer value while keeping competitors at bay. After years of successful results, they have become the best practices of industry leaders. Learning these best practices will help you approach business process management and continuous improvement with the same mindset and rigor that successful practitioners use to keep focused and sustain the drive toward achievement. Creating this awareness requires the following:

- *Understanding* how best to formulate a competitive strategy that is realistic, defensible, and achievable

- *Foresight* as to how people, business processes, and information technology can be structured to make them more effective, adaptable, and valuable
- *Techniques* to translate strategy into execution, creating a plan that aligns your resources to best achieve strategic objectives

OVERVIEW OF THE BEST PRACTICES
OF INDUSTRY LEADERS

Industry leaders achieve such awareness when they pay close attention to how well they run their business. They do so by continuously analyzing and practicing how best to do the following:

- Formulate business strategy by:
  - Analyzing competition.
  - Focusing operations.
  - Managing performance.
  - Adapting to change.
- Organize people and empower and motivate them to successfully execute strategy.
  - Through workforce collaboration.
  - Using personal, group, and collaborative objectives.
- Reveal performance measures and controls to help achieve strategic objectives.
  - Through process modeling and analysis.
  - By managing events, exceptions, commitments, and resolution efforts.
- Structure information technology to ensure strategic achievement.
  - Through information acquisition, assessment, and dissemination.
  - Using a "process-centric" systems approach.
  - By practicing information technology portfolio management.
- Align strategy, people, processes, and technology.
  - By learning how to ask and answer the right questions using derivative analysis techniques.

Each of these best practices will be discussed in succession, revealing important relationships that are often overlooked in many process and quality improvement programs. Understanding these relationships and how to influence them for competitive advantage will provide the foresight necessary to begin aligning resources with strategy. Then by asking and answering the right questions, the qualities needed for your resources to support your chosen strategy will be derived. Derivative analysis will help you identify and modify specific elements of organizational behavior, business process design, and information technology needed for execution.

USING BEST PRACTICES TO INNOVATE AND COMPETE

All organizations seek an edge that improves business results and keeps them ahead of competitors. Best practices represent valuable lessons learned by organizations that describe how to structure resources effectively and efficiently to achieve objectives, overcome challenges, and surpass competitors. Some question their value, arguing that if best practices are openly available to all, how can they be used to create competitive advantage? Certainly your competitors can pursue similar best practices.

Indeed, competitors are likely to duplicate best practices. However, all but the most aggressive rivals are also likely to fall short in their efforts. Why? For three reasons. First, many organizations believe they do not have the resources or talent to learn and implement best practices. They often consider such efforts to be too complex and time consuming, and thus avoid the attempt. Second, those that pursue best practices more often try merely to meet, rather than exceed them. They fail to see best practices as the bar that sets the standard from which innovation begins. These organizations make little effort to learn from others who have succeeded or failed. They do not create competitive advantage, but simply "reinvent the wheel." In other words, as the philosopher and novelist George Santayana noted, "Those who cannot learn from history are doomed to repeat it." And third, only aggressive industry rivals understand the multiplier effect created when related best practices are successively combined.

As is shown in our discussions in Section I, competitive advantage is determined by how well organizations align multiple resources into a system or operating model designed to execute strategy. This requires preparation, forethought, and discipline to learn the best practices used within an industry and by competitors and to understand their interrelationships. Such knowledge can then be used to surpass each best practice and combine their advantages to innovate new and better ways to improve and compete, ultimately forging a leadership role. The best practices discussed in this book can individually contribute to business performance improvement; but collectively they can create formidable competitive advantage when management is committed to do so. Your first step in this education process is to learn how industry leaders craft highly competitive business strategy.

1

How to Compete: Competitive Strategy

A benchmark work against which most industry-leading organizations form and judge their business strategy is found in *Competitive Strategy: Techniques for Analyzing Industries and Competitors* published in 1980 by The Free Press. In it, Professor Michael Porter of the Harvard Business School defines competitive strategy as a broad formula for how a business needs to compete, what its goals should be, and what policies will be needed to carry out these goals.

Competitive Strategy is comprised of three parts. The first part introduces how to structure competitive analysis by first understanding the five fundamental forces of competition that act on an industry. Also discussed are three generic competitive strategies and techniques to analyze competitors in an industry. The second part builds upon these analytical techniques, considering how to develop strategy within specific types of environments, such as concentrated or fragmented industries, mature industries, and industries exposed to global competition. In the final part, Porter uses this analytical structure to examine how best to address critical strategic decisions that organizations may face, such as those of vertical integration, capacity expansion, entering new markets, or divesting existing ones.

For our purposes, I will focus on some of the topics Porter introduces in the first part of his book. There he presents the techniques to assess competitive position and shows how to use this information to formulate strategy. He begins by introducing the classic approach to developing competitive strategy.

COMPETITIVE STRATEGY: THE CLASSIC APPROACH

The classic approach to competitive strategy consists of a combination of *ends* (or mission, goals, objectives) for which the organization is striving, and the *means* (or policies, tactics, procedures) by which they are achieved. These are illustrated in Figure 1.1, the "wheel of competitive strategy."

The hub of the wheel represents the organization's goals, defining broadly how it wants to compete and its specific economic and noneconomic objectives. The spokes of the wheel represent the operating policies or functional areas that must be structured to achieve these objectives. Management is responsible for specifying the key operating policies that collectively guide the overall behavior of the organization. Using the classic approach, formulating competitive strategy then involves considering four key factors that determine the limits of what the company can successfully accomplish, as illustrated in Figure 1.2.

FIGURE 1.1

Wheel of competitive strategy. (Reprinted with the permission of Free Press, a Division of Simon & Schuster, from *Competitive Strategy: Techniques for Analyzing Industries and Competitors*, p. xxv, by Michael E. Porter ©1980, 1998 by The Free Press. All rights reserved.)

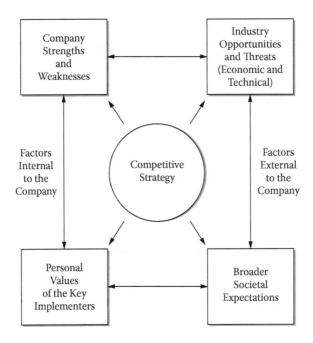

FIGURE 1.2
Context in which competitive strategy is formulated: the classic approach. (Reprinted with the permission of Free Press, a division of Simon & Schuster, from *Competitive Strategy: Techniques for Analyzing Industries and Competitors*, p. xxvi, by Michael E. Porter ©1980, 1998 by The Free Press. All rights reserved.)

Here Porter explains that the company's strengths and weaknesses are defined by its profile of assets and skills, such as financial resources, technology profile, and brand recognition (among others) relative to competitors. Personal values are the motivations and needs of key executives and personnel responsible for implementing the strategy. Strengths and weaknesses, when combined with values, define the internal limits to competitive strategy. External limits are defined by opportunities and threats presented by the industry in which the company chooses to compete and by broader societal and governmental influences. In other words, the internal and external limits define what the organization is willing and unwilling to do to compete.

The appropriateness of a competitive strategy can be determined by testing the proposed goals and policies of the strategy against these internal and external limits. To optimize a competitive strategy using the classic approach, Porter recommends an evaluation process whereby organizations consider three lines of questioning:

1. What is the business doing now, what is its current strategy, and what are the implied assumptions and data upon which the current strategy is based?
2. What is happening in the environment as determined by analysis of the industry, competitors, societal influences, and strengths and weaknesses of the organization?
3. What should the business be doing, meaning, how do the original assumptions hold up to a current analysis of the environment, and what are the feasible strategic alternatives given the findings of this analysis?

Porter believes that answering the questions posed by the classic approach requires "penetrating analysis" and is the purpose of *Competitive Strategy*. He begins his structural analysis of industries stating that the essence of formulating a competitive strategy is to relate an organization to its environment.

FIVE FORCES MODEL OF INDUSTRY COMPETITION

Porter argues that the state of competition in an industry is influenced by five basic competitive forces, as illustrated in Figure 1.3. The collective strength of these forces determines the profit potential in the industry as measured in terms of long-run return on capital invested. The key to developing strategy is for an organization to analyze the underlying sources of these competitive forces so that it can determine its relative strengths and weaknesses. The goal of competitive strategy then is to use this knowledge to find a position in the industry where the organization can best defend itself against these forces or can influence them in its favor.

The five forces noted in *Competitive Strategy* include (Porter, 1980, pp. 3–33):

1. The potential of new entrants, or the threat of new companies entering the market exploiting new or emerging technology that creates a quality or price advantage, eliminating what was once was assumed to be a barrier to entry.
2. The rivalry of industry competitors. Addressing how companies position themselves against one another in matters of pricing,

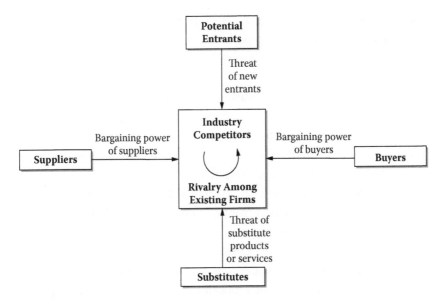

FIGURE 1.3
Porter's five forces driving industry competition. (Reprinted with the permission of Free Press, a division of Simon & Schuster, from *Competitive Strategy: Techniques for Analyzing Industries and Competitors*, p. 4, by Michael E. Porter ©1980, 1998 by The Free Press. All rights reserved.)

advertising, customer services, new product introductions, warranties, and so on.

3. The availability of substitutes representing alternative or new products or services that come to the market that create the risk of customer flight.
4. The bargaining power of buyers, or customers, that trends toward acquiring products and services as inexpensively as possible.
5. The bargaining power of suppliers, that trends toward selling their products or services at prices as high as possible.

New Entrants

The threat of entry by new competitors to capture and gain market share depends on the barriers to entry that exist in the industry and the reaction from the existing competitors that the newcomer can expect. If the barriers are high or the newcomer can expect strong retaliation from entrenched competitors, then the threat of entry is low.

Barriers to entry include (Porter, 1980, pp. 7–17):

- *Economies of scale.* Enabling per unit cost declines with increasing volume per a defined period. It forces the new entrant to enter the market on a large scale, risking a strong reaction from existing competitors.
- *Product differentiation.* Creating brand differentiation and customer loyalty that stem from past advertising, customer service, product features, or being first to market.
- *Capital requirements.* The need to invest larger financial resources in order to compete, creating a barrier to entry.
- *Switching costs.* Barriers are created if buyers face one-time costs associated with switching from one supplier to another.
- *Access to distribution channels.* Barriers are created if a new entrant needs to secure access to existing distribution channels.
- *Cost disadvantages independent of scale.* Established firms may have cost advantages not replicable by new entrants. Examples of this include: proprietary product technology, favorable access to raw materials, favorable locations, government subsidies, advanced knowledge, or experience.
- *Government policy.* Creates a barrier when it can limit or foreclose entry to industries.

Intensity of Rivalry

Rivalry among existing competitors is the result of a number of structural factors including (Porter, 1980, p. 17–23):

- Numerous or equally balanced competitors.
- Slow industry growth necessitating the need to maintain or expand market share.
- High fixed or storage costs pressuring firms to fill available capacity.
- Lack of differentiation or switching costs where products or services are viewed as commodities.
- Capacity increased in large increments requiring economies of scale. Can be disruptive to the industry's supply/demand balance and creates the risk of overcapacity and price cutting.
- Diverse competitors, such as foreign entrants or sole proprietor businesses that are indifferent to subnormal rates of return on invested capital, cause rivalry. Foreign firms may "dump" product on a market

and smaller owner-operator firms managing a "life-style" company simply don't need the return rate required of larger established firms.
- High strategic stakes where market presence and market share rivalry create the potential to sacrifice profitability.

Pressure from Substitute Products

The greater the number and availability of substitute products or services that can perform the same "function" as those currently in use threaten incumbents in an industry. This limits the potential for returns of an industry by placing a ceiling on the prices firms in the industry can possibly charge.

Bargaining Power of Buyers (Customers)

A buyer (or buyer group) is powerful if (Porter, 1980, pp. 24–27):

- It concentrates or purchases large volumes relative to supplier sales.
- The products purchased represent a significant fraction of the buyer's costs or purchases.
- The products it purchases are standard or undifferentiated.
- It faces few switching costs.
- It earns low profits creating the incentive to lower purchasing costs.
- It poses a threat of backward integration whereby the buyer places pressure on suppliers by suggesting that they will create the product or perform the service in-house.
- The products being bought are unimportant [have little to do with] to the quality of the buyer's products or services.
- The buyer has full information, giving it greater negotiating leverage.

Bargaining Power of Suppliers

A supplier is powerful if the following circumstances are true (Porter, 1980, pp. 27–28):

- It is dominated by only a few companies and is more concentrated than the industry in which it sells.
- It does not contend with substitute products.
- The industry of the buyer is not an important customer of the supplier.

- The supplier's product is critical to the buyer's business.
- The supplier's group's products are differentiated or have high switching costs.
- The supplier (or supplier group) poses a threat of forward integration, meaning it can potentially enter the buyer's business.

Here, Porter also points out that the labor employed by a firm (its workforce) can be viewed as a competitive factor similar to the effect of powerful suppliers. When labor wields considerable negotiating leverage for wages and benefits, the costs and profit of the firm's product or services are affected.

Porter uses the term "structural analysis" as the means by which an organization diagnoses the underlying causes of each of the forces affecting competition (structure). Once diagnosed, the organization is in position to identify its strengths and weaknesses relative to the industry. For example, where does the firm stand against substitutes, sources of entry, barriers, and coping with rivalry?

DETERMINING A DEFENSIBLE POSITION

An effective competitive strategy then takes offensive or defensive actions in order to determine a defendable position against the five competitive forces. This involves a number of possible approaches (Porter, 1980, pp. 29–33):

- Positioning the firm to exploit its strengths and diminish the importance or relativity of its weaknesses in the industry
- Influencing the balance of the forces by taking an offensive stand to alter their causes
- Exploiting change in the industry that influences the forces such as economies of scale or increasing capital requirements, improvements in differentiation, and so on
- Diversifying into new markets that exploit the organization's strengths relative to competitors

As part of the five forces model, Porter identifies many factors that influence the competitive environment in industries. His use of this structural analysis creates the framework that organizations can use to identify rapidly the features that determine the nature of competition and where the bulk of an organization's analytical and strategic attention should be focused.

Porter then offers the benefits and risks associated with three generic competitive strategies to cope with these forces. Here organizations can (Porter, 1980, pp. 34–46):

1. Strive for overall cost leadership, whereby they exploit economies of scale, aggressively pursue cost controls, avoid marginal customer accounts (customers with little to no profit potential), and minimize costs in areas such as research and development, services, sales force, advertising, and so on.

2. Differentiate products or services such that industrywide they are perceived as being unique. When differentiation creates brand loyalty, customers become less sensitive to price, helping minimize competitive threats or substitutions.

3. Focus, whereby a company channels effort and resources toward servicing a particular target very well, such as a customer segment, product line, service, geography, and the like. The goal here is to narrow the strategic target, serving it more effectively and efficiently than the competition.

Porter cautions firms against being "stuck in the middle." This is a term he uses to describe a firm that fails to "... develop its strategy in at least one of the three directions. This firm lacks the market share, capital investment, and resolve to play the low-cost game, the industry-wide differentiation necessary to obviate the need for low-cost position, or the focus to create differentiation or a low-cost position in a more limited sphere." Firms that are stuck in the middle risk low profitability. They must make a fundamental strategic choice and be prepared to make the necessary investments through a sustained effort to extricate itself from such a position. To help make such a choice, determine a defensible position, and thus craft a competitive strategy, Porter next recommends using the five forces model to analyze competitors.

COMPETITOR ANALYSIS

Porter notes that "Competitive strategy involves positioning a business to maximize the value of the capabilities that distinguish it from competitors." Crafting strategy should be based on as comprehensive an understanding of competitors in an industry as is possible given a firm's resources. But the need for knowledge about competitors and the rigor with which it is pursued can vary by organizations and be influenced by industry dynamics, staff availability, and competencies, and the interests (or lack thereof) of its management. Porter acknowledges with trepidation that many firms fail to commit proper resources or structure practices necessary to maintain accurate competitive intelligence. Nevertheless, the need exists and is necessary for proper strategic planning.

To simplify the effort, he offers a framework comprised of four diagnostic components to structure competitive analysis (Porter, 1980, pp. 47–74):

1. Future goals—What drives the competitor? Considered at multiple levels of management and dimensions, including organizational structure, systems used, etc.
2. Current strategy—What is the competitor doing and what can it do?
3. Capabilities—What are the competitor's strengths and weaknesses?
4. Assumptions—What assumption does the competitor hold about itself and what assumptions about the competitor are held within the industry?

The outcome of such competitor analysis produces a "competitor response profile." It includes the research findings, but more important, the conclusions seek to reveal how a competitor would respond to dynamics in its industry. Or perhaps they reveal how each competitor might react to your organization's strategic drive. Therefore, conclusions drawn from each profile must include competitor reactions and suggest possible countermeasures by addressing questions such as:

- Is the competitor satisfied with its current position?
- What likely moves or strategy shifts will the competitor make?
- Where is the competitor vulnerable?
- What will provoke the greatest and most effective retaliation by the competitor?

Sufficient knowledge of an organization's chief rivals is required to craft a competitive and defensible strategy within a market or industry. Porter believes that organizations need to create some form of competitive intelligence system, arguing that competitor analysis is too important to be handled haphazardly. He notes that there is a variety of ways organizations can perform this function, ranging from dedicated competitive intelligence groups as part of a planning department to solitary coordinators who informally compile competitive data.

BUILDING ON PORTER'S BEST PRACTICES

The driving force behind any process management and improvement initiative is the business strategy of an organization. Porter's *Competitive Strategy* (1980) defines the essential best practices an organization should adopt to formulate or assess its business strategy. Using a common-sense approach, Porter reveals how an organization can analyze its industry, its competitors, and itself to create and secure competitive advantage. It is recommended reading for organizations that are struggling competitively or need deeper knowledge of the factors that influence strategy to determine how best to align resources for execution.

Although Porter's approach is extensive and can be used to postulate many strategic options, he narrows the possibilities of how to begin preparing for execution by defining three generic strategies:

- Cost leadership
- Differentiation
- Focus (on a buyer group, product line, or geography)

He describes possible implementation approaches for each, but with caution. Porter notes, "Sometimes the firm can successfully pursue more than one approach as its primary target, though this is rarely possible. . . ."

Indeed, proper execution (and fundamental business logic) requires organizations to address all three strategies to some degree. A cost leadership strategy can fail if cost controls diminish product or service quality to the point where customers begin to flee. So too, price premiums for differentiated products are elastic. Buyers are willing to pay only so much before seeking substitutions. A strategy of focusing on a group, product line, or geography may require low cost or differentiation to establish a foothold. Market and competitive dynamics challenge organizations to sustain such advantages. In each case, to establish or maintain a leadership position something else must also be perceived to be of value to customers.

Porter offers the following reason as to why pursuing more than one approach is challenging. "Implementing them successfully requires different resources and skills. The generic strategies also imply different organizational arrangement, control procedures, and inventive systems. As a result, sustained commitment to one of the strategies as the primary target is usually necessary to achieve success."

Many industry leaders would argue that they do, indeed, address more than one strategic target simultaneously. But how? Porter's argument rings true. Different strategies do require different organizational structures, systems, processes, and controls to be effective and competitive. So, the questions then become not what is the primary target strategy requiring sustained commitment, but to what degree are other strategies also required to achieve and maintain a leadership position, and how does such an approach affect an organization's ability to execute?

Porter introduces a means to analyze this in his book *Competitive Advantage: Creating and Sustaining Superior Performance*, first published in 1985. Here, he expands on his earlier work to address execution in more detail by describing the importance and structure of value chains.

A *value chain* is a collection of activities—performed across multiple business functions, such as manufacturing, marketing, procurement, and services—that design, produce, market, deliver, and support an organization's product or service, as illustrated in Figure 1.4.

Value is defined as the qualities, functions, or attributes for which a customer is willing to pay. Here Porter offers another unique and comprehensive analytical framework, this time to determine how individual firms create competitive advantage. They do so by eliminating activities that do not add value, streamline those that enable value, and optimize those that are directly responsible for adding value. Ultimately, competitive strategy drives the structure of a firm's value chain that, in turn, determines the activities and linkages between activities (both internal and external) that structure processes required for execution. Competitive advantage is created when organizations integrate the processes in their value chains in the best way possible.

But value is determined differently by different customers. Different value requires different activities that then determine the structure of

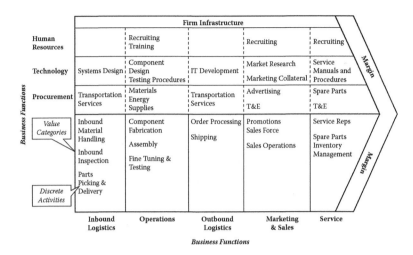

FIGURE 1.4
Porter's value chain. (Adapted and reprinted with the permission of Free Press, a division of Simon & Schuster, from *Competitive Advantage: Creating and Sustaining Superior Performance,* pp. 46, 47, by Michael E. Porter ©1985, 1998 by The Free Press. All rights reserved.)

a value chain and the degree to which primary and other strategies are needed. It is impractical to be all things to all people, however, competition dictates the need to be at least some things to most people.

To determine how industry leaders address more than one strategic effort requires us to build on Porter's concepts and techniques. We need to understand how a value chain can do the following:

- Focus operations to deliver one type of customer value while still addressing minimum thresholds for other types of customer value.
- Manage performance using measurement systems to track the creation and delivery of primary customer value while also tracking threshold performance for all other forms of customer value.
- Adapt to a modified or new strategy, or value-chain structure, when explicit customer needs change or when unanticipated needs emerge.

All these challenges are addressed in turn here in Section I.

To determine how best to focus operations on one type of customer value while addressing minimum thresholds for others, we next introduce the best practices found in *The Discipline of Market Leaders* by Michael Treacy and Fred Wiersema (1995).

2

How to Focus Operations: The Discipline of Market Leaders

Michael Treacy, a lecturer on business strategy and founder of Treacy & Company (a Boston-based management consulting firm), and Fred Wiersema, founder of Ibex Partners (specializing in strategic and management team alignment), through their work with CSC Index, coauthored *The Discipline of Market Leaders: Choose Your Customers, Narrow Your Focus, Dominate Your Market* published in 1995 by Perseus Books. In it, they state that setting strategy and direction requires organizations to create a focused response to new rules of competition, which in brief are

1. Put unmatched value of one chosen kind in the marketplace.
2. Meet threshold standards in other dimensions of value.
3. Make the proposition better every year.
4. Build a superior operating model to deliver on the promise.

Treacy and Wiersema argue consistently with Michael Porter (Chapter 1) that no company can be all things to all people. "It must instead find the unique value that it alone can deliver to a chosen market."

Companies that become industry leaders share a common trait: they understand and exploit their specific source of value to customers. The strategy of these companies emphasizes excellence and requires focus in one of three *value disciplines* (Treacy and Wiersema, 1995, pp. 33–43):

- Operational excellence
- Product leadership
- Customer intimacy

The authors postulate that there are three important truths that characterize the world of competition (Treacy and Wiersema, 1995, p. 19):

1. Different customers buy different kinds of values. Companies cannot hope to be the best in all dimensions of value; they must choose their customers and narrow their focus.
2. As value standards rise, so do customer expectations. So to stay ahead, a company must always be moving ahead.
3. Producing an unmatched level of a particular value requires a superior operating model, or a "machine" designed specifically to deliver that value.

The *dimensions of value* include (Treacy and Wiersema, 1995, p. 20):

- Price
- Product quality
- Product features
- Service convenience
- Service reliability
- Expert advice and support services

After studying 80 market-leading companies, Treacy and Wiersema (1995, pp. 20–21) noted that their customers tended to fall into three categories:

- Customers that viewed product performance or uniqueness as the pivotal component of value
- Customers who valued personalized service and advice
- Customers who prefer lowest total cost

They also observed that market leaders tend to excel in delivering extraordinary levels of one particular value and the customers recognize them for it. These companies do so by creating a set of expectations in the customer's mind that competitors must strive to meet or exceed.

NEW RULES OF COMPETITION

The coauthors discovered that market leaders abide by four new rules that govern their actions (Treacy and Wiersema, 1995, pp. 21–28):

1. *Rule 1:* Provide the best offering in the marketplace by excelling in a specific dimension of value.

   Customers generally distinguish among different types of value and are not likely to demand all value dimensions. For example, customers who value product quality may be less sensitive to price. Those seeking superior service and advice may be less impressed with product features and so on.

2. *Rule 2:* Maintain threshold standards on other dimensions of value.

   Although Porter, Treacy, and Wiersema are correct to some degree that "you cannot be all things to all people," Treacy and Wiersema believe you must be at least some things to many people. A company cannot allow performance in other dimensions to fall, such that it impairs the attraction of superior value. For example, if a company focuses on the value dimensions associated with customer intimacy (such as service reliability and expert advice), it cannot let the remaining dimensions of value (such as price, product quality, and product features) falter. Market leaders are always under attack from two perspectives:
   - Competitors that focus on the same dimension of value
   - Competitors that increase customer expectations on the secondary dimensions of value

   To sustain market leadership, it is not enough simply to be today's superior value. A company must deliver superior value consistently and continuously over time. To remain in front, a market leader must ensure that its operating model (or "machine" used to deliver value) improves faster than its competitors'.

3. *Rule 3:* Dominate the market by improving value year after year.

   When a company focuses its efforts and resources on delivering and improving one type of customer value, it can almost always deliver better performance as compared to a competitor that divides its efforts and resources among more than one. This requires the company's operating model to be superior to its competitors. Creating a highly competitive operating model becomes more evident once a company has decided upon which customer value to focus. For example, superior product performance might require an operating model based on strong research and development funding or rigorous quality testing. Low cost might require the operating model to emphasize superior supply chain planning and management. Customer intimacy might drive the need for the operating model to include aggressive customer research investments and superior relationship management techniques.

4. *Rule 4:* Build a well-tuned operating model dedicated to delivering unmatched value.

The operating model is responsible for raising and resetting customer expectations. Improving it makes competitive offerings less appealing. The operating model becomes the ultimate competitive strategy to deliver and sustain customer value, which in turn builds shareholder wealth and employee satisfaction.

Treacy and Wiersema compare their theory against the accepted wisdom of other popular management models that stress, for example, the importance of understanding *core competencies* (harkening to Porter's competitive analysis techniques on a company's strengths and weaknesses) or creating *learning organizations* (postulated by the balanced scorecard theory that will be discussed next). They conclude that few of these generally accepted theories get to the heart of what sustains success in a competitive marketplace. For example, considering the concept of core competency, many competitors in a market will have similar core competencies in manufacturing, engineering, marketing, or sales. Apple and Dell are both competent at bringing personal computers to market, but this alone does not help firms balance the management of core and secondary processes, structure, and culture necessary to achieve market leadership.

OPERATING MODELS

Treacy and Wiersema argue that success is far more multifaceted. Different value disciplines require different operating models and as such define unique operating models for each of the three disciplines of market leaders. Each operating model has common components but with different attributes defining effort and focus. The common components include the core processes, culture, organization, information technology, and management systems, as illustrated in Figure 2.1. The attributes defining the effort and focus of each component are then uniquely tailored.

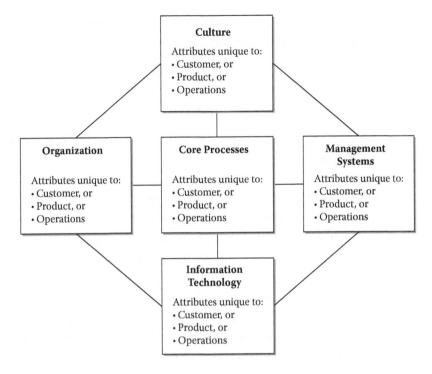

FIGURE 2.1
Treacy and Wiersema's operating model. (Adapted from Treacy, M., and Wiersema, F., *The Discipline of Market Leaders*, Perseus Books, Cambridge, MA, 1995, p. 90. With permission.)

Operational Excellence Operating Model

In *The Discipline of Operational Excellence* operating model (Treacy and Wiersema, 1995, pp. 47–64):

- *Core Processes* are streamlined and optimized to minimize cost and effort, focus on end-to-end product supply, and provide basic service. They are enabled using standard no-frills fixed assets.
- *Culture* is part of disciplined teamwork that is process focused with a conforming "one-size-fits-all" mindset that avoids waste and rewards efficiency.
- *Organization* is centralized with highly skilled talent at the core of the company. Operations are standardized, simplified, and tightly controlled, leaving few decisions to employee discretion.
- *Information Technology* is integrated, based on low-cost systems that exploit proven technologies.

- *Management Systems* focus on "command and control" techniques, compensation is tied to cost and quality, and profitability is tracked on a transaction basis.

Product Leadership Operating Model

In *The Discipline of Product Leadership* operating model (Treacy and Wiersema, 1995, pp. 85–100):

- *Core Processes* include: invention, product development and commercialization, market exploitation, and disjointed/flexible work procedures.
- *Culture* supports the creation and development of concepts and is future driven with an experimentation "outside the box" mindset and an attack "go-for-it" win attitude.
- *Organization* is structured such that high skills abound in loose-knit, ad-hoc, organic, and cellular structure to stimulate discovery and creativity. This helps the organization to adjust to new entrepreneurial initiatives and redirections when attempting to reveal innovative new products while working in unexplored territory.
- *Information Technology* is based on person-to-person communications systems and collaboration technologies that enable cooperation and knowledge management.
- *Management Systems* are results-driven and control overall product life-cycle profitability. They support risk-oriented ingenuity, measuring and rewarding new product success; individual innovation is encouraged; failed experimentation is unpunished.

Customer Intimacy Operating Model

In *The Discipline of Customer Intimacy* operating model (Treacy and Wiersema, 1995, pp. 123–142):

- *Core Processes* focus on solution development and implementation, whereby the customer understands exactly what is needed, what is happening, and that the solution gets implemented properly. Relationship management, including customer acquisition and development is coveted; work procedures are flexible and responsive.

- *Culture* is customer- and field-driven with a "have it your way" mindset that embraces specific rather than general solutions and thrives on deep and lasting customer relationships.
- *Organization* is based on entrepreneurial client teams with high-skill levels in the field who are available to the customers. Decision making is delegated to employees who work closely with the customer.
- *Information Technology* focuses on customer databases linking internal and external information with knowledge bases built around expertise.
- *Management Systems* focus on revenue and "share of wallet" metrics and are geared toward creating results for carefully selected and nurtured customers. Rewards are based, in part, on client feedback, and overall the lifetime value of the customer is analyzed as a critical performance measure.

Defining Value

The Discipline of Market Leaders concludes by challenging managers to define precisely the exceptional value that the organization offers customers and describe the operating model that delivers this value. Many managers struggle with such explanations, because they have not considered their business from such a perspective. As guidance, Treacy and Wiersema suggest that the best way to craft and articulate these messages requires three rounds of disciplined assessment and deliberation (Treacy and Wiersema, 1995, pp. 169–176):

1. In the first round, the management team must come to an understanding of where the organization currently stands and why. The coauthors suggest the following questions for deliberation:
   a. What are the dimensions of value the customer cares about?
   b. Where does the company stand relative to its competitors on each of these dimensions?
   c. Where and why do they fall short?
2. In the second round, managers must develop realistic, alternative value propositions and operating models. Questions to deliberate include:
   a. What would customers perceive as unmatched value?
   b. Could competitors quickly better that value?

    c. What kind of operating model would deliver the value proposition at a profit?

    d. What change would the company have to implement?

3. In the third round, the management team must commit to one operating model and deliberate the following questions:

    a. How would the operating model work?

    b. What change initiatives must the company launch?

    c. How must the company restructure?

    d. How will the company manage these changes and maintain its focus?

    e. How will it manage the associated risks?

Treacy and Wiersema's assessment approach to defining *exceptional value* asks questions similar to Porter in *Competitive Strategy* (1980). However, Porter's reasoning and analytic techniques go to considerable depth in each of these topics. But the important message to be taken from Treacy and Wiersema here is how the customer's dimension of value shapes the structure of the operating model of the company.

Their concept of an operating model is a simple and elegant way to begin thinking about how you must structure resources to support a chosen value discipline, and, in effect, business strategy. It should be deliberated prior to any more detailed value-chain assessment as prescribed in Porter's *Competitive Advantage*, which can go into considerable detail broadly identifying the resources and activities needed to deliver value.

BUILDING ON TREACY AND WIERSEMA'S BEST PRACTICES

The best practices presented in *The Discipline of Market Leaders* teach us the importance of focus when formulating business strategy. Treacy and Wiersema present a logical progression from Porter's best practices. Porter offers techniques to analyze industries and competitors for crafting competitive strategy. Treacy and Wiersema's conclusions channel such analysis, encouraging the operational discipline necessary to execute. By focusing on one of three value disciplines (product leadership, customer intimacy, or operational excellence), the coauthors teach us to think about how resources (core processes, culture, organization, information technology, and management systems), represented in the form of an operating model, need to be identified and aligned to achieve the business strategy sought.

The operating model, therefore, must be structured to enable superior performance of the chosen primary value discipline while maintaining threshold standards for secondary dimensions of value. However, to guide this design properly and ensure consistent execution of all value dimensions, we need to build on the best practices presented in *The Discipline of Market Leaders* by detailing:

- An analytic technique that will help identify, structure, and align the specific resources required to deliver the strategic discipline sought.
- Improved methods for performance measurement such that threshold levels for all dimensions of value (primary and secondary) can be managed and maintained to keep competitors at bay.

Derivative analysis is the structured analytic technique used to identify, structure, and align resources. It is explained and demonstrated later in Section III, entitled, "How to Align Strategy and Resources to Improve Execution, Adaptability, and Consistency."

Addressing the maintenance of threshold standards requires consideration of how best to measure thresholds to manage their performance. Not just across all customer value dimensions as defined by Treacy and Wiersema, but across the entire organization. A balanced view of management and performance measurement is critical to strategic achievement. This is best demonstrated through the best practices identified in *Balanced Scorecard* by Robert Kaplan and David Norton (1996).

3

How to Manage Performance: The Balanced Scorecard

After working with several pioneering technology and manufacturing companies, Robert Kaplan, a Harvard Business School professor, and David Norton, president of a management consulting firm, found that performance management was defined very narrowly, focusing almost exclusively on financial measures. They concluded that financial performance alone was insufficient to measure accurately an organization's achievement and total value, and that a broader approach was needed.

In their book, *The Balanced Scorecard: Translating Strategy into Action,* published in 1996 by Harvard Business School Press, Kaplan and Norton defined a *scorecard* model, whereby in addition to financial measures, organizational performance should include measures from a customer perspective, an internal business process perspective, and a perspective measuring employee innovation and learning.

Sometimes referred to as the four perspectives model, the name "balanced scorecard" was chosen to reflect the need for organizations to manage using a balanced assessment of performance measures. A good scorecard, therefore, includes a mix of core outcome measures common to most strategies, and performance drivers that reflect the uniqueness of a particular strategy. The measures and drivers selected should distinguish between long- and short-term objectives, between financial and nonfinancial measures, between lagging and leading indicators, and between internal and external performance perspectives. Ultimately, all measures need to be tied back to financial performance. Originally conceived as a performance measurement system, executives using it encouraged the authors to further its potential as a strategic management system. More on this later in our discussion on strategy maps.

Early on, Kaplan and Norton believed that sustainable competitive advantage, both near-term and long-term, requires organizations to exploit intangible assets that are not necessarily reflected in financial measures. They believed that intangible assets possess unique hidden potential to do the following (Kaplan and Norton, 1996, p. 3):

- Develop customer relationships, improve customer loyalty, and open new markets.
- Introduce innovative products and services to targeted segments.
- Produce customized products at low cost.
- Mobilize employee skills, and motivate them for continuous improvement in quality and process execution.
- Uniquely deploy and exploit emerging information technology to drive strategy and enable sustained competitive advantages.

To realize the potential of intangible assets, organizations must consider a new set of operating assumptions (Kaplan and Norton, 1996, p. 4):

- "Silo" departments must yield to more efficient, cross-functional organizations that share information for improved intelligence, efficiency, and specialization.
- Simple message exchange with customers and suppliers will be inadequate in some cases, driving the need for integrated information systems and process flows with external parties.
- Customers will require unique solutions and products based on their strategy and competitive landscape. Organizations must be able to respond quickly and effectively to these needs.
- Domestic boundaries no longer exist; all companies can compete on a global scale.
- Innovation and evolution of products, services, and product life-cycle management must accelerate and be tightly coupled with an understanding of the competitive landscape and customer needs.
- All employees possess unique talents; organizations must exploit their expertise and cycle this energy back into the organization to learn and respond dynamically to opportunity and change. As knowledge workers, employees serve a far greater purpose and offer superior value to an organization.

As organizations seek to transform themselves based on these assumptions, they look to a variety of improvement initiatives such as the following (Kaplan and Norton, 1996, p. 6):

- Total Quality Management
- Just-in-time (JIT) production and distribution systems
- Lean manufacturing
- Activity-based costing
- Customer-focused organizations
- Others

However, many of these initiatives are also measured narrowly by quarterly and annual financial reports anchored to an aging accounting model. *The Balanced Scorecard* represents a new performance measurement system, and ultimately, a strategic management model, one derived from an organization's vision and strategy, and also accounts for value derived from intangible assets. It is based on the belief that cause-and-effect relationships exist among the four measurement perspectives: financial, customer, internal business process, and learning and growth. Each aids the other in realizing their respective measures, and thus the strategic objectives of the organization. To understand cause-and-effect relationships from *The Balanced Scorecard* perspective, think about the four perspectives in the following way:

1. Invested capital (as measured in dollars, a financial measure)
2. Leads to the early development of an innovative, high-quality product (as measured by time to market, an internal business process measure)
3. That satisfies a unique customer need (as measured by customer satisfaction, a customer feedback measure)
4. When produced using an improved manufacturing process (as measured by production cycle time and inventory turns, an internal business process measure)
5. Developed by motivated employees (as measured by employee satisfaction, an innovation and growth measure)
6. Yields better than expected results (as measured by market share, a customer growth measure)
7. Satisfying investor requirements (as measured by the return-on-invested capital, a financial measure)

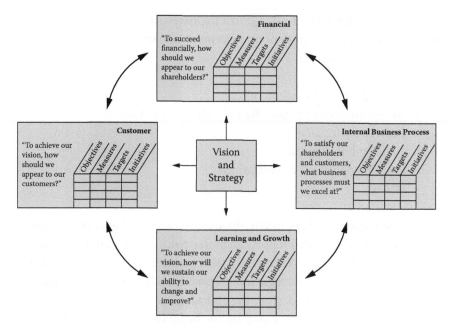

FIGURE 3.1

The balanced scorecard. (From Kaplan, R.S., and Norton, D.P., *The Balanced Scorecard,* Harvard Business School Press, Boston, MA, 1996, p. 9. With permission.)

This scenario demonstrates a basic cause-and-effect model highlighting how different business perspectives influence one another. *The Balanced Scorecard* emphasizes the need to develop strategy, share it with all employees, and measure results as a holistic system. Financial or statistical measures from a departmental or organizational perspective are simply too narrow. Organizations that don't pay attention to cause-and-effect relationships among the four perspectives may be at a competitive disadvantage. Figure 3.1 illustrates an example of a balanced scorecard demonstrating these relationships. To better understand the balanced scorecard, let's take a closer look at each of the four perspectives.

PERFORMANCE MEASURES FROM A FINANCIAL PERSPECTIVE

An organization's financial objectives will differ depending upon its business life-cycle strategy. Business life-cycles can be broadly defined, but to keep the explanation simple, Kaplan and Norton discuss the financial objectives of three typical life-cycle strategies: growth, sustain, and harvest.

Growth businesses commit resources to develop and enhance new products and services, construct and expand production facilities, invest in systems and infrastructure, develop relationships, enter markets, and nurture customers. They typically operate with negative cash flows and low current returns on invested capital. Financial objectives will measure percentage growth rates in revenues and sales growth by targeted markets, customer groups, or geographies.

Businesses operating with a *sustain* life-cycle strategy are required to earn attractive returns on invested capital and to maintain or grow market share. Investment is channeled to process management and continuous improvement. Managers are asked to maximize income and operate profitably. Return-on-investment, return-on-capital employed, and value-added measures are used to evaluate financial performance.

Businesses operating with a *harvest* life-cycle strategy are mature and warrant little incremental investment. Emphasis is on maintaining operations profitably. Any investment is expected to yield short-term returns. Financial performance is measured by reduction in working capital requirements and cash flow improvement.

For each of these life-cycle strategies, the coauthors identify three traditional financial themes that drive business strategy, as illustrated in Figure 3.2.

		Strategic Themes		
		Revenue Growth and Mix	**Cost Reduction/ Productivity Improvement**	**Asset Utilization**
Business Unit Strategy	Growth	Sales growth rate by segment Percentage revenue from new product, services, and customers	Revenue/employee	Investment (percentage of sales) R&D (percentage of sales)
	Sustain	Share of targeted customers and accounts Cross-selling Percentage revenues from new applications Customer and product line profitability	Cost versus competitors' Cost reductions rates Indirect expenses (percentage of sales)	Working capital ratios (cash-to-cash cycle) Return-on-capital-employed by key asset categories Asset utilization rates
	Harvest	Customer and product line profitability Percentage unprofitable customers	Unit costs (per unit of output, per transaction)	Payback Throughput

FIGURE 3.2

Measuring strategic financial themes. (From Kaplan, R.S., and Norton, D.P., *The Balanced Scorecard*, Harvard Business School Press, Boston, MA, 1996, p. 52. With permission.)

1. *Revenue growth and mix* across product or services lines, customer markets, and pricing strategies.
2. *Cost reduction and productivity improvement*, but not to the point where expenses are a burden that must be contained and eliminated over time. Rather the output of the expenses, such as indirect and support resources, should be measured to demonstrate increased efficiencies and as such are valued as assets to the organization.
3. *Asset utilization* and strategy to improve working capital, accounts receivable, accounts payable, and inventory management. A key measure of working capital efficiency is the cash-to-cash cycle that helps organizations understand how long it takes from the time they buy goods and pay labor until the time cash receipts are received from customers.

Organizations choose financial objectives from the themes that facilitate strategy and measure performance. Depending on the life-cycle of a strategy, revenue, cost, or asset management becomes the priority. The scorecard helps executives to specify the metrics by which long-term performance will be evaluated by highlighting the variables associated with business life-cycle success.

This is a traditional approach to financial performance measurement. The critical message that the coauthors emphasize is that to best realize financial objectives, an organization must understand and control how the cause-and-effect relationships of the other perspectives influence financial results. In other words, every measure selected in the scorecard should be part of a cause-and-effect relationship that, when complete, achieves the financial objectives being sought. In the cause-and-effect scenario stated earlier, the last relationship was a measurement of the financial result.

PERFORMANCE MEASURES FROM A CUSTOMER PERSPECTIVE

In the customer perspective, the observations of Kaplan and Norton bring into focus the findings of Porter. As in *Competitive Strategy*, organizations identify the customer and market segments in which they choose to compete. Organizations identify value propositions and deliver to targeted customers and markets. In *The Balanced Scorecard,* success of the value propositions is determined through five core customer outcome measures (Kaplan and Norton, 1996, p. 67):

1. Market share
2. Customer retention
3. Customer acquisition
4. Customer satisfaction
5. Customer profitability

Beyond aspiring to delight customers, organizations must translate their mission and strategy statements into specific market segments and customer-based objectives. Echoing Treacy and Wiersema, Kaplan and Norton also believe there must be a focused effort in each targeted segment. They note that some managers sometimes object to this focus, thinking that anyone willing to pay for goods and services is a good customer. Kaplan and Norton dismiss this attitude as short-sighted, arguing that it runs the risk of doing nothing well for anyone. The essence of business strategy is not just choosing what to do; but also choosing what not to do. Boundaries help focus resources to create distinguishable value propositions. This concept of defining boundaries is also reflected in the best practices found in *The Adaptive Enterprise* by Stephan Haeckel, which is discussed in more detail later.

The customer perspective of *The Balanced Scorecard* reflects other messages found in *The Discipline of Market Leaders.* Both observe that different customers have different needs for different types of value. Some customers require absolute rock-bottom price from suppliers, others seek innovative solutions, still others require knowledgeable advice, and so on. In *The Balanced Scorecard,* the relative strength or weakness of a value proposition drives the outcome of each of the five core customer measures. Realizing the desired outcome for customer acquisition, for example, demands that prospective customers perceive the organization's value proposition to be differentiated from those of competitors. The attributes of value, therefore, need to be addressed to drive the desired outcome. Kaplan and Norton (1996, pp. 73–77) organize the attributes of value propositions into three categories:

1. Product/service attributes encompassing functionality, price, and quality.

2. Customer relationships garnered from the tangible results of commerce transactions, such as timely responses, delivery, and professionalism.
3. Image and reputation reflecting intangible factors that attract customers and create loyalty as garnered from advertising, image and brand, and the perceived quality of the good or service.

Formulating strategy and performance measures, therefore, from the customer perspective of *The Balanced Scorecard,* requires organizations to do the following:

- Target customer and market segments.
- Differentiate value propositions across the three value categories: product services attributes, customer relationships, and image and reputation.
- Focus marketing, operational logistics, and product and service development efforts to achieve success as determined by the five core customer measures: customer acquisition, customer satisfaction, customer retention, customer profitability, and market share.

PERFORMANCE MEASURES FROM AN INTERNAL BUSINESS PROCESS PERSPECTIVE

From the internal business process perspective, Kaplan and Norton believe that performance measurement systems for many organizations focus too heavily on departmental measures. *The Balanced Scorecard* approach emphasizes the measurement of integrated processes across an organization. Cost, quality, throughput, and time measures should be defined for processes that span multiple departments, such as procurement, production planning and control, order fulfillment, and others. Indeed, this model can be externalized to include customers, suppliers, and other partners.*

---

* Cross-organizational process design affects workforce behavior and ushers in a new way of thinking about how individual, group, and organizational objectives are managed and achieved. This is explored in detail in Chapter 6.

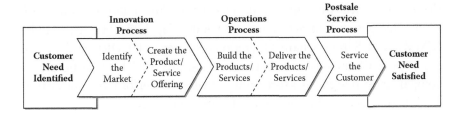

FIGURE 3.3
Internal business process perspective, the generic value-chain model. (From Kaplan, R.S., and Norton, D.P., *The Balanced Scorecard*, Harvard Business School Press, Boston, MA, 1996, p. 96. With permission.)

Organizations should focus on cross-organizational processes that are most critical for achieving customer and shareholder value. Management and measurement of these processes should be addressed by looking at them as end-to-end value chains that start with customer need and end with customer satisfaction.

All businesses have unique ways of creating customer value. But Kaplan and Norton highlight common denominators that define a generic value-chain model, as illustrated in Figure 3.3. They suggest using this generic model as a starting point and template for organizations to model their unique performance measures for business processes.

In contrast to Porter's depiction of a value chain as an analytical construct to define, then analyze, value categories and activities, Kaplan and Norton's value chain is a generic, high-level process representation. It starts with *innovation* processes, where customer needs and markets are identified, and then products and services are designed to meet these needs. It proceeds to *operations* processes where products and services are crafted and delivered, and concludes with *post-sale services* to ensure that customer needs are met, and if not, engages corrective actions to result in customer satisfaction.*

Kaplan and Norton believe operations and post-sale services processes are important but view them somewhat generically in *The Balanced Scorecard*, only briefly reviewing the activities and performance measures unique to each. They advise pursuing other established business improvement initiatives such as total quality management (TQM) that use well-defined scientific practices and measures. In recent years, other business process management and improvement methods have matured to offer

---

* Kaplan and Norton expand and refine their thinking about value-chain structure and internal business processes in a later book, *Strategy Maps* (2004), which we discuss shortly.

the process measurement details missing in *The Balanced Scorecard*. Methodologies such as Six Sigma, ISO 9000, Capability Maturity Model (CMM), and Supply Chain Operations Reference (SCOR) model from the Supply Chain Council, among others, are used by leading global companies to design, measure, and manage the performance of critical quality management initiatives and business processes.

The coauthors do describe in detail various techniques used in the innovation process to perform and measure market and customer research, applied research, and product R&D. Here, their message emphasizes the need for organizations to understand and anticipate customer need. To realize ambitious customer objectives, *The Balanced Scorecard* illustrates through several examples the need for organizations to develop internal business processes that capture a deep understanding of customer needs, requirements, challenges, and desires, and (similar to Treacy and Wiersema's calling) the need to be recognized by the customer that this knowledge is sufficient and accurate. Lacking such processes and such knowledge can cause the customer to seek alternatives. Lacking such recognition can cause misunderstanding, confusion, and frustration, potentially harming the relationship.

This assumes, of course, that the customers in fact know what they need. Sometimes customers are uncertain about the outcomes they seek, knowing only that they need innovative solutions. In these circumstances, the organization must possess sufficient intelligence and knowledge of the environment to anticipate the need, suggest such innovation, and be recognized for its expertise.

In any case, organizations must use their internal business processes and the employees closest to the customer to build constantly upon their knowledge of the customer and the market. Organizations must master customer solution development processes and analyze them to reveal new and unique processes that support a known need, or produce innovative value in the eyes of the customer. This level of effort propels organizations to outperform competitors and creates distinctive and sustainable competitive advantage.

PERFORMANCE MEASURES FROM A LEARNING AND GROWTH PERSPECTIVE

In the learning and growth perspective of *The Balanced Scorecard*, resourceful and motivated employees drive achievement in the other three perspectives. Organizations that focus solely on financial objectives often treat investments to motivate and improve people as expenses to be eliminated when financial performance declines. *The Balanced Scorecard* stresses the importance of investing in the future. That includes investing in the capabilities, productivity, and motivation of employees and measuring the outcome of these investments by determining the rates of employee (Kaplan and Norton, 1996, p. 129):

- Satisfaction
- Retention
- Productivity

Most organizations should and do measure employee satisfaction, retention, and productivity, and influence behavior with targeted incentives. All can be measured in several ways. Employee satisfaction is typically measured by retention or the rate of staff turnover. The simplest and most common measure of productivity is revenue per employee. But managers indifferent to such workforce measures sometimes make simple tactical changes to improve the outcome without really improving the results. For example, outsourcing some functions may improve employee productivity measures simply because there are fewer employees on the books. This doesn't mean that productivity actually improves or that customer objectives are being met.

Ideas for improving the customer experience and realizing customer objectives must increasingly rely on input from the employees closest to both the customer and the organization's internal processes. Employees must be engaged so that their minds and creative capabilities can be applied to achieve customer and organizational objectives. Here, Kaplan and Norton acknowledge the importance of aligning people, processes, and technology to support strategic objectives. To do so, organizations must consider investment in three categories that enable learning and growth (Kaplan and Norton, 1996, pp. 127–146):

1. Employee capabilities—as customer needs change, internal processes must respond, and investment is needed to apply employee knowledge and creative skills to help facilitate change, retrain and re-skill employees if required to realize evolving objectives.
2. Information system capabilities—investment is needed to support the workforce by providing it with strategic information necessary

to be knowledgeable about changing conditions and to be responsive to customers.

3. Motivation, empowerment, and alignment—methods and practices to motivate, empower, reward, and align the efforts of employees across the organization are required to achieve customer and organizational objectives.

Kaplan and Norton note that most organizations have devoted little effort to measuring the outcomes or drivers regarding employee skills, strategic information availability, and organizational alignment. Efforts that advance, retrain, or re-skill employees are often overlooked when developing strategic objectives. Exposing strategic information that can potentially affect employee job performance is inadequately planned. Aligning individuals, teams, and departments or groups with the organization's strategy to drive long-term objectives is inconsistent and sporadic.

Organizations must shift workforce thinking and behavior. Merely executing planned processes and reacting to customer requests is inadequate. Rather, organizations should proactively anticipate customer needs, and then market an expanded set of products and services to them. This may require retraining, new skills, or realignment of the organization and its resources. *The Balanced Scorecard* offers techniques and measures by which transformation can be assessed. Those of note include:

- *Strategic job coverage:* An analysis that maps the skills required of employees by job families, such as sales, services, and operations. It helps determine the extent to which these skills match what is needed to exceed customer perspective measures, the result of which may be to assign new roles and responsibilities or require new skills or retraining.
- *Strategic information availability:* An analysis of the information used by employees, measuring its quality, accuracy, and timeliness critical to enhance knowledge, improve judgment, and make decisions relative to each job family.
- *Percentage of business processes achieved:* An analysis of business process execution that meets performance measures. Those that don't achieve target rates may suggest that employee execution is lacking, requiring renewed focus on workforce skills and capabilities for those processes.

- *Percentage of key employees aligned to the scorecard objective:* An analysis of how business strategy and scorecard practices are disseminated throughout the organization. The key principle of the scorecard is to align all aspects of an organization to reach strategic objectives. Top-heavy concentration of objectives at executive and managerial levels should be avoided with responsibilities dispersed to key employees in the job families that most influence value-chain performance and customer satisfaction.

Aligning an organization to a shared vision with common direction requires communication and education programs, so that all employees understand the strategy and required behaviors to meet it. The strategy then needs to be translated into personal and team objectives to drive that behavior. *The Balanced Scorecard* permits and enables all employees within an organization to understand its strategy and shows how individual action influences the "big picture" perspective across financial, customer, business process, and learning and growth perspectives. Reward systems then need to be established to motivate the behavior. This too is discussed in Chapter 6.*

STRATEGY MAPS

As noted earlier, Kaplan and Norton developed the four perspectives model as a performance measurement system. But over time, it became something more. After 12 years of experience garnered from developing balanced scorecards with more than 300 organizations, the authors learned how it can be used as a tool to describe and implement an organization's strategy. They found that it provided a language that can be used by management teams to discuss the direction and priorities of their organization's value creating assets and processes. In describing how organizations create value, Kaplan and Norton observed that, "They can view their strategic measures, not as performance indicators in four independent perspectives, but as a series of cause-and-effect linkages among

---

* This discussion on performance measures from each of the four balanced scorecard perspectives provides high-level guidance, alerting you to how they should be structured. Specific key performance indicators (KPIs) must be selected to track and manage strategic objectives. This topic is addressed in more detail in Chapter 7 when we discuss how to manage execution.

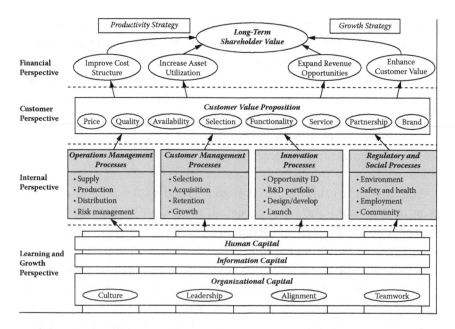

FIGURE 3.4

A strategy map represents how the organization creates value. (From Kaplan, R.S., and Norton, D.P., *Strategy Maps,* Harvard Business School Publishing Corporation, Boston, MA, 2004, p. 11. With permission.)

objectives in the four Balanced Scorecard perspectives." The representation of these linkages can be visualized in what Kaplan and Norton refer to as a *strategy map.*

A strategy map, as described by Kaplan and Norton in their book *Strategy Maps: Converting Intangible Assets Into Tangible Outcomes,* published in 2004 by Harvard Business School Press, is "... a visual representation of the cause-and-effect relationships among the components of an organization's strategy...," as illustrated in Figure 3.4. It "... provides a uniform and consistent way to describe that strategy, so that objectives and measures can be established and managed. The strategy map provides the missing link between strategy formulation and strategy execution."

Kaplan and Norton envision this illustration as a template to be used as a checklist of a strategy's elemental components and interrelationships. They believe that for a strategy to succeed, it must address each element represented in the template. Organizations choosing to use a strategy map to help formulate and explain strategy should use the following principles to guide its creation (Kaplan and Norton, 2004, pp. 10–13):

1. Strategy balances contradictory forces.

   For example, strategy must describe a balance between goals to control cost to improve short-term financial performance versus long-term goals that may require investment to achieve long-term revenue growth. Trade-offs between contradictory forces such as this must be identified and planned.

2. Strategy is based on a differentiated customer value proposition.

   As with Porter and Treacy and Wiersema, Kaplan and Norton discuss differentiation in *Strategy Maps* using generic examples that include total low cost, product leadership, complete customer solution, and a new value proposition known as "system lock-in," which are attempts by organizations to create standards that are adopted by complementary solutions providers to expand market share. They cite Microsoft and Intel as examples pioneering such value. A strategy must enable and explain some form of differentiated value.

3. Value is created through internal business processes.

   Processes describe how an organization will implement its strategy. Kaplan and Norton refine their earlier thinking on value-chain structure to describe four generic process clusters: operations management responsible for producing and delivering products and services; customer management that establishes, nurtures, and leverages customer relationships; innovation processes responsible for developing new products, services, and partnerships; and regulatory and social processes that satisfy government and societal expectations. A strategy must call out the "critical few processes" necessary for execution (more on this shortly).

4. Strategy consists of simultaneous, complementary themes.

   This means that each cluster of processes delivers "benefits" at different times. For example, operations management processes deliver short-term results, producing products or services or controlling costs. Customer relationship processes generate increased sales over a slightly longer term, as prospects begin to buy in to value propositions. Innovation processes generate longer term benefits still. Investment trial and error is typically required before new innovations begin to pay off. Finally, benefits derived from regulatory and social processes may yield good will affecting the brand or avoiding litigation. This is more difficult to measure, but nevertheless, critical to an organization's strategy. In this principle, Kaplan and Norton emphasize, "Strategies should be balanced, incorporating at least one strategic theme from each of the four internal clusters. By having strategic themes for enhancing processes in all four clusters, the organization realizes benefits that phase in over time, generating sustainable growth in shareholder value."

5. Strategy alignment determines the value of intangible assets.

Here, Kaplan and Norton structure intangible assets of the fourth perspective, learning and growth, into three categories:

a. *Human Capital* that includes the workforce, their skills, knowledge, expertise, and talent

b. *Information Capital* that includes data, information, IT systems, and infrastructure

c. *Organizational Capital* that includes culture, leadership, teamwork, and knowledge management

Kaplan and Norton emphasize aligning these intangible assets with strategic (the critical few) processes using "targeted approaches" that they refer to as strategic job families (first introduced in *The Balanced Scorecard*), a strategic IT portfolio, and an organization change agenda. Each strategic process should define the critical job families and IT resources necessary for execution while adopting a culture that is aware of the strategy, its goals, and the cause-and-effect relationships of its assets. These targeted approaches are the means by which Kaplan and Norton propose aligning people and technology to support the chosen strategy and execute the strategic processes structured across the four process clusters. Collectively, they enable "organizational readiness" that is able to respond to change as is required to execute strategy.*

A strategy map is an excellent tool to put strategy, execution, measurement, people, processes, and technology in perspective. It reveals the components and relationships of each, managing them as assets to achieve what is planned.

Business process management and continuous improvement initiatives cannot be pursued in isolation of the assets and components that constitute

---

* In *Strategy Maps*, Kaplan and Norton discuss the components and behavior of organizational capital. They define it as "the ability of the organization to mobilize and sustain the process of change required to execute the strategy." Doing so requires that culture, leadership, organizational alignment, and teamwork must focus on the customer, spawn creativity and innovation, and deliver results. Behavior of the organization must be based on an understanding of the organization's strategy and values, foster accountability and communications, and emphasize teamwork. Specific techniques will be discussed to do this in Chapter 6 and in Section III, that will detail a unique approach to align people, processes, and technology to support strategy.

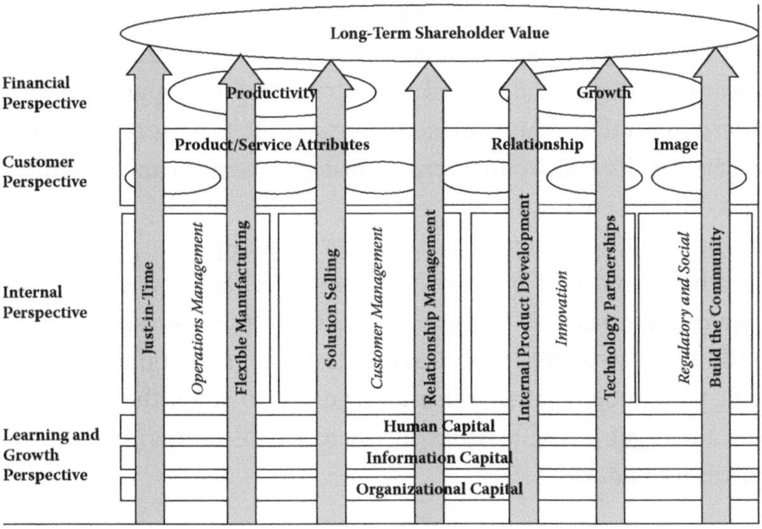

FIGURE 3.5
Strategic themes based on value-creating processes. (From Kaplan, R.S., and Norton, D.P., *Strategy Maps,* Harvard Business School Publishing Corporation, Boston, MA, 2004, p. 50. With permission.)

a strategy map. However, focus is required on the "critical few processes" that are essential for strategic execution. Similarly, Treacy and Wiersema's operating model calls for a focused group of "core" processes. Kaplan and Norton emphasize that processes in the internal and learning and growth perspectives derive how value is created and delivered, and how strategy is implemented. The authors state, "Executives practicing the art of strategy must identify the critical few processes that are the most important for creating and delivering the differentiating customer value proposition." Kaplan and Norton refer to these critical few processes as "strategic themes."

Strategic themes are the means to define focus. The coauthors advise that balancing a strategy requires an organization to ". . . incorporate at least one strategic theme from each of the four internal [process] clusters." Figure 3.5 illustrates how several strategic themes are structured to span the four scorecard perspectives and the four process clusters of a strategy map, in this case for a manufacturing operation.

Each strategic theme then must be defined and structured to state the specific objectives sought from each of the four scorecard perspectives, identifying the specific measures to be managed and tracked for each objective, and prescribing action plans that identify specific strategic initiatives for each measure sought.

A strategic initiative is a call to action by the organization to structure a set of activities to achieve desired measurable results for each of the four perspectives. They are designed and structured to support short- and long-term objectives of a strategic theme specific to a process cluster. The aggregate results within and across strategic themes can determine the success or failure of a strategy.

At this point, let's step back, summarize, and put in perspective the logic, advice, and best practices offered by Kaplan and Norton in *The Balanced Scorecard* and *Strategy Maps*. Then, the discussion continues to build upon what has been learned thus far in Section I to describe specific techniques that enable organizations to adapt their assets, processes, and organizational behavior when circumstances change or when opportunity knocks.

SUMMARIZING KAPLAN AND NORTON'S BEST PRACTICES

- The balanced scorecard helps an organization to identify a performance measurement system, enabling it to fully exploit its tangible and intangible assets to achieve a chosen strategy. It does so by defining and tracking performance measures across four perspectives: financial, customer, internal business process, and learning and growth. A scorecard is comprised of a mix of the following:
  - Financial and nonfinancial measures
  - Core outcome measures common to most strategies
  - Performance drivers that reflect the uniqueness of a particular strategy
  - Long- and short-term objectives
  - Lagging and leading indicators
- A balanced scorecard also begins to demonstrate the cause-and-effect relationships that exist across the organization's asset structure (tangible and intangible) that affect a chosen strategy. These cause-and-effect relationships need to be understood to manage what is necessary to achieve the performance and outcomes desired. Ultimately, the cause-and effect relationships must translate to the desired financial results.

- Aligning and structuring assets to execute a chosen strategy is best facilitated using a strategy map. A strategy map identifies a checklist of an organization's assets across the four perspectives of a balanced scorecard, defines four generic process clusters (operations management, customer management, innovation, and regulatory and social), and illustrates the cause-and-effect relationships that are necessary to create and deliver customer and shareholder value.
- The "chosen few" strategic processes necessary to create and deliver value should be organized within strategic themes. Strategic themes identify and help structure organizations' assets, processes, and performance measures as building blocks upon which execution is enabled.
- Strategic themes clarify what is necessary to structure the value-creating processes across the four-process cluster: operations management, customer management, innovation, and regulatory and social. They drive the definition, targets, and priority of the various balanced scorecard measures that structure a set of outcome measures and performance drivers to be tracked and managed across the four perspectives.
- For each measure called for, a strategic initiative or specific action plan is put in place to achieve the targets sought.

Figure 3.6 illustrates how a strategy map, balanced scorecard, and strategic initiatives in the form of an action plan are structured for a strategic theme within the operations management process cluster, in this case for a low-cost airline.

BUILDING ON KAPLAN AND NORTON'S BEST PRACTICES

Kaplan and Norton offer us a clear vision and commonsense techniques to formulate strategy and align resources for execution. To facilitate the change necessary to support execution, the coauthors offer targeted approaches in the learning and growth perspective to create the organizational readiness necessary to mobilize and sustain the process of change. They advise that human, information, and organizational capital be identified, trained, and disciplined to adopt a culture of change necessary to

Strategy Map		Balanced Scorecard		Action Plan	
Process: Operations Management **Theme: Ground Turnaround**	Objectives	Measurement	Target	Initiative	Budget
Financial Perspective Profits Grow Revenues — Fewer Planes	▪ Profitability ▪ Grow revenues ▪ Fewer planes	▪ Market value ▪ Seat revenue ▪ Plane lease cost	▪ 30% CAGR ▪ 20% CAGR ▪ 5% CAGR		
Customer Perspective Attract and Retain More Customers On-time Services — Lowest Prices	▪ Attract & retain more customers ▪ Flight is on time ▪ Lowest prices	▪ # repeat customers ▪ # customers ▪ FAA on-time arrival rating ▪ Customer ranking	▪ 70% ▪ Increase 12% annually ▪ #1 ▪ #1	▪ Implement CRM system ▪ Quality management ▪ Customer loyalty program	▪ $XXX ▪ $XXX ▪ $XXX
Internal Perspective Fast Ground Turnaround	▪ Fast ground turnaround	▪ On ground time ▪ On time departure	▪ 30 minutes ▪ 90%	▪ Cycle time optimization	▪ $XXX
Learning and Growth Perspective Strategic Job Ramp Agent Strategic Systems Crew Scheduling Ground Crew Alignment	▪ Develop the necessary skills ▪ Develop the support system ▪ Ground crew aligned with strategy	▪ Strategic job readiness ▪ Info system availability ▪ Strategic awareness ▪ % ground crew stockholders	▪ Yr. 1–70% Yr. 3–90% Yr. 5–100% ▪ 100% ▪ 100% ▪ 100%	▪ Ground crew training ▪ Crew scheduling system rollout ▪ Communications program ▪ Employee stock ownership plan	▪ $XXX ▪ $XXX ▪ $XXX ▪ $XXX
				Total Budget	**$XXX**

FIGURE 3.6

How a strategic theme defines processes, intangible assets, targets, and initiatives. (From Kaplan, R.S., and Norton, D.P., *Strategy Maps,* Harvard Business School Publishing Corporation, Boston, MA, 2004, p. 53. With permission.)

align assets and processes, and foster the teamwork necessary to achieve strategic objectives.

Indeed, salient advice, but, how does leadership best "train and discipline" its organization to properly respond when unanticipated events occur, problems arise, or unique opportunity presents itself? For example, the strategic initiatives called for in a strategy map must execute flawlessly, or at least perform very well. Their aggregate performance, or lack thereof, is tightly coupled to overall strategic execution, performance measurement, and outcomes. They are typically executed in lower levels of an organization where constant managerial oversight of the workforce is inefficient and impractical. How can workforce behavior at all levels be structured to maintain consistent execution and properly respond to problems, change, or sudden opportunity?

To instill a culture of change and organizational readiness called for by Kaplan and Norton, oversight and decisions must be performed locally by an empowered and motivated workforce, equipped with the proper tools to maintain consistent execution and take reasoned and proper action when they sense that it is necessary. This requires rules of engagement that define how organizational structure and workforce behavior react under a range of circumstances. This is best accomplished using sense-and-respond techniques that enable the organization, workforce, and business processes to adapt as necessary, which brings up the next discussion—how to adapt by using techniques described in the book, *Adaptive Enterprise,* by Stephan H. Haeckel (1999).

4

How to Adapt: Adaptive Enterprise

Over the past several decades, IBM has researched how organizations in diverse industries sensed and responded to change. Stephan H. Haeckel, the director of strategic studies at IBM's Advanced Business Institute, outlined some of the key findings of this work in his book *Adaptive Enterprise: Creating and Leading Sense-and-Respond Organizations*, published in 1999 by the Harvard Business School Press.

Haeckel believes that the only kind of strategy that makes sense in the face of unpredictable change is a strategy to become adaptive. Speed to market, customer intimacy, operational excellence, and organizational agility, however important, are not adaptive strategic objectives in and of themselves. Adaptation requires more than agility. It requires appropriate organizational response to change.

In this environment, Haeckel argues that planned responses are not sufficient. Being agile enough to go to market based on predictions of what customers want is too risky in competitive environments. Unpredictability implies that the organization and organizational behavior must be driven by current customer requests, expressed and anticipated (recall a similar discussion in *The Balanced Scorecard*, Kaplan and Norton, 1996), rather than by firm plans to "make-and-sell" offerings based on market predictions.

A sense-and-respond organization does not attempt to predict future demand for its offerings. Instead, it identifies changing customer needs and new business challenges as they happen. Adaptation based on customer needs means dispatching capabilities on demand using a modular organizational structure, as opposed to scheduling them efficiently in advance.

Traditional command and control managerial techniques are not designed for such responsiveness. Instead, leadership must redesign the organizational model. It must have purpose, boundaries, and structure that translate the noise and confusion typically associated with change into meaning. It must define and empower key roles within the organization and instill behavior about how and when it is to adapt, under what circumstances, and within what defined limits (a concept similar to that expressed in *The Balanced Scorecard,* where Kaplan and Norton call for training and discipline to be structured for strategic job families). This organizational context is the foundation upon which a sense-and-respond organization exists.

SENSE-AND-RESPOND ORGANIZATION

Haeckel defines a sense-and-respond *organization* as a collection of capabilities and assets managed as an adaptive system. Sense-and-respond *behavior* is the triggering of an organization's operations by the requests of individual customers. The sense-and-respond *model* represents the techniques designed for producing this behavior economically on a large scale.

The best practices garnered from *Adaptive Enterprise* critical to facilitating these sense-and-respond traits require organizations to do the following:

1. Organize information (from customers, competitors, markets, etc.) in a specific way to support its productive use by key roles (people) in the organization. This practice is called the "adaptive loop."
2. Structure the assets and capabilities of the organization into a system of modules that can be opportunistically assembled to create new "one-off" value chains capable of unique responses. This structure enables a "modular organization."
3. Replace top-down "command and control" management with a governance system that empowers employees to make business commitments for specific purposes, within defined bounds, throughout the organization. Here, interactions, rather than the actions, of an organization are managed as modular capabilities using a method called "commitment management protocol."

ADAPTIVE LOOP

The behavior of a sense-and-respond organization is described in terms of a four-phase adaptive loop. Here, individuals and organizations first sense change in their environment or are exposed to direct opportunity. Next, they must interpret these changes in the context of their experience, aims, and capabilities, separating threats from opportunities and discarding irrelevant information. They then decide how to respond, guided by the governance provided by leadership, and finally act if no new information changes the decision to respond. The progression from sensing, to interpretation, to decision, to action becomes an iterative loop as the adaptive system monitors the results of its previous actions, as illustrated in Figure 4.1.

Leadership is responsible for setting forth governing principles that define the organization's limits of action, including what its members must always do, or never do, in pursuit of the organization's purpose. This is to ensure that the decisions and actions made using the adaptive loop process lead to customer satisfaction and profitable business.

Essentially, this means giving key roles within the organization autonomous authority to decide whether to pursue new customer opportunity and act to win it, but within certain bounds. For example, consider a systems integration company that specializes in implementing and

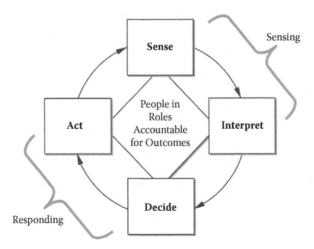

FIGURE 4.1
Haeckel's adaptive loop. (From Haeckel, S.H., *Adaptive Enterprise*, Harvard Business School Press, 1999, p. 76. With permission.)

customizing supply chain management software. Its salesperson "senses" that one of its existing supply chain customers has a new need for a custom human resources (HR) management system. Here, the basic opportunity (software implementation and customization) is consistent with the firm's purpose, but the expertise required of HR processes differs from its supply chain process expertise.

The leadership must make clear unambiguous rules as to whether the salesperson should pursue this business. If the goal of the firm is to invest in a new market, then the salesperson would have broadly defined rules of interpretation and decision. This would empower her with the flexibility to understand in more detail the customer need and negotiate to reach a decision. If the leadership states specifically that it will only focus on providing superior supply chain expertise, then the salesperson must let the opportunity pass.

Another way to think about the iterative process of the adaptive loop and the role of leadership is to think about how a proprietor of a small business would behave. Here, customers interact with the leader and decision maker directly. Consider the owner of a kitchen cabinet-making shop being asked by a homeowner to build an extension to make room for a kitchen expansion. The cabinetmaker has to interpret first if this is a business he wants to enter based on his business objectives or financial needs. If the answer is yes, then the scope of the extension, the skills, resources, tools, time, and subcontractors need to be considered. Here, the cabinetmaker begins negotiations of scope and price with an iterative question-answer-proposal exchange with the homeowner to better understand the need and to suggest available options. He decides to close the deal and acts to assemble the resources, having direct authority to make decisions and be accountable for the results.

Adaptive loop behavior characterizes many small and mid-sized organizations, but not all, and only a few large organizations. In growing or larger organizations, the customer will not have direct access to leadership. Haeckel observes that task-oriented employees typically do not have the authority or the proper motivation to react to new opportunity if it does not fit the model they understand how to serve. These companies sense a new opportunity but fail to respond, and hence lose it or the customer.

The proprietor knows instinctively how and when to marshal resources and put them to work based on experience and decision-making authority as the business owner. Similar guidance should be provided by leaders to those employees in an adaptive organization who interact with customers. Employees in these key roles must know without ambiguity, and with conviction, what they can and cannot do, and what they should and should not do. Here, Haeckel recommends appropriate caution. Sense-and-respond does not mean "listen-and-comply." In instances where organizations cannot respond profitably, the response should be "no-bid."

Change or opportunity in larger or distributed organizations may require resources from several parts of an organization. Different key roles in different organizational groups may be required to participate in the adaptive loop process. Interpretation, decisions, and action from multiple parties within an organization will require structure and governance. Here, leadership must also specify how employees interrelate to achieve the organization's purpose.

MODULAR ORGANIZATION

In sense-and-respond organizations, business functions are modularized to create capabilities that when used in combination can respond to a much broader spectrum of customer requests. Haeckel believes that when organizations successfully dispatch these modular capabilities, they can achieve large-scale, low-cost, rapid customization, a basic requirement and objective for sense-and-respond organizations.

In the *Adaptive Enterprise,* the term *protocol-oriented modularity* is used to explain modularization. This means employees in key roles empowered to interpret, decide, and act in one business function are likely to do so with similar employees in key roles representing other business functions. Here, protocol, or organizational behavior and discipline, are structured using formal yet flexible interaction techniques to guide participants in the adaptive loop process. To illustrate this, consider the prior example of the supply chain systems integration firm that "sensed" an HR opportunity.

Assume here that the firm's leadership is pursuing a growth strategy and has expanded its purpose to include implementation and customization services for HR applications. The salesperson who sensed the opportunity now begins further interpretation. Discovery on her part creates more questions, requiring the participation of other key employees in the firm. Among them, a project manager from the professional services group and a lead software designer from engineering. Each represents different parts of the firm and is responsible for his own commitments and outcomes. Interpretations by all result in the decision to act and close the deal. The unique customer requirements identified through the adaptive loop process (sense, interpret, decide, act) now define the scope of the project and the deliverables of each business function within the firm.

Organizational modularity was created by empowering the salesperson to reach across organizational disciplines and acquire the unique expertise needed to analyze the opportunity. Each business function in this adaptive organization identified people in key roles who were empowered to interpret, decide, and act within the boundaries that were defined by leadership. When each was satisfied that he or she can act profitably, they agreed to their respective commitments and were able to close the deal.

Haeckel emphasizes that modular organizations require its leadership to pay close attention to how interlocking sets of commitments are negotiated by business functions. As organizations adapt to changing conditions, they will need to negotiate new commitments or renegotiate older ones with internal, as well as external parties. Haeckel observes that shifting patterns of interdependent commitments can cause confusion and complexity. Abrogating confusion and deciding how commitments are met falls to those making the commitments, within the limits defined by governing principles. This requires leadership to structure a consistent means for people to define, negotiate, and execute commitments with each other. Here, Haeckel introduces the proven, but not widely known concept called *commitment management protocol.*

COMMITMENT MANAGEMENT PROTOCOL

The commitment management protocol is a tool that helps organizations govern sense-and-respond practices. It is introduced in the *Adaptive Enterprise* referencing the work of Fernando Flores, a workflow analyst and software entrepreneur, and Alan Scherr, an IBM fellow. Haeckel uses it to make the point that human accountability is often the missing dimension of business process design.

Modular organizations enable various business functions to plug-and-play with one another as illustrated earlier. When the adaptive loop process concludes and commitments are agreed to by employees, they should then be measured based on outcomes rather than tasks. Haeckel states that how goods and services are delivered (the tasks) is of little consequence to customers as long as the expected quality is delivered on time and within budget (the outcome).

Indeed, outcomes are a priority. However, to improve execution, efficiency, and consistency, Haeckel's premise needs to be expanded. Employees and business functions should be measured based on outcomes and tasks. How well goods and services are delivered (the efficiency of task execution) is of great consequence to organizations. It directly affects profitability and whether the customer recognizes superior value as compared to competitors (recall earlier discussions on Porter, Treacy and Wiersema, and Kaplan and Norton). Indeed, the effective and efficient execution of tasks is the purpose driving business process management and continuous improvement.

A critical success factor for business process management, therefore, requires that consistent governance and structure be applied to commitments made as a result of the adaptive loop process. In sense-and-response organizations, tasks are dynamic; they can change with each opportunity. The commitment management protocol is a technique designed to structure ad hoc responses to unanticipated events or requests and reach agreement and commitment from among the participants involved. When faithfully applied, it brings clarity to processes that otherwise might be rife with ambiguity and misunderstanding. This technique applies equally well to stable repeated processes and negotiations with external parties.

The commitment management protocol is illustrated in Figure 4.2. It consists of four task phases (define, negotiate, perform, and assess) and seven communications (offer, request, agree, report, accept, reject, and withdraw).

The commitments made as a result of this protocol must be authentic. The parties must mean what they say and will be held responsible and accountable to meet the outcome or deliverables as defined and to which they agree. At each action, the task or communication should be recorded and signed off by representative participants with the authority to do so.

This protocol is important, because it represents a very basic, yet important business process in and of itself. It defines how to negotiate and record commitments, outcomes, and deliverables made by employees (or external parties) to avoid ambiguity and confusion. It helps set proper expectations and can be used to build or improve relationships. It addresses the missing dimension of human accountability in many business process designs by holding people to their commitments. It can be implemented in something as simple as an e-mail exchange, or it can be automated and managed using

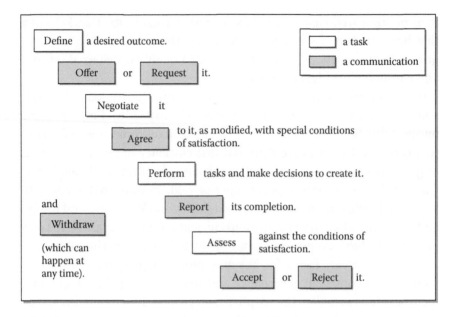

FIGURE 4.2

Commitment management protocol. (From Alan Scherr and Fernando Flores cited in Haeckel, S.H., *Adaptive Enterprise,* Harvard Business School Press, Boston, MA, 1999, p. 149. With permission.)

various business applications, workflow technology, or business process management suites. On the topic of technology, Haeckel touches briefly on how to automate processes to support sense-and-respond capabilities, but only at a conceptual level that he refers to as "manage by wire." Through analogy and example, he describes the principles and advantages of information availability through automation, but does not detail the techniques needed to model and analyze sense-and-respond processes or develop an information technology strategy to support them. These topics will be discussed shortly.*

BUILDING ON HAECKEL'S BEST PRACTICES

The *Adaptive Enterprise* introduces a critical and challenging dimension to formulating business strategy. Haeckel instills the need for organizations to include adaptability that reacts to events and customer

---

* Accountability and responsibility are discussed further in Chapter 6. The information technology available to automate a commitment management protocol is discussed in Chapter 8.

needs as they are anticipated or occur. Fulfilling demand based on predictions of what the market needs is too risky. He describes a sense-and-respond organization as one that reacts to change or opportunity using an adaptive loop analysis process. Business functions form a modular organization where employees in key roles are empowered to make and manage commitments with one another, within well-defined boundaries, using a formal commitment management process. These techniques enable organizations to adapt to change or new opportunity more rapidly than competitors.

Building on Haeckel's best practices requires us to take all that we learned about business strategy and use it to help craft a strategic plan that, in turn, provides the blueprint required to structure and align resources for proper execution of a chosen strategy.

SECTION I CONCLUSION: STRATEGIC PLANNING—A PROCESS, NOT AN EVENT

Considering these best practices collectively, most executives would conclude that they must do all simultaneously. Commanding competitive knowledge (*Competitive Strategy*, Porter), focusing operations (*The Discipline of Market Leaders*, Treacy and Wiersema), measuring performance from multiple perspectives (*The Balanced Scorecard*, Kaplan and Norton), and quickly responding to change or customer need (*Adaptive Enterprise*, Haeckel) are the very definition of a highly competitive business. Collectively, these best practices represent a comprehensive summary of the knowledge required, and the decisions executives must make to craft and execute successful business strategy.

Figure 4.3 illustrates how these best practices interrelate and ultimately drive the structure of the people, processes, and information technology required to execute strategy and deliver customer value. All of these works have their critics and detractors; our goal here is not to debate about who is "right" or "more right" in their views on strategy. Each work offers an important perspective that, when considered collectively, helps guide your thinking about the following:

- The business(es) you choose
- The goals you seek

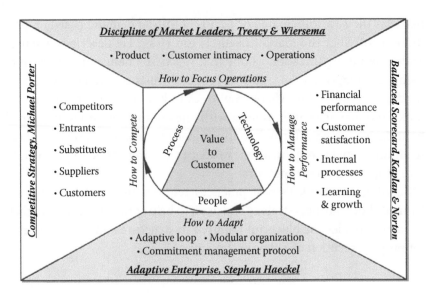

FIGURE 4.3
Collective best practices used in strategic planning.

- How you create and deliver value
- How you distinguish yourselves competitively
- How you structure your operating model to deliver customer value and achieve goals
- How you measure performance and outcomes
- How you react to opportunity and change

Using these best practices in this way helps organizations to structure the line of reasoning necessary to formulate a highly competitive business strategy rich in customer value. They help organizations that struggle with poor performance to answer fundamental strategic planning questions:

- Were my objectives realistic and achievable?
- Did I misunderstand or underestimate the challenges?
- Did I have enough of the right resources?
- Was my strategy correct given my resources, challenges, and objectives?

And, as a result, master the visceral business concepts such as competition, execution, measurement, control, and adaptation to change to form the foundation for your organization's strategic plan.

Formulating, analyzing, and adjusting business strategy should not be an event; it must be a continuous process. All the authors emphasize an ongoing commitment to learning and adapting. But making such a commitment requires resources and effort. How can this be achieved while maintaining an already overburdened workload?

Part of the answer lies in how effective we are in structuring and aligning our resources. When done properly, business strategy and execution can become synchronous, adjusting continuously by an empowered workforce and savvy leadership using technology to monitor and share strategic information related to customer satisfaction, business process, and financial performance. These best practices can then become inherent to all job functions and managerial practices without necessarily requiring extra effort. Nevertheless, effective strategy requires continuous reviews with leadership and management, scheduled periodically using a predetermined strategic planning calendar on a monthly, quarterly, semi-annual, or annual basis. Strategy and performance reviews must become part of a strategic planning process that systematically examines strategy and strategic achievement along the same line of reasoning as it was formulated. This is done by analyzing how effectively your organization:

- *Competes:* Reviewing the lessons learned from *Competitive Strategy*
- *Focuses operations:* Reviewing the lessons learned from *The Discipline of Market Leaders*
- *Manages performance:* Reviewing the lessons learned from *The Balanced Scorecard*
- *Adapts to change:* Reviewing the lessons learned from *Adaptive Enterprise*

Such initiatives should be managed as part of a continuous process improvement program where strategy must be translated into action. Execution requires you to select and structure specific resources needed by the strategy chosen.

* * *

This brings us to Section II where the best practices and the line of reasoning used by industry leaders to structure and align people, processes, and technology to translate a strategic plan into reality will be discussed.

Section II

Execution—Best Practice Use of Strategic Resources

Achieving strategic objectives is all about execution. Execution, too, has been a well-studied topic by business academia and corporate leadership. The best-selling book *Execution: The Discipline of Getting Things Done* (2002, p. 22) by Larry Bossidy (former chairman and CEO of Honeywell International) and Ram Charan (senior advisor to Fortune 500 executives) offers this definition:

> Execution is a systematic process of rigorously discussing hows and whats, questioning, tenaciously following through, and ensuring accountability. It includes making assumptions about the business environment, assessing the organization's capabilities, linking strategy to operations and the people who are going to implement strategy, synchronizing those people and their various disciplines, and linking rewards to outcomes. It also includes mechanisms for changing assumptions as the environment changes and upgrading the company's capabilities to meet the challenges of an ambitious strategy.

Essentially, Bossidy and Charan summarize all the best practices discussed in Section I. Execution then means putting these best practices to work in your organization.

When preparing to execute your strategy, it is best to learn how highly effective organizations structure their people, business processes, and information technology (strategic resources) for execution. In this section the best practice structure of each strategic resource will be discussed in succession.

- The discussion about people addresses how to empower and motivate the workforce and introduces the concepts of *workforce collaboration and collaborative objectives* as means to help successfully execute business strategy.
- The discussion on business processes involves how to include human accountability and responsibility in the process designs that support workforce collaboration, and introduces effective techniques to control, measure, and manage the performance and outcomes of tasks, activities, and collaborative objectives. Here, we also begin our discussion on the value and importance of process modeling and analysis.
- The discussion on information technology outlines the capabilities that business systems need for a workforce to collaborate, have ready access to strategic information, measure performance, and manage outcomes as called for by business strategy and business process designs.

5

How to Structure Organizational Behavior for Strategic Execution

Organizations that execute effectively view their people as assets. They believe that static, lethargic, unmotivated employees can be a burden to an organization. When employees are treated as assets and knowledge workers, rather than as "labor" that incurs expense, they add considerable value to an organization. They become a workforce, an asset empowered and motivated to achieve results.

EMPOWER AND MOTIVATE

Empowering the workforce means:

- The business strategy and objectives are widely disseminated. They are not kept secret. If something requires secrecy, it is part of another agenda or represents future effort.
- Employees know who the customers are and the value they seek.
- Employees know the value their organization brings to customers and how it compares to each of its most competitive rivals.
- Employees are knowledgeable about the business strategy and aware of the strategic objectives for the entire organization, not just group or individual goals.
- When asked, employees can articulate the business strategy and objectives.

- Employees understand the business processes, outcomes, and measures of which they are a direct part, and for which they are responsible as process stakeholders.
- Employees understand how their actions, or inactions, affect other stakeholders of their business process and other business processes that they may influence or affect.
- Employees always have access to the strategic information they require to perform the business processes for which they are directly responsible and those that they affect.
- Employees always have access to the reporting and measurement systems that track the measures for which they are directly responsible and those that they affect.
- Employees have tools to rapidly acquire, assess, and disseminate information with relevant business process stakeholders, management, and leadership as required when change or opportunity is sensed, and interpretation, decision, and action are required.
- Employees have access to management and leadership freely as required when they sense strategic objectives or performance measures are threatened or they discover unique opportunity.
- Employees are held responsible and accountable to continuously and consistently track, manage, and achieve the outcomes and tasks assigned to them.

Motivating the workforce means that leadership and management do the following:

- Demonstrate that employee satisfaction, retention, and productivity measures are important by providing the necessary resources and investments to develop and sustain a superior workforce.
- Make available educational resources for training, retraining or re-skilling, and continuous improvements.
- Involve employees in decisions and provide recognition for achievement and awards for exceptional performance.
- Set realistic and achievable individual, group, organizational, and other goals that may be required.
- Craft a straightforward and unambiguous incentive system that rewards achievement when goals are met or exceeded, including proper incentives for "stretch" goals. Confusing or complex incentive systems must be replaced.

- Encourage and reward initiative that rapidly acquires, assesses, and disseminates information with relevant business process stakeholders, management, and leadership as required when change or opportunity is sensed, and interpretation, decision, and action are required.

Empowering and motivating organizational behavior is a common theme in the books discussed in Chapters 1 through 4. For example, in *The Discipline of Market Leaders,* Treacy and Wiersema discuss organizational behavior as part of the cultural and organizational components of an operating model. In *The Balanced Scorecard,* Kaplan and Norton discuss this as part of the learning and growth perspective of performance measurement. Haeckel's *Adaptive Enterprise* offers the adaptive loop process and the commitment management protocol as techniques to govern organizational behavior. When empowered and motivated, the workforce practices sense-and-respond behavior. Put another way, all of these works emphasize the importance and need for the workforce to collaborate to achieve business objectives and seek new ways to deliver and enhance customer value.

WORKFORCE COLLABORATION

In many organizations, the quality of workforce collaboration is overlooked. When a business process is designed and an IT system is put in place to run it, leadership and management often take for granted that the workforce collaborates effectively.

Workforce collaboration influences all aspects of value discussed thus far (customer intimacy, product leadership, cost advantage, personalized service, knowledgeable advice, etc.). The collaborative initiative across functional groups and skilled individuals determines the quality of customer value and the timeliness of its delivery, indeed, more so than any other single process of an organization. The degree to which a workforce collaborates, and the processes and systems the organization puts in place to do so, directly determines its success (or failure). Workforce collaboration should be considered a value-added process and a critical asset to an organization's value chain.

The importance of this is also demonstrated by Porter in the article "What is Strategy?," published in the November–December 1996 issue of the *Harvard Business Review.* There he argues that competitive advantage through strategic positioning is a more sustainable approach than continually trying to improve operational effectiveness. He states, "While operational effectiveness is about achieving excellence in individual activities or functions, strategy is about combining activities" (p. 70). To Porter, "Competitive advantage grows out of the entire system of activities. The fit among activities substantially reduces cost or increases differentiation" (p. 73).

In other words, how well an organization executes the "entire system of activities" and how well these activities "fit" with one another, determine the strength and advantages of its value chain. Porter acknowledges that this can be a challenge: "Achieving fit is difficult because it requires the integration of decisions and actions across many independent subunits" (p. 74).

Fit is determined by many factors that influence how well an organization synchronizes the flow of information, materials, and capital within its value chain to achieve strategic objectives. But overcoming the challenge of integrating the "decisions and actions across many independent subunits" (p. 74), rests squarely on how well a workforce collaborates and on the processes and systems used to do so. Effective organizations encourage workforce collaboration by first instilling a collective attitude toward performance measurement and achievement. They do this by crafting and using *collaborative objectives.*

Collaborative Objectives

A collaborative objective is an end (or goal) that requires activities and tasks to be performed by several functions that span an organization's value chain. It is a cross-organizational business process. For example, Figure 5.1 illustrates a generic order-to-cash (O2C) business process that spans several departments.

The departments represented in this process map include the following:

- *Sales:* Responsible for customer relationship management, closing deals, and processing orders.
- *Procurement:* Responsible for buying supplies.
- *Operations:* Responsible for receiving supplies and fulfilling orders.

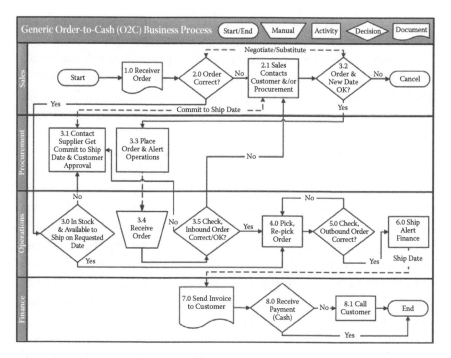

FIGURE 5.1
Generic order-to-cash business process map.

- *Finance:* Responsible for billing and collections. A collaborative objective assigns responsibility and accountability for specific performance measures of the overall O2C process to each functional department. If the overall performance measure is not met, any incentive tied to its achievement is lost to all.

Individual and group objectives to manage performance are common. Few organizations, however, reliably track and manage the end-to-end value-chain performance of business processes. It becomes critical to do so under a variety of conditions, particularly in situations where time is of the essence, such as in just-in-time manufacturing, when working capital is needed through cash receipts, or when a customer need is urgent.

Failure by one stakeholder in one department affects the success of others, not just for the collaborative objective, but for individual and group objectives as well. For example, if the operations department rejects the acceptance of a critical supply and fails to promptly alert the procurement and sales groups, the fulfillment of a customer order can be delayed. This can affect cash receipts, which in turn, affect the individual and group goals for day's sales outstanding (DSO), procurement efficiency, and accounts receivable objectives.

Creating collaborative objectives requires organizations to bolster traditional performance measures. Typical management by objectives (MBOs) defined for individual and group performance must also include objectives that track and measure cross-organizational performance. Using our example, a collaborative objective measuring the timing between tasks, while holding all stakeholders accountable for the overall O2C process, can improve motivation and performance results. Rewards tied to a collaborative O2C objective would motivate the operations group to ensure collaboration with procurement and sales. Procurement and sales would be motivated to be on the lookout for delays from other stakeholders, prompting action if they sense that a collaborative objective is at risk. In this example, the collaborative objective would be managed by control processes and IT tools that track timing thresholds, alerting relevant stakeholders via a collaboration tool (such as e-mail or mobile device) when performance measures vary or exceed acceptable limits.

Making collaborative objectives work in an organization requires all stakeholders in any business process to be aware of their roles and goals as well as the roles and goals of other stakeholders. As advised by Kaplan and Norton, they must understand the cause-and-effect relationships that exist within and between the business processes they affect. They must also understand the impact their actions or inactions have on key performance indicators (KPIs) and outcomes at the individual, group, and organizational levels. This awareness, coupled with proper incentives, motivates stakeholders to acquire and disseminate information rapidly across the organization when they sense change, opportunity, or risk.

The best way to demonstrate the importance and value of this behavior is to think about the crew of a large ocean-going vessel. Command, navigation, sonar, radar, helm, engineering, and safety officers all must receive and disseminate information instantaneously for the ship to avert danger and safely arrive in port. Failure to acquire information, disseminate it to relevant stakeholders, and react in the event of an anomaly (such as "Iceberg ahead!") can produce disastrous consequences. Here, incentives to promote such behavior are obvious. In business, when functional groups and process stakeholders are governed and rewarded by collaborative objectives, similar actions can be taken to protect the results of individual, group, and organizational goals when something happens, or doesn't happen.

Understanding the cause-and-effect relationships among process stakeholders and motivating collaborative behavior begins with properly defining the roles and goals of a workforce. A simple and effective technique for doing this is known as RACI.

MANAGING RESPONSIBILITY AND ACCOUNTABILITY

RACI, or the *RACI matrix,* is a popular technique used to organize cross-functional team members involved in project, program, or portfolio management; it works equally well in business process management. RACI is an acronym representing responsible, accountable, consulted, and informed. Also known as the responsibility assignment matrix (RAM) or the linear responsibility chart (LRC), it is used to determine who is responsible for project or process execution, who is accountable for decisions and outcomes, who is consulted for advice, and who is informed as to progress and outcomes. It is a simple and straightforward technique that can be used to help clarify all the "roles and goals" of each stakeholders in a business process. Figure 5.2 is a sample RACI matrix for a generic, process improvement project.

The RACI matrix illustrates stakeholder roles respective to one another. Haeckel (1999) alerted us in *Adaptive Enterprise* that many business process management initiatives fail to include human accountability in process design. Creating a RACI matrix for each business process, or cluster of processes, begins to address this oversight.

Defining the roles of key stakeholders in such a way helps structure collaborative objectives to align organizational behavior with a business strategy. RACI is an important first step toward these ends, but it doesn't illustrate cause-and-effect relationships among process stakeholders. Doing so requires a deeper understanding and analysis of how value is created and delivered to customers, and how organizations respond when opportunity is sensed, change occurs, or objectives are at risk.

Here we begin our discussion on the role business process design plays in executing strategy, and the value and importance of process modeling and analysis.

BPMethods The PRACTICE Method™ for Business Process Analysis & Improvement

RACI Matrix

Program/Project Name

R = Responsible, A = Accountable, C = Consulted, I = Informed

Process Improvement Team: A = Decision Maker, R = Executes

Phase	Description	Step	Deliverables	Sponsor	Business Process Owner	Program Manager	Project Manager	Process Developer	Lead Stakeholder	IT or Subject Matter Expert	Stakeholder(s) (1-n)
1	Plan	1.0	Business Objectives	A	R	C	I	I	I	I	
		1.1	Participant Org. Chart	A	R	C	I	I		I	
		1.2	Program Charter	A	R	C	I				
		1.3	Program Announcement	A	R	C	I	I	I	I	I
2	Research	2.0	As-is Process Model	C	A	R	R	R	C	C	C
		2.1	KPI Selection	C	A	R	R	I	C	C	
		2.2	Interview Questionnaire	I	R	A	R	I	C	C	C
		2.3	IT Readiness Assessment	I	C	A	R	I	C	R	C
3	Analyze, Correct, Test	3.0	Process Analysis Findings	I	C	R	A	R	C	C	C
		3.1	To-Be Redesign & Correction	C	C	A	C	R	C	C	
		3.2	Test & IT Requirements	C	A	R	R	C	C	R	
		3.3	ROI Analysis > Decision	A	C	R	R	C	C	C	
4	Implement, Control	4.0	Systems Implementation	A	R	R	R		C	R	
		4.1	Training Plan		A	C	R		C	C	
		4.2	Re-Analysis & Control	I	A	R	R	R	C	C	
5	Extend	5.0	Continuous Improvement Plan	A	R	R	I	I	I	I	I
		5.1	Process Inventory Analysis	A	R	C					C

FIGURE 5.2

RACI matrix for generic business process improvement project.

6

How to Structure Business Processes for Strategic Execution

How well an organization executes is largely determined by how well its business processes are designed. To be effective as strategic resources, business processes must do the following:

- Create value for which customers are willing to pay.
- Support the desired organizational behavior needed for a strategy by facilitating workforce collaboration, accountability, and responsibility.
- Be designed to include techniques to measure, manage, and control the desired performance outcomes of the activities and tasks that comprise the process.

Designing these qualities into business processes requires the following to be defined:

- A mix of core outcome measures common to most strategies, and performance drivers that reflect the uniqueness of a particular strategy used to track and manage execution (as advised by Kaplan and Norton)
- The control techniques needed to make corrections when performance or outcomes vary

To properly do so, organizations must distinguish between various types of processes, because the design of each addresses different strategic needs.

DEFINING PROCESSES

A basic definition of a *process* is a logical sequence of activities that transforms input into output or results. Other definitions add details about the technicalities of execution. More accurate definitions describe a process as a means to create value. Indeed, processes are much more than just sterile transactions. They are how we do business with customers, partners, and suppliers; how we establish and nurture relationships; how we make, service, and fix things; how we share knowledge to create new things; how we make decisions, solve problems, or do something that has never been done before. And in the end, processes provide the means for us to make money and get paid.

Processes viewed in this light take on new meaning. In fact, they take on several meanings. A proper extended definition of a process, therefore, is the following.

(1) *Process* is a logical series of related activities that converts input to results or output. (2) *Value-added extension* is designed to create or deliver customer value or shareholder value through efficiency. (3) *Asset extension* is an asset that affects the quality of a product, service, or brand to uniquely satisfy customer needs and differentiates its executor from competitors.

Innovative leaders and managers elevate the status of processes from sequential activities to value-adding assets. They then seek to use them to create competitive advantage. They do so by differentiating the various types of processes that comprise their value chain and operating model and focus on controlling the quality and consistency of their performance outcomes.

Operating, Support, and Management Processes

Processes that can create competitive advantage are those that directly contribute to the creation of value, support it in some way, help make decisions, control variance, or solve problems. These types of processes generally fall into three high-level classes.

Operating Processes

Operating processes create, add, or deliver value for which customers are willing to pay. They develop, make, sell, and deliver products and services. They are typically designed to execute an organization's stated business strategy. Depending on your strategy, examples of operating processes can be product manufacturing, raw material refinement, sales order processing, customer services, or rendering repair and warranty services.

Support Processes

Support processes do not directly create products or services but are necessary to facilitate or assist the execution of operating or management processes. Examples of processes that support operating processes are supply procurements, inventory replenishment, and machine maintenance. Examples of processes that support management processes are administrative, typically associated with finance, accounting, sales, or human resources.

Management Processes

Management processes provide the means to measure and control quality and ensure the desired performance outcomes. They help make decisions, control variance, and resolve problems. They help guide the organizational behavior needed for a strategy by facilitating workforce collaboration, accountability, and responsibility.

To be effective in maintaining quality and desired outcomes, management processes need to be able to sense when outcomes are at risk, interpret options, decide, and then engage an appropriate response. Doing this reliably requires forethought, agility, and structure. Industry leaders prepare for this by distinguishing two types of management processes: decision-making and control processes.

Decision-making processes are management processes that define objectives, study alternatives, analyze available data, and reflect on intuitive beliefs. They interpret findings and compare alternatives to form a conclusion or make a choice upon which the organization may act. Examples of decision-making processes include strategic planning, selecting new suppliers, acquiring or merging with another organization, or how best to restructure during trying economic conditions.

As are many processes, decision-making processes are diverse and subjective, but uniquely so because they are strongly influenced by the personalities and culture of the organization's leadership and management teams. This makes them difficult to standardize and automate, especially when new people fill key leadership and management roles.

Moreover, different decisions often warrant different approaches. Most organizations and management teams have unique professional skills and organizational structure designed to assemble information and interpret options for decisions. For example, some decisions by large retailers regarding how best to market to consumers may be derived from a process of rigorous data acquisition and statistical analysis of historic consumer behavior. In contrast, entrepreneurial management teams or visionary leaders may make similar decisions based on "gut feeling," sensing what they believe to be correct with minimal data analysis or further market inquisition.

Industry leaders optimize decision-making processes through the strength, quality, and talent of the leadership and management teams, the structure and frequency of communication and collaboration, and the quality and availability of relevant information.

Control processes are management processes that engage corrective action and resolve problems. They keep performance outcomes on track using dynamic sense-and-respond techniques such as those introduced by Haeckel and discussed in Section I. These techniques enable organizations, in many cases, to prepare predetermined responses. Properly designed control processes execute with discipline and structure guided by rules of engagement and policies that enable the workforce to interpret options, make decisions, and solve problems quickly. This makes control processes less susceptible to wavering styles of management and easier to standardize and automate.

Most organizations understate or misunderstand the value and importance of control processes to support execution and enable competitive advantage. For this reason, they warrant closer examination.

Control Processes

A *control process* is a series of activities and tasks performed to adjust or correct a business process (operating, support, or other management process), or its outcome, when performance measures vary, exceed acceptable thresholds, or when new opportunity is presented. Examples of control processes include escalation procedures that accelerate responses to customer complaints; quality control processes that make corrective actions when errors or defects are discovered; and collaborative processes that respond to something unexpected by interpreting options, deciding what needs to be done, and then taking action.

Any number of events can cause outcome and performance measures to vary from expected results. An *event* is something that happens or doesn't happen (but is supposed to) during a process. It can be either anticipated or unanticipated. The design of control processes will depend upon whether the events are known or anticipated, or unknown or unanticipated. Therefore, there are two general types of control processes.

Known or anticipated events that cause a process to vary, or place performance measures at risk, are *exceptions*; controlling them calls for *exception control processes*. Unknown or unanticipated events that cause a process to vary, or place performance measures at risk, present a greater challenge. Resolution demands diligent workforce collaboration; controlling such events calls for *resolution control processes.*

Exception Control Processes Exception control processes are control processes that correct known and anticipated events, the "Oh, here we go again!" problems that occur during normal operations. They are engaged when either an IT system or the workforce senses that an event has exceeded, or threatens to exceed, a predetermined measurement threshold. All other relevant systems or stakeholders are alerted to the event, and they, in turn, execute a prescribed series of predetermined activities and tasks, usually performed sequentially, to make the necessary corrections. For example, inventory levels falling below an acceptable level trigger an alert to a purchasing manager in an online exception report. She then knows to contact a supplier for a rush order. In another example, an event alerts a customer service representative (CSR) via e-mail that a new order has been received but with errors. He then knows to call the customer or the salesperson to make the necessary corrections within the timeframe thresholds determined for such an event.

Resolution Control Processes Resolution control processes determine how best to correct unknown or unanticipated (the "Didn't see that coming! What do we do now?") events, or properly respond to a sudden and unexpected opportunity. ("The customer will double the order if we can ship it TODAY?") Sometimes referred to as "case management," they typically require dynamic collaboration of multiple functional groups, subject matter experts, and stakeholders accessing one or more internal and external information system. Resolution control processes establish the rules of engagement that coordinate the organization's behavior to interpret the event or opportunity and decide how best to act. The rules of engagement help manage resolution attempts within prescribed boundaries and record actions taken and commitments made, and hold accountable and responsible the stakeholders involved. (Recall the discussion in Chapter 3 on the adaptive loop process and commitment management protocol introduced by Haeckel.) For example, if a labor strike threatens contractual obligations with an established customer, or if an important customer suddenly places an order for a product that exceeds the available inventory and manufacturing capacity, alternative sourcing efforts may be required to maintain the relationship.

Control processes are also part of a broader managerial discipline designed to manage an organization's risk. *Event management* is a form (or subset) of risk management that coordinates control processes, workforce behavior, information technology, and business policies to prevent or control adverse effects of process variance on an organization and its strategic objectives. It is discussed in greater detail later in this chapter.

Control Processes and Competitive Advantage

Many organizations fail to plan for failure. Meaning, they do not know what to do when things go wrong. Control processes are unheard of or take a back seat in overall BPM strategies. Other organizations embed control processes in operating or support processes where they are overlooked. This prevents them from being scrutinized uniquely with rigor, causing them to become insufficient in their resolve. For example:

- If the input required of an activity (accounts receivable)
- Is awaiting the output of another activity (the check is in the mail)
- And there is no timing threshold to alert and prescribe action if the output is delayed (a control process)
- The business process could unknowingly stop because no control is in place ("Hey, did they ever pay us?")
- Affecting several outcome measures such as day's sale outstanding (DSO), accounts receivable (AR), working capital, and others

A business rule identifies the timing threshold (e.g., if no input after 10 business days then trigger an alert to a process stakeholder), and the alert (DSO exceeding timing threshold) triggers a prescribed action (call the customer). But, sometimes business rules are mistaken as control processes. In this example, an event triggers the timing threshold, sending an alert to a customer service representative so they know to call the customer. Great, but if the CSR is unaware of the appropriate control activities necessary for exception or resolution management, performance measures can remain at risk. In this case, the CSR needs to know more than just to call the customer when a business rule is triggered. He also needs to know how to respond when a call is made to inquire about the payment. For example, if the customer response is, "Oh, our system was down. I'll make certain we get it out today." The CSR completes an exception process (this is a known and anticipated event) and makes the appropriate system entry resetting the DSO alert.

But, if the customer response is, "Oh, I was wondering when you where going to call; we have no intention of paying" (an unknown and unanticipated event), the CSR needs to initiate a resolution management process that:

- Interprets this event
- Engages the persons held accountable for its outcome (the owner of DSO measures and others) who
- Decides what to do, agrees on how to do it, records the agreement for tracking and analysis purposes
- Acts to successful conclusion (as prescribed by the *adaptive loop process* and *commitment management protocol* discussed in Chapter 3).

Formal resolution management processes are practically nonexistent in most organizations. They typically happen on the fly and without regard to the performance impact on the rest of the organization. As noted in Chapter 5, many organizations overlook the quality and effectiveness of workforce collaboration. To wit, you may have seen a placard hanging as a testament to such oversight in a colleague's cubicle or office,

Lack of planning on your part does not constitute an emergency on my part.

Often management will implement generic collaboration technology such as e-mail, instant messaging, portals, workflow suites, Web 2.0 services (social media), conferencing systems, and various mobile solutions assuming their use alone will drive the necessary resolve among stakeholders. Indeed, these are all valuable capabilities and assets to stakeholders, but their mere presence does not ensure or guide the organizational behavior necessary to drive strategic achievement or competitive advantage.

Sometimes management will rely solely on the reporting and analytic capabilities of their business applications as a means to control and resolve. Again, useful tools, but they need to be configured correctly, aligned with relevant business processes, and linked with alerting and messaging tools to be effective.

Control processes must be considered as unique and distinct from operating, support, or other management processes. When designed and tested with rigor and coupled with properly configured collaborative, reporting, and analytic technology, they can enable considerable competitive advantage. Why? Because many of your competitors will overlook or underestimate the need to do this.*

Business Rules and Process Controls

Control processes are specialized and designed to help organizations stay on plan when strategic objectives are at risk or performance measures begin to vary. Like many other processes, they are governed or influenced in some way by business rules. Business rules enumerate an organization's rules of engagement, defining the boundaries within which it is necessary or acceptable to do business. They act as thresholds triggering other operating, support, or management processes as required by business strategy or process design.

Creating customer value and enabling competitive advantage requires organizations to manage and control business rules as adeptly as they need to manage business processes. However, managing business rules as strategic assets is an allusive art for many organizations because rules frequently change.

Business rules are broadly defined from many perspectives. Your organization will structure rules to govern operations, manage resources, control risk, adhere to policies, comply with government regulations, and fulfill business commitments. Each business function, such as finance, IT, operations, human resources, sales, and so on, will have unique rules that are likely to change. Indeed, different leaders and managers will reprioritize and redefine business rules as opportunities, regulations, and risks dictate. The way in which business rules are implemented and

---

* Proper IT configuration requires the ability to alert relevant process stakeholders, making available the necessary information required to manage the event. How to enable this process-centric approach to IT architecture is discussed in Chapter 7.

enforced can also vary, using automated systems, the workforce, or both. Controlling the diversity and dynamics of business rules requires that they, too, be properly classified, defined, and organized in ways similar to business processes.

In general, business rules are measures, conditions, or constraints that define and govern execution, or the behavior of activities and tasks; they assert control and influence further action. Business rules may result from, or be a subset of, business policy. A business policy is a declaration or statement of guidelines that govern business decisions. Policy statements are often insufficient to form the design of a process or an automated system. Business rules specify the details of how policy is enacted and enforced, thus influencing process design.

Regardless of a formal definition, business rules and the policies that drive them are what you describe them to be for your purposes. They must be easily articulated and understood to avoid ambiguity on the part of those held accountable and responsible for their implementation in systems, and their execution in practice. To make this point, consider the following business rule, "Orders require approval." The process stakeholder controlled by the rule must interpret this rule. What type of orders? Orders for services? Orders for products? Both? Approval by whom?

An unambiguous business rule is a definitive declarative statement such as, "All service orders over $100,000 must be approved by the senior sales VP in charge at the time the order is received." In this latter description, little is left for interpretation.

The management and governance of business rules are not exclusive to business process management. Indeed, business rules exist outside business processes. Examples would be those governing ethical behavior, conditions of employment, or statements of a belief or policy such as, "We are an equal opportunity employer." For our purposes, however, I focus on the management and governance of business rules as they pertain to business processes.

Business rules help to control a process, as noted earlier, but they are not "control processes" themselves. As you recall, a "control process" is a sequential or dynamic series of activities and tasks designed to take corrective action. *Process controls,* on the other hand, are business rules mandated by management that are embedded within, or called upon during, the execution of a process, activity, or task to ensure the organization achieves its performance objectives, mitigates risk, or complies with other obligations as required.

Process controls can take on several forms. They can:

- Establish *thresholds* or *conditions* that govern behavior or respond to an event. For example, "All requisitions exceeding $10,000 must have senior VP approval" (a rule that governs behavior). "Upon receipt of a requisition exceeding $10,000, alert the senior VP for approval" (a rule that responds to an event).
- Define *actions* required before the process can resume. For example, "Check credit rating of customer."
- Call for *reviews* or *oversights* structured to ensure quality or mitigate risk. For example, "Evaluate supplier response time and compare to obligations established in service level agreement." "Report findings to supplier in quarterly performance reviews."

Process controls are frequently used for internal and external auditing to help organizations comply with government regulations such as the Sarbanes–Oxley Act. In addition, well-documented business processes and well-defined process controls are required to earn certification from quality management standards bodies such as the International Organization for Standardization (ISO 9000 et al.).

Later in this chapter I discuss techniques you can use to assign the proper value to business rules so they can be properly used to enable process controls and manage process performance. I conclude the discussion here on process definition by noting a means to prioritize your business processes.

Core and Noncore Processes

Many works published on business strategy and process management define a class of process known as *core*. For example, various definitions and descriptions of value chains declare operating processes to be core processes, uniquely distinguishing operating processes from support or management processes. They argue that operating processes are core because they generate products and services, or create value, whereas support and management processes simply help ensure that operating (core) processes function. In many of these same works any discussion of management and control processes is often vague, overlooked, or ignored.

I have chosen to explain process classes as I have because I believe it is important to distinguish their unique purpose and role. As assets, they create and deliver value, and should enable competitive differentiation and advantage in some way. Moreover, your business strategy is supposed to be unique. It should enable you to differentiate your organization (value chain and operating model) from your competitors in the eyes of the customers you seek. To do so, it is imperative to prioritize processes and classify them as you see fit, consistent with your unique strategy.

Therefore, I do not identify core as a "class" of high-value operating processes, rather core processes are a "priority." A core process is any process your organization deems critical to the creation and delivery of customer and shareholder value and enables some form of competitive advantage. Core processes can be operating, support, management, or control processes. Recalling the discussion in Chapter 2, Treacy and Wiersema describe core processes to be any process that is central to the organization's operating model.

Processes not central to your operating model are noncore. Core processes demand commitment, ownership, investment in performance enhancement, and optimization. Noncore processes demand control, restraint, and evaluation for necessity and purpose. To enable competitive advantage, core processes must be managed as assets to ensure consistent performance and outcomes. Noncore processes should be kept to a minimum by consolidating or eliminating them, thus minimizing their potential to create risk or liability due to lack of proper attention or oversight.

Preparing to Organize Processes as Assets

To this point, I have discussed how to classify processes at a high level as value-adding assets. Each class is defined by specific abilities. In review:

- *Operating processes* are those that are critical to creating and delivering products and services.
- *Support processes* enable or facilitate operating or management processes in some way.
- *Management processes* guide decisions and control outcomes.
- *Control processes* are specialized management processes expressly and purposely designed to take corrective action and resolve problems. There are two types:

- *Exception control* processes correct known or anticipated events.
  - *Resolution control* processes correct unknown or unanticipated events.
- *Business rules* guide process execution and control. When codified within, or called for by a process, activity, or task, business rules become *process controls*.
- *Core processes* are priorities because they are deemed by an organization to be critical to the creation and delivery of customer and shareholder value, or enable some form of competitive advantage. They demand commitment, ownership, investment in performance enhancement, and optimization.
- *Noncore processes* require control, restraint, oversight, and evaluation for necessity, purpose, and efficiency.

Classification helps determine which processes are critical to achieving objectives and which play secondary roles. It is an important practice needed to structure a BPM initiative and prioritize processes for improvement, streamlining, consolidation, or decommissioning.

But, classifying and organizing the dozens and potentially hundreds of processes used to run day-to-day operations can be daunting. Few organizations even list the processes they use, much less define them within classes. Managing processes as value-adding assets therefore requires a pragmatic means to identify and evaluate them.

MANAGING PROCESSES AS A PORTFOLIO OF ASSETS

Portfolio management is a general technique used to control and optimize the efficiency of, and returns from, many diverse assets. Each asset is continuously evaluated. When necessary, structural adjustments are made to an asset that help increase its individual value and, consequently, to the portfolio of assets as a whole. It is a common technique practiced in finance where it manages the balance and returns of diversified stocks, bonds, and other securities that collectively determine the overall value of a financial portfolio.

Portfolio management is also used by many industry leaders to manage a diverse range of IT assets. IT portfolio management creates an inventory of existing IT assets and uses it to do the following:

- Reprioritize and rebalance diverse IT investments (including projects, architecture, infrastructure, systems, applications, resources, etc.).
- Eliminate redundancies while maximizing reuse.
- Optimally schedule personnel and other resources.
- Measure project plans, costs, schedules, risks, returns, and benefits from development through postimplementation.

IT portfolio management is discussed in more detail in Chapter 7.

Business Process Portfolio Management

Business process portfolio management uses similar principles, but focuses on how to improve the returns from diverse business processes that comprise an organization's value chain such as those associated with the following:

- Creating and sustaining customer and supplier relationships
- Developing and managing products and services
- Controlling administrative functions such as finance, human resources, and regulatory requirements

To create a competitive advantage industry leaders engage in a systematic approach by taking stock of business processes as value-adding assets and continuously assessing them for strategic value and effect.

Business process portfolio management provides techniques and tools used to document and evaluate business processes as assets, and manage their ongoing performance improvement. It reveals the core business processes that yield the greatest strategic value and financial returns, and it exposes noncore processes that do not. It provides clarity of vision, helping organizations to pinpoint investments in enterprise resource planning (ERP), supply chain management (SCM), customer relationship management (CRM), software-as-a-service (SaaS) subscriptions, and BPM Suites: the IT portfolio necessary for process execution. It ensures early and substantial returns from business process improvement projects and lays the groundwork for highly effective continuous process improvement programs.

Business Process Portfolio

The primary tool used in business process portfolio management is the portfolio itself. A business process portfolio is a classification system and common data repository used to inventory, document, and manage detailed information about business processes. Information captured and managed within a portfolio includes activities, tasks, performance measures, and resource requirements that comprise a process. It does not map or model workflow. Other tools and techniques are reserved for this purpose and are discussed later in Chapter 7. Rather, the portfolio assists management teams in evaluating process quality, effectiveness, and efficiency, thus revealing the core processes that require improvement, and exposing noncore processes that require consolidation or elimination.

A business process portfolio can be:

- As simple as a well-structured document shared among management team members, or throughout an organization, using content and document management technology
- A dedicated database
- An in-place enterprise resource planning system (if properly equipped)
- A business process management suite

A portfolio approach to business process management begins by taking stock or "inventorying" your organization's business processes.

Business Process Inventory

A business process inventory is a structured exercise designed to "take stock" of all the processes your organization uses to run its operations. It identifies and classifies business processes and provides a means to evaluate their quality. The processes inventoried can then be documented and managed in a business process portfolio.

The inventory exercise is accomplished through a facilitated discussion with members of your management team and business process owners. It elicits how they perceive the value and quality of various business processes and how well or poorly each process is being managed. Indeed, most organizations measure process performance quantitatively using key performance indicators (KPIs). However, the quality of how well a process is defined, documented, changed, evaluated for compliance and value, and so on is rarely assessed. In other words, a key reason to conduct a business process inventory is to assess the quality of management and execution for each process category, group, and individual process used by an organization. This provides the baseline knowledge needed to help you understand what is necessary to establish your organization's BPM initiative.

Introducing Business Process Reference Models

The diversity and complexity of business processes have created the need for standardization. Several reference models for business process design and performance management now exist. Developed by a range of industry consortia, nonprofit associations, government research programs, and academia, they are thoughtful representations of real-world operating environments. Many are crafted from the input of hundreds of organizations.

Process classification frameworks and reference models standardize process definitions and performance measures. They help organizations to evaluate and refine their value chains and operating models. They are particularly useful when they define regulatory or industry-specific processes, or when performance benchmarking against peers and competitors is desired.

Some standardized frameworks classify generic business processes that can be applied across industries such as APQC's Process Classification Framework (PCF) and the Value Chain Group's Value Reference Model (VRM). Some focus on certain types of processes such as software development, IT service management, or address interenterprise supply chain processes among trading partners such as the Supply Chain Council's SCOR model. Some have regional origins such as the European Foundation for Quality Management, and others define reference models for industry-specific processes such as ACORD (Association for Cooperative Operations Research and Development) for the insurance industry and related financial services industries, eTom (Enhanced Telecom Operations Map) for the telecommunications industry, AIAG (Automotive Industry Action Group) for the automotive industry, and RosettatNet used mainly in the information technology industry.

These and other standardized frameworks represent comprehensive bodies of knowledge, but they are not "out of the box" value chains. They are designed as models that can be used by organizations to evaluate the business processes critical to their strategy. They are intended to help create competitive advantage by facilitating analysis of business process design, execution, and performance.

Without such models, conducting a business process inventory can be daunting. Essentially, they can be used as a checklist. The classification system provided by the chosen framework can be adapted by the organization as they see fit: by department, function, and group, or what-have-you. For example, organizations can use APQC's PCF to inventory the processes in the framework they use, flag those they don't use, and add processes unique to it—thus reconciling the framework—to represent its value chain. This greatly simplifies the effort needed to inventory and classify processes from scratch.

After choosing or creating a custom classification model, your management team should evaluate the quality, or lack thereof, of each process category, group, or individual process; analyze the findings; and determine what is to be done with the core and noncore processes.

BPMethods (www.bpmethods.com), a professional services firm specializing in BPM and continuous improvement, developed an inventory and evaluation system for this purpose. Process quality can be assessed across several standardized evaluation criteria. This is accomplished by answering basic multiple choice questions about each process during a facilitated discussion. The answers help expose how well processes are aligned with a business strategy. For example, processes thought by your management team to be critical to a product leadership strategy should be evaluated as follows:

- "Core" in value
- "Routine" in use
- "Formal" in managerial discipline
- "Full" or "semi" automated with
- "Detailed" documentation

However, if your management team qualitatively assesses the processes critical to a product leadership strategy as being supportive in value, occasional in use, informal in discipline, manually executed, and undocumented, then we have revealed a possible inconsistency. There may be rational reasons explaining and justifying why core processes to a business strategy are managed this way. If acceptable, then they should be noted as comments in the business process portfolio. If not, the business process inventory helped reveal a critical area in need of alignment and improvement.

The following describes each evaluation criterion in detail, followed by options for what steps should be taken next for the evaluated process, and prescribes how to analyze your findings to draw proper conclusions.

Evaluation Dimensions

1. VALUE: What *value* does the process afford the organization? (Secondary, low, not-used processes, and most outsourced processes are noncore.) Answer choices include:

   a. *Core:* Core processes are those your organization deems critical to the creation and delivery of customer and shareholder value, and that enable some form of competitive advantage. Core processes can be operating, support, managerial, or control processes. They are not a class or type of process, but a priority.

   b. *Secondary:* Secondary processes are noncore, meaning they do not directly create or deliver value. However, they may (1) enable competitive advantage; (2) contribute to the execution of operating, support, and management processes; or (3) be specialized or helpful to a business function or group.

   c. *Low:* Low-value processes are noncore and used to perform some esoteric function. They may be necessary under certain circumstances, or their purpose is unclear to stakeholders. They are the "We have always done it this way" processes that may create more cost and risk than value.

   d. *Outsourced:* Secondary or low-value processes executed by a third-party business process outsourcer (BPO).

   e. *Not Used:* Processes listed in a reference model but are unused should be scrutinized to determine the reasons why. If the reasons are explanatory and justified, then no further evaluation is required. However, if these processes are typical to an industry, mandated by regulation, or used by competitors to create value or advantage, then they require further analysis.

   f. *Not Applicable:* These are processes listed in a reference model that have no relevance within the industry or organization.

2. TYPE: For each process or activity, determine the asset type. Answer choices include:

    a. *Operating:* Operating processes are directly responsible for adding, creating, or delivering value for which customers are willing to pay.

    b. *Support:* Support processes do not directly create or add value but are necessary to facilitate or assist the execution of operating or management processes.

    c. *Management:* Management processes provide the means to measure and control quality and ensure the desired performance outcomes. They help make decisions, control variance, and resolve problems.

    d. *Exception:* Exception control processes correct for known and anticipated events or anomalies.

    e. *Resolution:* Resolution control processes correct for unknown and unanticipated events or anomalies, or guide the response to sudden opportunity.

3. USE: For each category, group, process, and activity determine its use. How frequently is the process used? Answer choices include:

    a. *Routine* processes are used in day-to-day operations.

    b. *Periodic* processes execute on a scheduled timetable.

    c. *Occasional* processes execute when circumstances require.

    d. *Unknown* requires clarification.

    e. *New process* is required for a strategic initiative.

4. COMPLEXITY: Determine the complexity of the process. To how many decisions or business rules is the process subject? (Refer to "Dealing with Complexity" later in this chapter to learn more.) This question is important, because it is used to prioritize improvement projects. Answer choices include:

    a. *Simple* = Task-oriented procedure with few decisions or rules.

    b. *Low* = Workflow-oriented procedure with several decisions and rules.

    c. *Moderate* = Workflow-oriented process with (potentially) dozens of decisions and rules.

    d. *Complex* = Dynamic process with dozens to hundreds of decisions and rules.

    e. *Highly complex* = Expert system with hundreds to thousands of decisions and rules.

5. DISCIPLINE: Determine the discipline used to design and manage the process. Answer choices include:

  a. *Formal:* Structured processes systematically designed and rede-signed at scheduled intervals; using process mapping, modeling, or business process analysis (BPA) techniques and tools. Their performance measures are consistently tracked and managed. When anomalies occur, corrective action is taken, and the findings are fed back into the process design and performance tracking systems.

  b. *Informal:* Structured processes manually designed and infrequently redesigned. If design tools are used, they are likely to be static process mapping tools such as whiteboards or simple diagramming software. Performance measures are occasionally tracked and managed, or not at all. When anomalies occur, corrective action is taken, usually in the form of a manual workaround, and findings are seldom fed back into its redesign.

  c. *Rely on third party:* The design, management, and execution of the process is outsourced to a BPO service provider. Your organization has little to no input.

6. AUTOMATION: Determine the state of automation. Answer choices include:

  a. *Manual:* Manual processes are executed solely by the workforce without use of information technology. Input and output are exchanged through structured stakeholder collaboration using direct interaction or paper-based exchanges.

  b. *Semi-automated:* Semi-automated processes are executed using a combination of technology and stakeholder collaboration. Input and output are exchanged directly with other business applications, information systems, other forms of automated technology, stakeholders with access to automated systems, or paper-based exchanges among stakeholders, business functions, or groups.

  c. *Fully automated:* Fully automated processes are executed solely by technology. Input and output are exchanged directly among business applications, information systems, or other forms of automated technology. They require no workforce interaction unless a control process requires interaction to manage exception or resolution efforts.

  d. *Rely on third party:* The design, management, and execution of the process is outsourced to a BPO service provider. Your organization may initiate the process through some form of trigger or data exchange, but it has little to no influence on its execution or performance.

7. DOCUMENTATION: Determine the status and quality of how well the process is documented. Answer choices include:

   a. *Detailed:* Detailed process documentation includes descriptions of the process and composite activities and tasks, input and output, key performance indicators, business rules, control processes, maps workflow, and simulation results from modeling tests. Identifies process owners, constituent business functions, groups, and stakeholders. Lists resources required for execution, such as IT systems and business applications. Refers to and defines the procedures for creating training documentation and collateral.

   b. *Satisfactory:* Process owners and stakeholders know process documentation shortcomings (as compared to detailed process documentation) but see no current need to update or address as part of a process improvement project.

   c. *Unsatisfactory:* Process owners and stakeholders believe the documentation is inadequate and advise action to be taken to update or address as part of an improvement project.

   d. *Undocumented:* Requires further evaluation to determine reasons why, whether this is acceptable, or if remedy is required via a process improvement project.

8. TRAINING: Note the state and quality of the training available for the category, group, process, or activity. Answer choices include:

   a. *Sufficient* means the quality of training successfully educates the workforce of what is required.

   b. *Insufficient* means that the quality of training does not educate the workforce as to what is required, creates confusion, consumes too much time, or is otherwise outdated.

   c. *Not available* means that no training exists.

   d. *Not necessary* means that the complexity is either simple or low, negating the need for formal training, or is highly complex, whereupon training is impractical.

   e. *Rely on third party* means the training is outsourced and is sufficient.

9. EFFECTIVENESS: Determine the relative effectiveness of the process as it executes its activities and tasks and the degree to which it

contributes to desired performance measures and outcomes. Answer choices include:

a. *Very Effective* (merits a rating of 9–10 on a scale from 0 to 10, 10 being highest) means the process consistently performs in all aspects of execution, performance, and outcomes, and creates competitive advantage.

b. *Effective* (merits a rating of 6–7–8 on a scale from 0 to 10, 10 being highest) means the process executes reliably with little to no adverse effects on performance measures and outcomes.

c. *Unremarkable/Adequate* (merits a rating of 5 on a scale from 0 to 10, 10 being highest) means process execution is usually reliable and adverse effects on performance measures and outcomes are frustrating but manageable.

d. *Not Very Effective* (merits a rating of 2–3–4 on a scale from 0 to 10, 10 being highest) means the process does not execute reliably and adverse effects on performance measures and outcomes are unacceptable.

e. *Not At All Effective* (merits a rating of 0–1 on a scale from 0 to 10, 10 being highest) means the process is inconsistent or unpredictable in all aspects of execution, performance, and outcomes, and creates competitive disadvantage.

10. EFFICIENCY: Determine the relative efficiency of how well the process performs and how it makes use of or consumes time, resources, and costs. Answer choices include:

a. *Very Efficient* (merits a rating of 9–10 on a scale from 0 to 10, 10 being highest) means the process consistently conserves time, resources, and costs during execution and creates competitive advantage.

b. *Efficient* (merits a rating of 6–7–8 on a scale from 0 to 10, 10 being highest) means the process reliably manages time, resources, and costs.

c. *Unremarkable/Adequate* (merits a rating of 5 on a scale from 0 to 10, 10 being highest) means the process usually consumes time, resources, and costs as expected; overages are frustrating but manageable.

d. *Not Very Efficient* (merits a rating of 2–3–4 on a scale from 0 to 10, 10 being highest) means the process frequently consumes more time, resources, and cost than expected, and its execution and performance are unacceptable.

e. *Not At All Efficient* (merits a rating of 0–1 on a scale from 0 to 10, 10 being highest) means the process always or unpredictably consumes more time, resources, and costs than is expected, and creates competitive disadvantage.

Next Steps

- ACTION: Determine what action is to be taken with this process. Answer choices include:
  - *Improve* means to initiate a business process improvement project.
  - *Consolidate* means to combine like or redundant processes.
  - *Decommission* means that the process is irrelevant, is no longer supported by the organization, and steps should be taken to decommit or redeploy resources that support or enable it.
  - *Benchmark* means to initiate an industry comparison of process using a third-party benchmarking service.
  - *Re-evaluate* means that additional details are required to accurately evaluate the process.
  - *Design* means to plan, map, model, and simulate a new process.
  - *Outsource* means to initiate an evaluation of third-party BPO firms to execute this process.
  - *Insource* means to cease use of a third-party BPO for this process and bring it back in-house.
  - *None* means no action is required at the time of evaluation.
- TIMING: What *timing* should be specified if action is required? When should it occur? Answer choices include (revise these time frames as you see fit):
  - *Immediately* means right now.
  - *Near-term* generally means within one or two quarters or sometime within 180 days.
  - *Long-term* generally means greater than 180 days but within 1 year.
  - *Unspecified* means that the matter is to be addressed again in the next inventory exercise.

Analyzing Inventoried Processes

A business process inventory and evaluation exercise represents a qualitative assessment by process owners and stakeholders. The evaluation should identify the following processes:

- Those critical to the operations of the organization, and those that are not
- Those that are managed well, and those that are not
- Those that consume resources wastefully requiring them to be streamlined, consolidated, or eliminated
- Those that should be optimized (or at least improved) to support strategic objectives and performance requirements of the organization

Subsequent analysis of your evaluation answers should reveal inaccurate, incomplete, or conflicting responses and ensure that the reality of process structure and quality is in fact being exposed. The following analytical procedure will help you with such revelations, to draw conclusions, and determine next steps.

1. VALUE: Begin by analyzing the processes whose value is classified as core, followed by secondary, low, and outsourced processes. Alternatively, you may begin by analyzing the core processes that were evaluated as requiring immediate action. When complete, analyze the remaining noncore processes. Prioritize as you see fit. Not-applicable processes can be skipped.
   a. Please note that processes initially evaluated as "Not Used" should be re-evaluated at a later time to determine whether other industry rivals are using them to create competitive advantage. Indeed, your organization may not use all the processes identified in the reference model you choose. Some are industry-specific and simply not applicable. Others may focus on service-oriented industries (such as finance and insurance) and not apply to product-oriented industries (such as agriculture or aerospace) and vice versa. However, some processes capable of adding customer or shareholder value may have been overlooked by your organization. Your analysis should give you pause to step back and ask, "Why? Why are these processes not used?" The processes your organization deems unnecessary may be used by your

competitors to create differentiation and advantage. Re-evaluate these processes. Are they common industry processes? Do competitors make use of them? If so, do they create competitive advantage? Is your organization's competitive differentiation or advantage at stake or at risk? If the reasons why these processes are unused are justifiable, then no further evaluation is required. However, if these processes are typical to an industry, mandated by regulation, used by competitors to create value or advantage, or you do not know why, then they require further analysis.

2. TYPE: Note the type of each. Core processes are commonly classified by most organizations as operating processes. In many organizations operating processes are directly responsible for creating and delivering customer value. If your team has selected a support or management process as core, then confirm this assessment. It could be an error, it may reflect typical behavior within your industry, or it might be the source of unique competitive advantage. Discuss this further to determine the case. If this process is indeed a core support or core management process, consider how best to exploit it by flagging it for improvement, benchmarking, or both.

   a. Few organizations will identify an existing process as an exception control or resolution control. This is because control processes (as discussed earlier) are uncommon or take a back seat in many BPM strategies. Typically, controls are embedded in operating or support process designs where they can be overlooked. This prevents them from being scrutinized uniquely with rigor, thus they rarely are singled out in a business process inventory exercise. As you begin to understand the quality (or lack thereof) of your BPM efforts the presence or absence of exception and resolution control processes for other core processes will become obvious. Relevant business process owners should note whether sufficient control processes are in place for each of their core processes and call for their design.

3. USE: Note the use of each. Core processes are typically used routinely or periodically. Those classified as occasional or unknown should be discussed to determine why. Reassess the process, or agree upon the finding, and record its rationale in your business process portfolio.

4. COMPLEXITY: Note the complexity of the process (refer to the discussion "Dealing with Complexity" later in this chapter). Many core

processes are moderate, complex, or highly complex. Simple or low complexity processes are usually not core to an operation, but they can be. These answers may require clarification or justification to determine the legitimacy of the evaluation answer.

5. DISCIPLINE: Note the management discipline for each. Core processes create and deliver customer value or enable competitive advantage in some way. They are a priority and should be managed with formal discipline. If the process was evaluated as informal, then perhaps it is not a core process. Consider re-evaluating it or justifying why it is managed informally. Otherwise, flag it for requiring improvement.

   a. Core processes may be outsourced to a third-party BPO to enable competitive advantage of some sort, usually to exploit economies of scale, cost advantages, or when time to market is an issue. For example, product-centric organizations frequently outsource manufacturing of components, subassemblies, or even entire products, as is common with many consumer electronics companies. These relationships must be closely monitored to ensure quality and timely performance from the BPO; in these circumstances, your team should evaluate the core process as being managed as formal. If there is little discipline in managing the BPO relationship (meaning a core outsourced process was evaluated to be informal), then consider re-evaluating the process or flag it for some form of action.

6. AUTOMATION: Note the automation of each. Core processes are typically semi-automated; several may be fully automated. Core processes may be executed manually but with good reason that requires justification. Usually this means the process should be targeted for improvement (to be automated in some way) or other action.

7. DOCUMENTATION: Note how well each is documented. The quality of documentation for core processes should be detailed or at least satisfactory. Documentation plays a valuable role in ongoing management and improvement of processes. High-quality documentation also improves the outcomes from workforce training, process, and IT systems design. Core processes assessed as unsatisfactory or undocumented should be flagged for improvement. Otherwise, agree upon the finding and record the rationale in your portfolio as to why it is unnecessary. Possible exceptions include "highly complex" processes, but even then, high-level documentation and models should be available and evaluated as satisfactory.

8. TRAINING: Note the quality and availability of training. It is common to have well-established training programs in place for moderate to complex processes. Moderate or complex processes, evaluated as insufficient or not available training, may execute or perform poorly. Outcome measures and quality can be adversely affected.

9. EFFECTIVENESS: Note the perceived effectiveness. Core processes should be very effective with relative rankings for each as close to 10 as practical. Any core process rated as unremarkable/adequate or less should be further assessed and flagged for improvement. Otherwise, agree upon the finding and record the rationale in the portfolio as to why this is unnecessary.

10. EFFICIENCY: Note the perceived efficiency. Core processes should be highly efficient with relative rankings for each as close to 10 as practical. Any core process rated as unremarkable/adequate or less should be further assessed and flagged for improvement. Otherwise, here too, agree upon the finding and record the rationale in the portfolio as to why this is unnecessary.

The action recommended depends upon the answers above. All core processes should be periodically reviewed and managed within a continuous process improvement program. Therefore, they should be scheduled for periodic re-evaluation, benchmarking, or improvement. Noncore processes ranking as low in value, unsatisfactory, or undocumented with low effectiveness and efficiency evaluations, should be flagged for improvement (streamlining them, if necessary), decommissioning, consolidation, or elimination. Organizations seeking competitive advantage should also consider benchmarking all core processes, or at least as many core operating processes used routinely that are feasible and practical. Otherwise, agree upon the finding, and record the rationale in the portfolio as to why it is unnecessary. Benchmarking processes reveal weaknesses and strengths. They can help you determine how best to differentiate business strategy, realign resources, and guide investments to create competitive advantage.

- *Timing:* When should action be taken? Note inconsistency. For example, a core process executing manually and flagged for improvement, whose timing is unspecified, should be re-evaluated or justified and noted in the portfolio.

- *Comments:* Finally, ask the participants of the inventory and evaluation exercise to comment on the following:
  - Do the processes defined as core effectively support your business strategy?
  - Do they enable a competitive and efficient operating model?
  - If not, what and where are the disconnects?

Record any findings, rationale, or justifications for each evaluation as required, and note them in your business process portfolio.

A business process inventory and evaluation exercise should be a regularly scheduled event as part of your organization's strategic planning process. Doing so establishes a process life-cycle management technique and the foundation for a continuous process improvement program.

Classifying, evaluating, and documenting your business processes in a business process portfolio are critical first steps in establishing a BPM program.

* * *

The next discussion focuses on what is needed to manage process execution to ensure their performance and outcomes are consistent with your organization's chosen business strategy and the performance measures it seeks.

MANAGING PROCESS EXECUTION

Managing process execution requires techniques to measure and control the desired performance and outcomes. Maintaining performance will require automated control processes or the workforce to take action when results begin to vary. In either case, information about performance and variance from desired measures and outcomes must be made available as the process executes. This will require a means to manage events that affect execution as they occur.

Event management helps control variance and, as promised earlier, is discussed shortly. But before variance can be managed it must be detected. You must first define the key measures needed, assign target values to these measures, and establish the thresholds of tolerable variance. Maintaining control requires business processes to be designed so they can track the key measures, targets, and variance, and enable automated control processes or the workforce to know the following:

- When something happens that requires action
- When something doesn't happen that requires action
- When patterns of process behavior, performance, or outcome measures begin to change so proactive responses can be made
- How to solve expected variances or anomalies (the "Oh, here we go again!" opportunities or problems)
- How to collaborate to resolve variances and anomalies out of the ordinary (the "Didn't see that coming! What do we do now?" opportunities or problems)
- How to organize dynamically, make commitments across the organization, and track their execution reliably

This requires organizations to establish a performance measurement system and then describe techniques to make corrections when necessary.

Performance Measurement

Business strategy and strategic objectives must be translated into a performance measurement system that guides workforce behavior and process design. Critical to success is defining the necessary and relevant measures to track and manage. On the importance of doing so, Kaplan and Norton (1996, p. 147) in *The Balanced Scorecard* offer this:

> The objective of any measurement system should be to motivate all managers and employees to implement successfully the business unit's strategy. Those companies that can translate their strategy into their measurement system are far better able to execute their strategy because they can communicate their objectives and their targets. This communication focuses managers and employees on the critical drivers, enabling them to align investments, initiatives and actions with accomplishing strategic goals. Thus, a successful Balanced Scorecard is one that communicates a strategy through an integrated set of financial and non-financial measurement.

In Chapter 3 I discussed the four perspectives model that describes Kaplan and Norton's balanced scorecard where they emphasized the importance of two types of performance measures:

- *Outcome measures* that are common to most strategies, such as financial ratios and market share attainment
- *Performance drivers* that are unique to a particular strategy, such as product durability and reliability measures, or economies of scale that enable cost leadership

A good performance measurement system, as Kaplan and Norton point out, ". . . therefore includes a mix of core outcome measures common to most strategies, and performance drivers that reflect the uniqueness of a particular strategy" (1996, p. 150). A balanced scorecard represents a means to craft such a mix of measures from the customer perspective, internal business process perspective, and learning and growth perspective, as well as the financial perspective. Figure 6.1 illustrates an example of a balanced scorecard demonstrating these relationships.

I call attention to this because many leaders and managers unwittingly underestimate, overlook, or take for granted the importance of selecting the correct performance measures to manage their chosen business strategy.

Strategic Objectives	Strategic Measurements	
	(Lag Indicators)	(Lead Indicators)
Financial F1 - Improve Returns F2 - Broaden Revenue Mix F3 - Reduce Cost Structure	Return-on-Investment Revenue Growth Cost Change	Revenue Mix

Customer
C1 - Increase Customer
    Satisfaction with Our Products
    and People
C2 - Increase Satisfaction "After the Sale"
	Share of Segment
	
	Customer Retention
		Depth of Relationship
		
		Satisfaction Survey

Internal I1 - Understand Our Customers I2 - Create Innovative Products I3 - Cross-Sell Products I4 - Shift Customers to Cost-Effective Channels I5 - Minimize Operational Problems I6 - Responsive Services	New Product Revenue Cross-Sell Ratio Channel Mix Change Service Error Rate Request Fulfillment Time	Product Development Cycle Hours with Customers
Learning L1 - Develop Strategic Skills L2 - Provide Strategic Information L3 - Align Personal Goals	 Employee Satisfaction Revenue per Employee	Strategic Job Coverage Ratio Strategic Information Availability Ratio Personal Goal Alignment (%)

FIGURE 6.1
Kaplan and Norton's balanced scorecard. (From Kaplan, R.S., and Norton, D.P., *The Balanced Scorecard*, Harvard Business School Press, Boston, MA, 1996, pp. 155, 157. With permission.)

Selecting Key Performance Indicators

For each process, organizations must select and execute against a set of key performance indicators. The KPI set should be carefully designed to include a mix of outcome measures and performance drivers necessary to monitor strategic achievement. The structure of the set should include KPIs that measure:

- Performance specific to each scorecard perspective
  - Financial
  - Internal business process
  - Customer
  - Learning and growth
- Factors critical to cost, quality, and schedule
  - The priority of these factors depends on the strategy chosen. For example, a business strategy that calls for product leadership is likely to emphasize KPIs measuring quality, closely followed by schedule, and then cost. Conversely, a business strategy calling for cost advantage may emphasize KPIs measuring cost control, closely followed by quality, then schedule.
- Short- and long-term objectives
  - There should be a careful balance of short- and long-term objectives to ensure plans remain on track. Properly selected and sequenced short-term KPIs can aggregate to long-term results. However, the two must be aligned. For example, a long-term goal of low-cost leadership should be supported by successive short-term goals to control costs. If short-term KPIs focus elsewhere, say on maintaining product quality, the long-term cost leadership goal may not be realized. In this example, a strategic initiative specifically designed to drive cost leadership over the long term must be implemented. It then must be decomposed into a sequence of short-term KPIs that track the gradual progress toward the desired long-term cost measure while maintaining current quality standards as a secondary dimension of value.
- Leading and lagging indicators.
  - Leading examples include sales backorders, volume of outstanding valid price quotes and proposals, number of extended warranties, commodities pricing, and working capital availability. Lagging examples include revenue measures, support costs, and

customer satisfaction. Here, too, a balance must be struck. Too much emphasis on lagging indicators may prohibit organizations from making rapid responses, or proactive corrections based on recent events. Too much emphasis on leading indicators may fail to sense major shifts or trends in cyclical or seasonal patterns.

Critical to competitive strategy and execution is identifying and controlling specific KPIs that measure unique performance drivers. These are measures specific to your strategy and determine how effectively (as compared to competitors) your organization delivers unique value to customers. Organizations that track performance measures in this way can create considerable competitive advantage.

From these perspectives, thousands of measures can be tracked. But measuring too many can be counterproductive, confusing the workforce and making it impractical to implement in IT systems. Too few can be incomplete and misleading. Tracking the wrong measures can be misguided. A properly balanced KPI set is required to be effective. It is best practice to keep the size of the set limited to the smallest number of KPIs necessary to sufficiently and effectively track and manage process performance and quality of outcomes. Many industry leaders select five to seven KPIs to monitor ongoing processes and operations. That number can contract for simple processes and expand for processes that are more complex.*

Figure 6.2 helps to explain how best to structure a KPI set by illustrating the relationships among the various types of measures. Each KPI relates to a scorecard measure from one or more of the four perspectives (financial, internal, customer, learning) and addresses the other measures stated above. When selecting specific KPIs, consider the following general rules to help get the results you seek.

General Rules about Selecting and Crafting KPIs

- The KPI's name should, by-and-large, be self-explanatory, describing what it measures and values.
- KPIs should be easy to explain and understand, well documented, and as such standardized to eliminate multiple definitions, ambiguity, or confusion.

---

* Problem solving and strategic planning will require sophisticated details; for these purposes, any or all KPIs should be analyzed at will to draw the necessary conclusions.

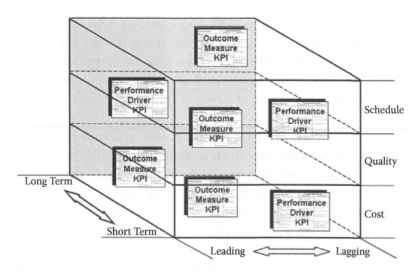

FIGURE 6.2
Illustration of a KPI set for a business process.

- Highly complex KPIs with many variables or open for interpretation make for poor KPI definitions and structure. For example, when "total costs" are called for in the KPI; the word "total" requires a specific definition and should be accompanied by a unique formula for its calculation.
- KPIs must be quantifiable.
  - Generalities as in "We need to speed up sales cycles!" and anecdotal observations such as "Customer calls seem to be getting longer," fail to indicate impact or instill any sense of urgency. Measurable results, when compared to thresholds for variance can define with certainty the degree to which effort, correction, adjustment, or change is required.
- KPIs must comply with the appropriate and relevant mathematical calculations and interpretations. For example, when variables used to calculate a KPI (let's say, speed) use different systems of measure (metric vs. English), a probe crashes rather than lands on Mars.
- KPIs can be long established or newly created for unique purpose. Indeed, new KPIs that measure performance drivers unique to a business strategy are necessary and encouraged to enable and sustain competitive advantage.
- To be effective, KPIs should measure performance that is within the span of control of the process and not be affected by events outside

the process. For example, the KPI "on-time departure," an outcome measure for a commercial aircraft, has a span of control that includes security, check-in, cargo loading, boarding processes, and flight checks. Even if all function smoothly, the outcome can be jeopardized by external factors such as inclement weather or volcanic ash. In this case, a similar KPI that measures performance within a span of control could be defined as "on-time departure in lieu of climatic conditions."

- • External events will be unavoidable; however, the point here is that selecting too many KPIs that require you to filter, evaluate, or explain away external events can be counterproductive. Any such reconciliation process consumes effort, diminishes the effect of the KPIs, and decreases management's ability to control and adjust the process.

- Process KPIs are usually not the same as, and should be distinguished from, an organizational goal or strategic objective. KPIs are a subset or part of a strategic initiative. Strategic objectives and organizational goals usually depend upon the performance of multiple strategic initiatives and processes.

- When the quality of process performance or outcome varies as measured by a KPI, the adjustment or correction should result in improved performance and outcomes, not simply to improve the value of the measurement.

- • Sometimes managers and stakeholders attempt to improve measurements without affecting quality or outcome. For example, when considering the remedies for an increase in the average time a customer is on a call with a CSR, a manager may attempt to shorten the call time (to bring the KPI back within compliance thresholds) by advising CSRs to "quick-kick" the call, or "side-step" some checklist questions, or to talk faster, or to hurry the customer, and the like. These tactics may bring the KPI back within threshold limits, but they also may diminish the customer's perception of value, thus affecting or potentially defeating other KPIs that measure customer satisfaction. Other remedies must be sought that maintain integrity of overall quality without adversely affecting related KPIs.

- KPIs must reflect the measurement sought, meaning the calculation accurately represents the data or variables that construct the performance or outcome measure.

This last bullet calls to attention the technical aspects of KPI selection and requires further explanation.

The data necessary to track such measures must be available and accessible as part of the existing information infrastructure, or capable of being accessible at a reasonable or justifiable cost. For example, a KPI measuring customer satisfaction (an outcome measure):

% of orders scheduled to customer request date

must be calculated using accurate order data including customer request dates and be compared with accurate actual customer receipt dates, not shipping dates. Shipping dates do not equal receiving dates due to potential delays in transportation or other such factors, or because the customer said so! The quality of this KPI is dependent upon the methods and techniques used to capture the customer receipt data. The data may or may not be available, and the accuracy may vary by customer, therefore potentially rendering the KPI inaccurate and useless in measuring overall customer satisfaction.

A solution would be to modify the data capture process and techniques, if economically justifiable. (Data capture can be challenging and expensive depending upon where the data exist if at all, and their format and other integration factors.) Alternatively, you could reassess the importance and need for the KPI, perhaps substituting it with another, or redefine the KPI to reflect the data captured and measured. This example reflects many of the challenges associated with accurately measuring KPIs. You need to be aware of such challenges to avoid or resolve them when you select KPI sets.

With a KPI set defined for your business strategy your next challenge is to control performance within desired thresholds. Measuring performance and outcomes has limited value if they cannot be corrected when they vary. This is accomplished through thoughtful process designs that track and measure your KPI set and can then apply various controls when events occur or when performance begins to vary. This leads us to our next discussion: how do we know when things are going wrong?

Measuring Variance

The essence of any KPI is the measure it tracks. But measurement without comparison to a desired outcome or analysis of variation over time fails to exploit its intrinsic knowledge fully. These are the roles of business rules: to know that something is happening as desired or know when something is changing that is not desired by comparing it to a target, a range, or over time. They define how organizations sense-and-respond to events and change.

In most, but not all endeavors, 100% reliability and accuracy are impractical. For these, we define degrees of variance that are acceptable given what we are trying to do. Some organizations maintain tight but attainable quality standards and become industry leaders built to last. Other organizations assign variance thresholds arbitrarily or without adequate forethought that, consequently, can diminish the perception of their quality and brand. An example of this is when a car manufacturer fails to observe an increasing trend in reports of car accidents caused by "unexpected acceleration."

Customer perceptions, shareholder expectations, competitive threats, and, indeed, governments exert constant pressure on organizations to engage in more thorough analysis to determine the least possible variance from a business rule in any performance measure. The benefits of such efforts contribute directly to customer and shareholder value, help enable competitive advantages, keep regulatory bodies at arm's length, and, indeed, protect an organization's strategic objectives.

The value assigned to KPIs and business rules should be based on a mix of top-down, bottom-up, and fundamental analysis of the factors affecting it. Top-down influences come from leadership and management teams who derive business rule targets necessary to support strategic objectives or to raise the bar, hoping to establish a new quality or performance standard. Bottom-up influence comes from process owners and stakeholders who help create and maintain steady-state processes from which they derive thresholds of business rule variance based on historic and current performance. Both should be based on reasoned analysis that together expose the reality of how things are done, concur on what must be done, and conclude realistic targets guided within narrow but achievable variance thresholds.

This is best exemplified by organizations successfully practicing Six Sigma. The combination of committed, top-down leadership and specialized, bottom-up talent (Black Belts, Green Belts) artfully use managerial and statistical analysis tools to create a design of experiments (DOE) that determines the best way to isolate variables, interpret interactions, and constrain variance that reduces error rates in manufactured goods to within 3.6 defects per million opportunities (DPMO).

Top-down targets are derived through analysis of industry, markets, and competitors, and are necessary to establish business strategy and align resources for execution. Bottom-up variances are often derived through statistical analysis techniques of which there are many, but those most commonly used include trend analysis and benchmarking.

Using Trend Analysis

Understanding the performance of each KPI and the business rules that govern it over time is just as important as measuring and comparing it to its target and threshold values. Long-term trend analysis captures historical data, measuring the frequency and severity of variance. It helps guide reactive responses for correction or improvement, but after the fact, much the same way as structural engineers and insurance actuaries help redefine building codes in earthquake zones.

Short-term trend analysis helps determine when things begin to vary or are about to exceed threshold limits. It helps guide proactive responses to mitigate risk and prevent adverse effects caused by a KPI exceeding its performance threshold, much the same way that a pressure release value prevents boiler explosions.

Trend analysis is also important to help understand whether threshold variances need to be adjusted, on occasion, due to known and expected patterns, for example, when seasonal and cyclical trends signal shifts in the business environment and buying patterns. Under these circumstances, threshold variance can and should be adjusted to reflect prevailing conditions and reality accurately.

However, this does not mean that there is no corresponding proactive or reactive response by an organization when known and expected patterns begin to influence KPI performance. A predictable pattern in one KPI may adversely affect other KPIs, for example, when the revenue from lawnmower sales begins to decline in late summer in New England. This is an anticipated event. The revenue from lawnmower sales KPI should be adjusted downward accordingly. Nevertheless, revenue (a key outcome measure) is declining. The proactive response is to begin selling snow blowers. A new KPI, revenues from snow blower sales, begins to be tracked. Here, business strategy reacts to trend analysis, structuring a combination, or set, of KPIs to maintain desired performance outcome: sustained revenue.

Sometimes trends are predictable, as our example demonstrates. Other times, trends are less revealing and present more of a challenge. For example, retailers in Florida know with some reliability how to order, and replenish, inventory for the Christmas season, but are uncertain how to do so for hurricane season. Each season reliably comes at the same time every year. Hurricane season starts in June and ends roughly in November. Christmas comes and goes in December. The impact of the Christmas season on consumer buying patterns can be reliably predicted; however, the impact of hurricane season on consumer buying patterns cannot. In the latter example, the retailer must make an educated guess (based on prior, but still unpredictable, hurricane behavior) about what (if any) emergency inventories will be required if a storm, or storms, make landfall. This example introduces the concept of *unpredictable variation* and how to prepare or accommodate for it.

Unpredictable variation is caused by random influences outside the control of the process. Examples include economic conditions, accidents/mishaps, new rivals entering the market, machine failure, supplier bankruptcy, hurricanes and other acts of God, and so on. Although the effect of the unpredictable variation on a process or processes (such as inventory replenishment) is—well—unpredictable at any time, the overall maximum magnitude of this variation can usually be estimated.

In the case of our Florida retailer, the magnitude of variation on the KPIs measuring inventory and customer satisfaction are at issue. Too much inventory pressures carrying costs and margins, whereas too little may lead to dissatisfied customers who flee to competitors. The magnitude of each variation can be estimated based on trend analysis of KPI performance during prior hurricane seasons to expose best- and worst-case scenarios. The decision to maintain or exceed acceptable inventory thresholds then becomes a management call based on the extent of the findings, the retailer's business strategy (cost advantages vs. customer satisfaction/churn), and the type and amount of risk the organization is willing to take as measured by these KPIs. A retailer concerned with customer satisfaction will create a predetermined exception control process to stock up, which is triggered before a hurricane is forecast to make landfall. A retailer concerned with inventory costs may do nothing, or have a similar control process but wait to trigger it when landfall probability exceeds 50%. Each makes his decision based on trend analysis, his business strategy, and his tolerance for risk.

Trend analysis of predictable or unpredictable variation helps establish realistic business rules and variance thresholds for performance measurement. By studying predictable variation, organizations can establish realistic business rules and formulate (in advance) control processes that manage exceptions when performance measures are threatened. By estimating the magnitude of unpredictable variation, organizations can prepare control processes for managing unknown and unanticipated variation using resolution management to contain performance variation and manage risk.

Variation of any degree drives the need for organizations to sense it rapidly and respond accordingly. This requires organizations to sharpen their sense-and-respond instincts (as prescribed in Chapter 4, "How to Adapt") and to have exception and resolution management control processes designed and in place as part of an overall event management capability.

There are, however, costs associated with maintaining tight performance tolerances. Preventing and correcting variation (quality control) requires effort and consumes resources. Being prepared to manage any type of variation (predictable or unpredictable) requires rules of engagement that define how far and to what degree an organization is willing to go to maintain process stability or bring performance variation in line when necessary. Underestimating what is required to maintain performance thresholds runs the risk of constant, and perhaps, intolerable variation. Overestimating what is required can be wasteful and costly. Determining how best to balance the effort leads us to the next common analytic technique: benchmarking.

Using Benchmarking

Benchmarking is a practice used within an industry or market segment to normalize business practices, processes, and performance measures. It facilitates the development of standards against which organizations may compare their operations and performance against peers and competitors.

Benchmarking helps determine how best to accomplish the following:

- Standardize and normalize business processes.
- Select and structure a performance measurement system.
- Define outcome measures (specific KPIs, KPI sets, business rules, and performance thresholds) common to an industry.

- Reveal performance drivers (specific KPIs, KPI sets, business rules, and performance thresholds) unique to a chosen business strategy.

In the context of business process management and improvement, it can reveal weaknesses and strengths, allowing organizations to adjust business strategy and realign resources accordingly. It can determine where to differentiate, thus guiding investment strategy to create competitive advantage.

In the context of business rules and maintaining performance thresholds, benchmarking can help determine how aggressive an organization needs to be to meet or exceed its peers and competitors. It can help organizations understand the degree to which they must prepare to manage variation, and determine what investment is required to keep it within acceptable thresholds.

To help you prepare how best to make quality control investments, consider looking into the benchmarking services associated with reference models discussed earlier (or another reference model of your choosing). However, benchmarking is not a panacea; it, too, has its pitfalls. Here are a few cautionary observations:

- Benchmark measures, themselves, may not accurately reflect reality. The benchmark may define mediocrity as a performance standard. Just because an organization outperforms the industry, does not mean it meets customer or shareholder expectations. Benchmarks themselves must be scrutinized to determine the degree to which they comply with what customers value and what shareholders require.
- Sometimes meeting a benchmark creates a false sense of security. Competitors sensing complacency will seize upon it by trying to increase customer expectations in areas where its rivals have dropped their guard.
- Sometimes benchmarks are assumed to be static. Indeed, some are slow to change, but do not assume they are static; keep current with changing benchmark parameters.
- Avoid using a benchmark exercise as a substitute for proper fundamental research and analysis of value chain design and core process structure. Benchmarks are not intended for this purpose; they are not "value chains in a box."
- Benchmarking should not allow, or create the perception of allowing, anticompetitive practices to develop.

- Sometimes a benchmark exercise becomes an end in itself. If results are satisfactory, the pursuit of performance improvement may stall. The point of benchmarking is not to pass a test but to determine over time where an organization stands against outcome measures common to its competitors (in an effort to beat them), and to determine performance drivers necessary for unique competitive advantage.

Trend analysis and benchmarking represent two common tools to help assign value to KPIs and business rules to measure and manage variation properly, design process controls, and prepare control processes. With a KPI set chosen and business rules designed to govern execution, we are finally prepared to discuss how to manage execution to ensure performance and outcomes are realized and maintained.

Performance Control via Event Management

Effective execution demands that an organization be vigilant regarding anomalies that can affect outcome measures and performance drivers. This requires timely monitoring of process execution, KPI measures, and thresholds, and exposing such data to all relevant information systems and workforce stakeholders, alerting them when an event occurs. An event is something that:

- Happens or doesn't happen during the execution of a process that can cause performance and outcomes to vary and requires action
- May or may not happen because patterns of process behavior, performance, or outcome measures begin to vary, requiring proactive response

Event management is a form (or subset) of risk management and a managerial discipline that helps leaders and management teams think broadly, enabling them to address all that is required to manage risk, execution, and performance to prevent or contain adverse effects of variance on an organization's business strategy and outcomes. It is also a superset of a technology-driven approach to performance control known as business activity monitoring (BAM). BAM is a means to provide real-time visibility into business activities, operations, and transactions of a departmental or cross-functional business process as they execute. In general, BAM can be considered a subset of event management because in most instances its focus is on the technology used to enable it. BAM uses a process-centric

IT architecture coupled with business intelligence dashboards (graphical user interface software) to expose performance measures to relevant process owners and stakeholders.*

As compared to BAM, event management is more comprehensive, addressing the issues of workforce behavior, collaborative objectives, and exception and resolution management that may or may not be supported or enabled by technology. Indeed, when technology fails, the workforce must take up the slack. Event management includes techniques to empower and motivate the workforce and align process stakeholders with the control processes and information resources needed to help maintain control, especially when technology fails. How events are managed will depend upon whether they are known or anticipated, or unknown or unanticipated. Each requires specific forms of management.

Exception Management and Resolution Management

Event management begins with an event. Anticipated and known events that cause a process to vary, or place performance measures at risk, are *exceptions*; managing them is called *exception management*. Unanticipated or unknown events that cause a process to vary, or place performance measures at risk, require unique resolution; managing them is called *resolution management*.

At this point in our discussion it is important to note that "exception management" and "resolution management" should not be confused with "exception control processes" and "resolution control processes" discussed earlier. An exception control process prescribes specific activities to control a single known or anticipated event. A resolution control process prescribes the rules of engagement and commitment management protocol to control a single unknown or unanticipated event, or events within a specified process category, group, or cross-functional domain such as in CRM. Exception and resolution management are forms of event management that address broadly all that is required including workforce behavior (empowerment and motivation via collaborative objectives), business policies and rules, and the IT infrastructure necessary to consistently manage multiple events to prevent the adverse effects of variance, with respect to the entire organization.

---

* Process-centric IT architecture is discussed a bit further in Chapter 7.

Exception management is somewhat predictable and can prescribe predetermined exception control processes, workforce behavior, collaboration, and escalation procedures for each known or anticipated event.

Resolution management (sometimes referred to as "case management") is more dynamic. The designs of resolution control processes require considerable flexibility. When an unknown or unanticipated event is sensed, the workforce must be empowered and motivated first to interpret the event and its implications, after which other collaborative and escalation efforts can occur, making most resolution management efforts unpredictable until they begin to unfold. Therefore, resolution management requires sense-and-respond techniques (as noted in Chapter 4) that call upon key members of the workforce to exploit a modular organization to do the following:

- Coordinate the collaboration of multiple functional groups, subject matter experts, and stakeholders accessing one or more internal and external information systems.
- Manage resolution attempts within established boundaries and rules of engagement.
- Define escalation policies that prescribe how and when to involve higher levels of management.
- Record actions taken and commitments made, and hold accountable and responsible the stakeholders involved in managing resolution responses toward an acceptable outcome.

Planning for event management requires an organization to carefully choreograph the relationship between the collaborative efforts of its workforce and the design of its information technology. The objective of such planning is twofold:

- To manage and track the event to proper conclusion
- To prevent any adverse effects of the event before they affect key performance measures

Doing so is not entirely determined by the choreography of a lightning-fast workforce or IT system responses. Rather, it is also predicated upon the KPI set chosen and the threshold values set for certain KPIs.

Earlier, several KPI types were identified, among them were *leading* and *lagging* indicators. Lagging KPIs, such as revenue and expense data or customer satisfaction scores, are revealed ad hoc or in periodic reports from information systems (after the fact where event management cannot prevent or control anomalies within the period being measured). Instead, corrections to lagging indicators must be made in subsequent periods during frequent and iterative strategic planning, organizational governance, and business process reviews. This is the role and purpose of leadership and management and is best executed through a continuous process improvement program.

But leading KPIs, such as quality control measures, process cycle times, and inventory replenishment, need to be exposed continuously or on demand so the workforce or various control processes can manage events before they negatively affect performance for the period being measured. This emphasizes the need to carefully select leading KPIs that are performance drivers unique to strategy and the need to structure information technology to support such measurement and event management.

Enabling Event Management

There are two critical components necessary to enable effective event management:

1. The ability to sense when an event occurs
2. The ability to respond appropriately given the nature of the event

Enabling event management requires:

- Carefully prepared control processes
- A process-centric IT architecture

Events must be sensed by the organization's workforce, through its information technology, or both. The quality of responses to events sensed solely by the workforce (without the need for, or use of, IT systems) is dependent upon the skills and training of individual employees. As discussed in Chapter 5, the workforce needs to be properly empowered and motivated, based on their role or function, to act within prescribed rules of engagement. When they sense a known event (an exception) that threatens performance measures, they engage the appropriate exception control processes. For example, when a physical quality control inspection of machined parts reveals diameters increasing toward threshold limits, this known and anticipated event calls for the operator to execute the following exception control process:

1. Record the variation
2. Alert the shop floor foreman
3. Stop production upon foreman's approval
4. Refer to the production run plan to determine proper calibration
5. Recalibrate the machine
6. Debrief the foreman as to the result of the recalibration
7. Resume production upon foreman's approval
8. Record the recalibration variance and any other steps taken for correction

Enabling such exception control is relatively straightforward. Here, the workforce senses the variance through consistent testing. The IT systems help facilitate the exception control process by exposing information to the workforce (in this case the machine operator referring to the proper calibration information), facilitate any collaboration efforts among stakeholders (between the operator and the foreman), or record and track remedies as called for by the exception control process. Later, management can analyze this and other similar events using trend analysis, benchmarking, or other statistical means to interpret the event data collected and determine whether preventive maintenance or replacement of the machine is required.

Many business processes rely on the workforce and the organization's IT systems for proper execution. The quality and effectiveness of responses to events sensed by IT rely heavily upon its technical capabilities and architecture. Ideally, IT systems should sense events when some performance threshold within a KPI set is at risk. This would trigger an alert to another system or process stakeholder to engage either an exception or resolution control process. Alerts to other systems are examples of fully automated control processes. Alerts to stakeholders who then engage various IT systems for responses are examples of semi-automated control processes.

For example, a laser scan that reveals a manufacturing defect and alerts a system to remove the part from the production line using a carefully timed blast of compressed air, is an example of a fully automated exception control process. The result: quality is controlled and production flow and throughput proceed uninterrupted.

In another example, an e-mail from an electronic data interchange (EDI) system that alerts a procurement officer to a price discrepancy between the

ERP system and an order acknowledgment returned from a supplier is an example of a semi-automated exception control process. The result: the procurement officer contacts the supplier, adjusts the data in the IT systems, and thus remedies the event.

In each case, the event, along with the corresponding corrections, must be recorded so that they can be tracked, managed, and analyzed to ensure performance measures remain within thresholds, and, if not, analyzed to assess how best to prevent or correct them if or when the event occurs again.

In cases when events trigger a KPI threshold, but the IT system has no corresponding control process, it must be smart enough to alert those stakeholders affected, for example, using BAM technology. They then interpret what has happened and engage exception or resolution management efforts as required.

If the events are known and anticipated, they engage the appropriate exception control processes. If no exception control process is prescribed, or the events are unknown and unanticipated, a resolution management must begin. Using the sense-and-respond techniques discussed in Chapter 4, empowered stakeholders take charge. They assemble resources from across the modular organization to execute an adaptive loop process to negotiate and resolve the event.

Resolution management calls for a dynamic and rigorous choreography of information acquisition, dissemination, analysis, and collaboration among those workforce members who are held accountable and responsible for its outcome. These cases require a collection of capabilities and assets managed to elicit sense-and-respond behavior whereby organizations do the following:

1. Manage information in a specific way to support its productive use by key roles (people) in the organization using the adaptive loop, a four-step, iterative process where an event and information about it are sensed and interpreted, enabling decisions to be made and acted upon.

2. Structure its assets and capabilities into a system of modules that can dynamically assemble, making them capable of unique responses. This structure represents a "modular" organization that allows the workforce to seek guidance and assistance from other parts of the organization unencumbered by hierarchical, geographical, or other governing boundaries.

3. Replace top-down, command-and-control management with a governance system that empowers key members of the workforce to make business commitments for specific purposes, within defined bounds, throughout the organization. Here interactions, rather than the actions, of the workforce manage modular capabilities using the commitment management protocol that facilitates a negotiations process among all participants to unknown or unanticipated events, recording the resolution agreed upon and the follow-through enacted. Events that cause empowered stakeholders to seek resolutions outside defined boundaries trigger escalation procedures that solicit input/approval from higher authorities within the organization.

Collectively, these capabilities and assets enable resolution management, and are critical elements of any event management system. Unknown and unanticipated events now have a formal and systematic process to be rapidly sensed, interpreted, decided, and acted upon to prevent—or at least minimize—adverse effects on outcome measures and performance drivers.

In either case (whether to engage exception or resolution management), the IT architecture must be able to expose critical data and information via reporting and analytic tools as necessary, and enable iterative collaboration and communication among stakeholders. It must be able to record, track, and manage the decisions and actions taken to ensure compliance, and assess the overall impact on process performance, outcome measures, and performance drivers. If the event was unknown and unanticipated, the IT systems must be capable of post-mortem analysis to determine how to create fail-safe protections for this now known event. Theses scenarios demonstrate the need for a process-centric IT architecture.

Process-centric IT architecture shares strategic information and assembles unique services dynamically to execute any logical series of activities and tasks across many disparate and distributed systems. It enables organizations to track and manage all the activities and tasks associated with a process and reports against all outcome measures and performance drivers (lagging and leading indicators, long- and short-term measures: as defined in KPI sets) associated with the process. To ensure such outcome measures and performance drivers are achieved, process-centric systems place priority on managing data, making strategic information available to all relevant stakeholders, measuring KPIs, and managing events.

Enabling event management will require your organization to include as part of its strategic planning the guidance offered in this chapter to accomplish the following:

- Define and manage business rules necessary to establish thresholds or conditions that define events.
- Devise techniques and the means to rapidly sense variance from thresholds, or conditions that require responses, using information technology and workforce collaboration processes.
- Craft rules of engagement that govern the boundaries within which relevant stakeholders are empowered to act.
- Establish escalation policies that prescribe how and when to involve higher levels of management.
- Facilitate workforce collaboration by enabling IT systems to record actions taken and commitments made to hold accountable and responsible the stakeholders involved in managing resolution responses toward acceptable outcomes.

All too often organizations invent corrective responses to events on the fly. There is no justifiable reason for reinventing the wheel every time an event requires correction. Organizations with constrained resources may find it difficult to initiate event management techniques or evolve toward a process-centric IT architecture. Nevertheless, the up-front investment is easily justified each time a newly created exception or resolution management technique is applied.

How to enable process-centric IT architecture will be discussed shortly in Chapter 7. However, its design and ability to support event management will require a deeper understanding of the business processes and control processes we are trying to create or improve. Overall, the best way to think this through is to visualize and measure processes.

Improving Execution through Process Modeling, Analysis, and Simulation

Executing successfully requires process design that does the following:

- Structures activities in a logical sequence to create and deliver customer and shareholder value while using resources efficiently
- Encourages and facilitates workforce collaboration

- Includes techniques to measure, control, and manage the desired performance outcomes of business processes using event management and corresponding control processes

It also requires the workforce to fully understand:

- How to properly execute the process in which they are stakeholders
- How to engage exception and resolution management when business process execution varies or outcomes are at risk
- The implications of their actions or inactions on the processes and stakeholders they directly and indirectly affect to help avoid errors

Peter Drucker, the renowned professor and management consultant, would argue that measurement and management go hand in hand. "You can only manage what you can measure" and "What's measured improves" are popular quotes attributed to him. But improvement does not occur solely as a result of measurement. Indeed, improvement comes from creative thought, testing assumptions, imagining extreme scenarios, and measuring these hypothetically to see what happens. It is preferable to use some form of model created in a "learning laboratory" before time, money, and resources are committed.

By inference, one could argue, the quality of management correlates directly to the quality of measurement. The more detailed and accurate a measurement the better its composite variables and outcomes can be managed. Quality management using Six Sigma demonstrates this correlation through its meticulous statistical analysis and experiments designed to determine how best to reduce quality defects to 3.4 per million opportunities (DPMO). Few would argue that measurement and testing are unnecessary practices. The question then becomes how much time, money, and resources do you invest to improve the accuracy of process measurement and analysis so you can manage better. One such area of investment is in the tools used to measure and analyze business processes.

Static media such as whiteboards, simple diagramming software like Visio, and spreadsheets remain the dominant means for process analysis. These tools are helpful and usually adequate for small process analysis teams modeling relatively straightforward or uncomplicated processes. But they lack the means to express and measure innovative options, and fail to precisely test assumptions; and they cannot realistically simulate the execution of a process design. Processes critical to creating customer value, maintaining a competitive edge or that are sufficiently complex are best measured and visualized using more powerful tools specifically designed for modeling and analysis.

Process modeling, analysis, and simulation are techniques that enable organizations to visualize process execution and study how improvement or new designs can affect performance and outcomes prior to spending money and effort based on untested assumptions. It also can help to solve business problems, expose blind spots in strategic plans that overlook the importance of certain resources required for execution, and can reveal potential conflicts among performance measures assigned to various business functions or groups for a given strategy.

It is best accomplished using software tools designed to diagram workflow and measure the economics of process designs. By economics, we mean measuring the resources, costs, and time consumed during the execution of a process. Some of these tools can also enable simulation of the process as it executes demonstrating quantifiable outcomes. Simulation and comparison of various process alternatives will help you select the best design.

Diagramming a process creates a map, or high-level flowchart, that illustrates the various activities, tasks, and relationships of participant functions, departments, or groups associated with the execution of a process. It is used as a starting point to be critical of the efficiency and effectiveness of business process execution. For example, Figure 6.3 visually illustrates the interdependencies of activities and tasks assigned to various stakeholders, alerting them to the cause-and-effect relationships that can impact individual, group, and organizational objectives.

Here, we see two sets of critical relationships that affect order-to-cash (O2C) performance measures: sales relationships with procurement and operations (in black), and operations relationship with finance (in dark gray). A notification delay by operations to sales that a supplier shipment was rejected (signified by the "No" triangle) can affect customer satisfaction measures. Sales needs to be alerted of this so they can recontact the customer, advise her of the issue, and, it is hoped, reset expectations or manage the relationship in some other way. Also, a failure to notify finance of a ship date can affect a collaborative objective to meet an O2C target timeframe, affecting all departments and stakeholders involved. These relationships may seem obvious in this simple example, but they are sometimes difficult to detect in more complex business processes. Awareness helps to prevent such delays. Motivation created through

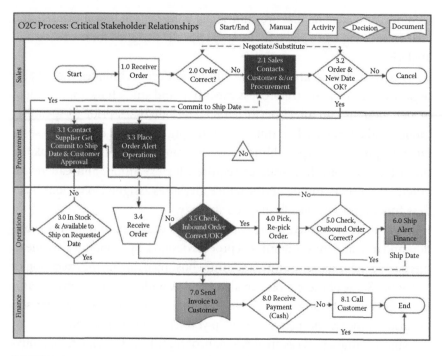

FIGURE 6.3

O2C process map and cause-and-effect stakeholder relationships.

collaborative objectives helps realize the desired performance outcomes of the entire process.

Modeling a process creates a detailed workflow diagram that expands upon a process map. It provides descriptions of subprocesses, activities, and tasks, including all input, output, decisions, and exceptions, as well as measurements of the resources consumed (such as time, labor/FTEs, material, capital, systems, etc.) during the execution of the process. Modeling enables detailed analysis via drill-down examination of processes, subprocesses, and activities, and provides the basis for process simulation. Simulation can test the outcome measures and performance drivers of various process alternatives using what-if scenarios to alter the process design. It offers an efficient means to test assumptions and choose the best alternative.

Unfortunately, most organizations do not understand the value of process modeling and simulation, overlook it, or execute poorly and become frustrated, dismissing further attempts. Usually, this occurs because the leadership and management:

- Think it is too difficult

- Lack adequate understanding of available process modeling and analysis tools
- Take for granted that process execution and organizational behavior are already aligned, and therefore have not considered it a priority

Any effort is "difficult" when we first attempt it or have no knowledge about how to do it. In recent years, process modeling and analysis tools have grown in their sophistication while becoming easier to use. They have come down considerably in price and are affordable to nearly all organizations, regardless of size. Process modeling capabilities are also being embedded in the latest versions of business application software and in more sophisticated enterprise application development or business process management suites.

In many organizations process execution and organizational behavior are frequently detached from each other. Various parts of an organization have diverse views of a business process, and therefore stress the importance of tasks and outcomes within a process differently. You may have heard the term "Throw it over the wall." This refers to a process handoff from one department to another, where the stakeholder has no idea what happens on the "other side of the wall" (the downstream department or stakeholder), nor cares because his task is complete. Process modeling and analysis enable the workforce to visualize relationships, as illustrated in Figure 6.3. When the workforce understands cause-and-effect relationships, and are motivated with incentives earned when collaborative objectives are achieved, they can modify their behavior accordingly to manage process execution, thus improving the consistency of performance outcomes.

Those organizations that have paid proper attention to process modeling and analysis have typically done so within the context of larger strategic enterprise initiatives. Many large organizations have pursued the benefits derived from continuous process and quality improvement programs, such as Six Sigma, TQM, and ISO 9000. These efforts have been rallying points that enable organizations to align business objectives, processes, and organizational behavior to improve efficiencies, productivity, and quality. However, they are costly, resource intensive, and require significant investment in specialized talent. Often referred to as "big bang" efforts, they have been outside the purview of many organizations.

Alternatively, well-run business process management and continuous improvement programs using process modeling and analysis tools can be equally effective as a rallying point for many more organizations, thus facilitating workforce collaboration and process alignment. Process modeling, analysis, and simulation help organizations:

- Create diagrams that model process flow from end-to-end, revealing the activities and tasks used to create and deliver customer and shareholder value, particularly valuable when designing or improving complex cross-functional processes.
- Promote a common understanding across functional groups, demonstrating cause-and-effect relationships and awareness among the workforce of the implications of their actions or inactions on other processes, groups, and stakeholders.
- Analyze process models qualitatively by visual examination, fostering discussion and debate that leads to consensus about how to make improvements.
- Simulate and analyze process models quantitatively by measuring the economics of various process designs, measuring the resources, costs, and time consumed or constrained during execution, and revealing expected performance before implementation.
- Design and analyze exception and resolution control processes to correct variances or anomalies that affect outcome measures or performance drivers.
- Simplify the alignment efforts of business and IT professionals by using process models to document common goals.

Process visualization and simulation are powerful techniques that organizations can use to save time and money before making commitments. It exposes cause-and-effect relationships that often go overlooked and can reveal how the workforce and various IT systems can be aligned to enable efficient execution.*

SELECTING PROCESSES FOR IMPROVEMENT

As discussed earlier, a business process portfolio provides a roadmap that identifies core processes requiring improvement and optimization

---

* See Appendix B to learn how to evaluate business process analysis software.

and noncore processes to be consolidated or eliminated. It categorizes processes that are required to execute business strategy, that are, or may become, problematic, or that must be continuously monitored for quality assurance or regulatory compliance. Generally, there are two reasons why processes are selected for improvement:

1. To solve a problem
2. To execute a strategic initiative (newly created, as part of a continuous quality assurance program or as government regulations require)

The priority given to any process improvement project must be dictated by what is needed to create and deliver customer value, closely followed by shareholder value (increased margins and profits) and other strategic objectives of the organization. However, when forced to choose among several options, other secondary factors will influence your selection. They include:

1. The level of effort required to improve the process
2. The investment returns expected

Common sense dictates selecting processes that have the greatest impact on improving customer value and strategic performance measures while using the least amount of resources. Making this determination may be difficult. It requires careful scoping of candidate processes for improvement to determine their relative complexity and potential for returns.

The discussion that follows demonstrates the obvious and not so obvious logic required for prioritizing and selecting processes for improvement.

Symptomatic versus Strategic Process Improvement

Obvious processes requiring improvement, redesign, or new design are those that solve a problem or help the organization execute its business strategy.

Symptomatic Processes

Processes that affect customer value and are deemed problematic must be dealt with expeditiously, kicking off an immediate analysis and improvement project. It is critical, however, to understand the source of the problem and assess what is required to resolve the problem(s). Fixing things consumes resources or diverts them from other processes. This creates opportunity costs that must also be considered when choosing to initiate an improvement project.

Symptomatic processes are existing business processes whose performance measures vary unacceptably, threatening or exceeding a prescribed performance threshold. They place desired outcomes at risk. It is important to note that variance or errors are usually not a problem, but rather a symptom of a problem that requires corrective action. Symptomatic processes first require analysis to determine the root cause(s). Examples include: when approvals for sales proposals from headquarters exceed a required 48-hour turnaround time, or when successive random product quality checks reveal increasing error rates. Each represents variance, but why the variance occurs is unknown without proper analysis. Sometimes the problem is obvious, such as "The sales VP is on vacation and didn't name a back-up decision-maker/signatory," or "A broken part in the packaging machine intermittently breaks product wrappers." Often the root cause is more difficult to decipher.

Problem solving requires resources with the necessary skills to interpret the cause(s) and implement a solution. The effort expended is usually proportional to the severity of the problem; often the greater the risk, the greater is the effort to fix it. Symptomatic processes whose risks outweigh opportunity costs should be prioritized for improvement.

Sometimes, problems (severe or otherwise) force hasty decisions that overlook opportunity costs. For example, imagine diverting your top salesperson away from a final multimillion dollar contract negotiation to help resolve an erroneous spare-part order worth only a few dollars. Stakeholders charged with problem solving (event management) must be wary of how their resource requests affect the rest of the organization. The resources diverted to solve one problem may create opportunity costs or worse, a cascading effect, creating successive problems elsewhere down the line in the process, system, or organization. When forced to grapple with multiple symptomatic processes, include analysis of potential opportunity costs or cascading effects among the proposed solutions. Select priorities that tackle the biggest problem, with the greatest returns, using the fewest resources, and the lowest opportunity costs or cascading effects.

Strategic Processes

Action plans designed to increase customer and shareholder value are *strategic initiatives* born from an organization's business strategy. Examples include a new product launch, expanding into a new facility, or targeting a new customer segment. They typically require several existing processes to be modified or supplemented, or they may require several new processes to be designed and implemented.

Core processes, and those required of a strategic initiative, are *strategic processes*. Selecting and prioritizing strategic processes for design or redesign must be predicated on their ability to achieve the performance measures and outcomes called for by the strategic initiative. Assumptions about expected results must be measured, simulated, and tested before resources are committed or restructured. This is best accomplished by identifying and classifying the necessary processes using your business process portfolio and then using the process modeling and simulation tools discussed earlier to test assumptions about the resources used, cycle times, and costs incurred during their execution. The simulation results of various process alternatives will help you select the best design necessary to achieve the desired outcomes.

Strategic initiatives typically launch an array of process designs and improvement projects. The processes most typically affected are those that span multiple departments, groups, and stakeholders, such as customer order processing, supply chain operations, or procure-to-pay processes. For example, a new product launch requires manufacturing to gear up; marketing and advertising to develop new campaigns; sales and service professionals to be trained; product catalogues, pricelists, and websites to be updated, and so on. External business-to-business (B2B) processes may also be affected, for example, when new suppliers must be approved and brought under contract; or when partners and distributors need incentive plans to carry and sell the new product, and so on.

Unless otherwise intended, strategic process design and or redesign should not adversely affect other existing strategic initiatives, performance measures, processes, or operations. Strategic processes carry similar cautions of symptomatic processes regarding opportunity costs and cascading effects. However, unlike symptomatic process improvement, which strives to minimize the effects of diverted resources, strategic initiatives usually require resources to be diverted or restructured in some way. Inevitably, this can cause adverse opportunity costs and cascading effects on other processes and parts of the organization. Moreover, in haste, or without proper due diligence, strategic initiatives produce redundant processes. An example of this would be when a division within an organization sets up a completely new order-processing system and website to market and sell the new product. Such redundancy increases operating costs, diminishes margins (shareholder value), and may confuse long-term customers.

Continuous Process Improvement Program

The proper approach to manage the complexity of symptomatic and strategic process improvement is to develop a formal methodology and commitment to continuous process improvement. A continuous process improvement program is a systematic managerial effort put in place to stay ahead of deteriorating process performance and align the resources required for strategic process development while minimizing risk. It coordinates the variety of improvement and development projects by routinely scheduling performance reviews for core processes based on the risk posed by diminishing quality or other implications spawned from new strategic initiatives. Using such an approach, new projects as called for by strategic initiatives can be assessed based on the collective results of expected returns weighed against opportunity costs. Resource conflicts that threaten adverse cascading effects are determined before changes or commitments are made, minimizing their effects.

In addition, a continuous process improvement program periodically schedules reviews of various categories of noncore processes to reassess their value and need. Often, the review and analysis of noncore processes is just as crucial as review and analysis of core processes. It provides a systematic way to eliminate unnecessary effort, freeing resources and lowering overall costs. Deeming processes as "noncore" does not mean they can be ignored. On the contrary, eliminating unvalued or undervalued processes, activities, and tasks is at the heart of all quality management methodologies (such as Total Quality Management, Lean, Six Sigma, et al.) and a crucial objective for any continuous process improvement program. Indeed, resources that become available when freed as a result of consolidating, eliminating, or otherwise decommissioning noncore processes may be able to be redeployed to support the designs or redesigns of core or strategic processes. This helps minimize opportunity costs and helps avoid cascading effects that can result from diverting or restructuring resources elsewhere.

* * *

Next, the selection criteria for process improvement that are less obvious is discussed. When several symptomatic, strategic core and noncore processes have been identified for improvement, they then should be evaluated based on their ability to deliver the greatest returns from the least amount of effort. Here, process complexity is examined.

DEALING WITH COMPLEXITY

Simple versus Complex Processes

Process complexity ranges from simple task-oriented procedures that are subject to very few rules, decisions, or branching paths, to highly complex expert systems subject to thousands of rules, decisions, and branching paths. Examples of simple processes include repetitive assembly tasks during manufacturing operations, or basic administrative tasks in day-to-day office operations. Examples of highly complex processes are how an aerospace engineer designs a new orbiter, or how a scientific researcher analyzes experimental data hoping to discover a new pharmaceutical drug.

At the low end, repetitive task-oriented processes are not likely to require detailed modeling and analysis using BPA tools. These processes have discrete tasks requiring few decisions. Many can be designed through a simple documentation exercise that enumerates and describes each step and action (a.k.a. a step-action chart). An example would be enrolling and initiating a new health club member.

If the process is slightly more complex such that its decisions and rules make a step-action list cumbersome to understand, it may be useful to map it using a simple workflow diagram. This helps visualize the logical sequence of activities and branching decisions while illustrating the interdependencies across participant stakeholders.

At the high end, complex processes are often too dynamic or unpredictable, rendering existing BPA tools inadequate. Highly complex processes are not only influenced by thousands of rules and decisions, but they are likely to be constituent to dynamic and evolving bodies of knowledge, making it impractical for process designers to keep ahead. These environments make detailed process modeling and analysis efforts costly and probably fruitless. Imagine trying to model the processes of the pharmaceutical researcher introduced earlier. The fields of biology and chemistry are dynamic, constantly changing, adding new findings, and discrediting others. Any attempt to model a research process would limit the availability of new knowledge to the process. Trying to capture the true dynamics associated with such research would be overwhelming. In these situations, it is best to hire "experts" and rely upon their collective wisdom, judgment, and learning discipline to afford the innovation and results sought.

Nevertheless, in environments with highly complex processes, it is useful to engage in high-level modeling. High-level modeling benefits participant stakeholders, and the organization at large, by establishing organizational policy, procedure, and protocol, identifying and managing available resources, and calling out critical business rules and boundaries governing the execution of the process.

In the middle are moderately complex processes governed by dozens, or perhaps hundreds of decisions, business rules, and branching paths. In many organizations, they execute the bulk of the work required in critical value-chain domains, such as product and services development, customer relationship management, supply chain operations, or administrative functions such as finance and human resources. Often, they reside in the realm of the knowledge worker or any stakeholder who is a participant in processes requiring the use of IT systems and information to perform his or her role.

Moderately complex processes are well suited to be mapped, modeled, analyzed, and simulated using currently available BPA tools. Figure 6.4 illustrates the practicality of process analysis considering increased degrees of complexity. Achieving consistent performance and competitive advantage may be difficult to sustain without engaging some form of business process analysis and performance improvement initiative. As process complexity increases, the risk of performance and outcome variance also rises. Figure 6.4 also helps demonstrate how various business process improvement projects can be prioritized. But it does not imply that all moderately complex processes can be improved with equal effort. Indeed, the effort necessary to improve processes of equal complexity can vary greatly.

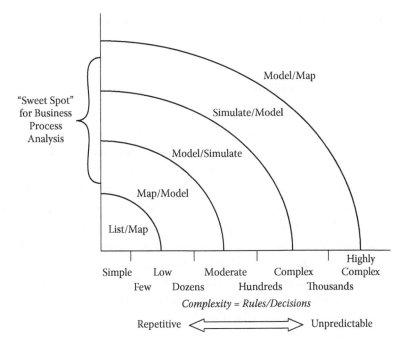

FIGURE 6.4
Process analysis and complexity.

Processes considered for improvement require further evaluation to determine the best returns from the effort. In general, priority should be given to those processes that are:

- Stable: Meaning that there is not likely to be major change in the near tem affecting the new process design or redesign; for example, if new ERP or accounting software is to be implemented within the next 12 months
- Aligned with strategic objectives: Meaning the process is, or affects, a priority, a core process that directly contributes to the creation of customer value, or the realization of shareholder value (margins and profits)
- Realistic and doable: Meaning the process improvement project can be initiated and executed within a prescribed timeframe (many organizations seek results in 1 quarter, 90 days) with each member of a project improvement team expending approximately three to five hours per week in their respective roles for planning, analysis, design, and implementation

Complying with this last criterion requires a closer examination of process complexity.

Assessing Process Complexity

When multiple processes have been identified for improvement, the priority should be driven by those that yield the greatest returns from the least effort. This requires an initial scoping exercise to evaluate other variables that affect the complexity of the process and an improvement effort. A useful tool for this purpose is a "complexity assessment matrix" illustrated in Figure 6.5. It is used in many IT organizations to help program and project managers evaluate multiple dimensions of complexity.

The complexity dimensions listed above are generic. They can be expanded, contracted, or replaced as required by the organization or depending upon the processes being assessed. The objective, however, is to create and compare complexity assessment matrices for each candidate process for improvement, selecting the process that yields the greatest returns with minimal effort.

	Low Complexity	←				→	High Complexity
Complexity Dimension		1	2	3	4	5	
Objectives	Clear				X		Vague
Business Climate	Stable		X				Uncertain
Financial Risk	Low			X			High
Technical Requirements	Clear				X		Vague
Organization	Centralized		X				Decentralized
Technology	Low-Tech.			X			High-Tech.
Urgency	Reasonable					X	Immediate
Geography	Local		X				Global
Team Members	Experienced			X			Inexperienced
Expected Benefit	Low				X		High

FIGURE 6.5

Complexity assessment matrix. (Adapted from Milošević, D.Z., Martinelli, R.J., and Waddell, J.M., *Program Management for Improved Business Results*, Wiley, Hoboken, NJ, 2007.)

7

How to Structure Technology for Strategic Execution

Structuring organizational behavior (as discussed in Chapter 5) and business processes (as discussed in Chapter 6) to properly execute your organization's chosen business strategy (as discussed in Section I) requires your information technology to properly support the following:

- The business processes designed to create customer value
- Tools to track and report KPIs for outcome measures and performance drivers
- Event management capabilities to define KPI performance thresholds and set up alerts
- Exception management control processes to manage anticipated events using prescribed activities and tasks
- Resolution management control processes guiding the workforce to interpret unanticipated events and make decisions about how best to act
- Managing alerts to ensure relevant stakeholders engage timely responses
- Periodic, ad hoc, and on-demand reports necessary to empower and motivate the workforce and track achievement of outcome measures, performance drivers, collaborative objectives, and overall strategic objectives

As a leader or manager of your organization, you may or may not have a good understanding of the software and technology used to run your business and whether it can support such capabilities. What follows is intended to help you review, assess, and understand the capabilities and limitations of your information technology. This knowledge is important because what your systems can and cannot do directly influence the return on investment from any proposed business process redesign and, consequently, your decision on how best to proceed.

Many business professionals are aware of their organization's software and what it does, such as a general ledger in an accounting software package, for example. But few may understand the effort and resources required to:

- Install the software
- Configure it for your organization
- Populate it with data
- Ensure data accuracy and reliability
- Integrate it with other systems or applications, if necessary
- Allow or restrict access by users based on their identity or role in the organization
- Establish and track KPIs
- Define threshold levels of performance
- Configure messaging and alerts
- Route workflow
- Extend access via mobile and other forms of collaborative technology
- Generate or limit access to reports
- Reconfigure all of the above when change occurs

These and other configuration and implementation details are determined in large part by the business processes they are designed to support, such as processing customer orders, accounts receivable, or accounts payable, for example.

More comprehensive systems, such as enterprise resource planning (ERP) software, have broader functionality and may support customer relationship management (CRM) processes, including marketing campaigns, or supply chain management (SCM) processes, such as inventory control. These systems have more complex configuration and design capabilities, often requiring specialized consulting services to set them up and modify them as required.

Your organization may have other IT infrastructure for application development and integration tools, or specialized systems to assist with document management, content management, and workflow control. Or you may have systems implemented years ago, systems that are no longer supported, or systems that were highly customized, making them difficult or costly to change.

Your organization may be using some of the more recent software-as-a-service (SaaS) or "Cloud" offerings, paying a subscription fee to access them using the Internet. SaaS/Cloud is a popular model for many small and mid-sized companies who prefer to avoid the cost associated with in-house IT systems support. Finally, your organization may be planning to use other recent entrants to the market such as a business process management suite (BPMS) that combines process modeling with application development and integration.

The point here is that you already have invested considerable money and effort in the information technology you use to run your business. When initiating business process management and continuous improvement, it is prudent and economical to try to exploit fully the resources in place before recommending to higher authorities the need for incremental investment. Besides, those authorities are going to ask you if you assessed whether current resources can handle the proposed improvements anyway, so you will be required to do your homework.

PREPARING FOR PROCESS IMPROVEMENT

Business process improvement often requires changes to your IT systems and business applications. Some IT resources are more flexible than others. Success requires an understanding of the capabilities and limitations of your existing IT investments. The feasibility, resources, time, and cost needed to adapt these systems should be measured early to test feasibility and set proper expectations in the eyes of decision makers. Surprises often kill process improvement projects. Doing so helps you demonstrate how best to exploit fully the capabilities of your IT resources to deliver value, create efficiency, improve quality, and enable competitive advantage.

Before beginning an improvement or redesign project for a selected process, the in-place IT system(s) used for its execution should be identified. Often, there is more than one. For example, many organizations have more than one purchasing system. Or, the purchasing process uses separate systems for different parts of the process. One system is used for requisitioning, another for procurement, yet another to exchange data with suppliers, and a final system to manage payments.

In any case, you need a general understanding of the resources, time, and costs associated with making fundamental changes to in-place systems.

Not only does this help you test the feasibility of change, but it also allows you to capture the baseline data that, when compared with resulting data from a business process analysis using BPA software, will enable you to perform an accurate and reliable return-on-investment (ROI) analysis of a proposed process improvement investments.

To assess IT readiness, business professionals must know the answers to specific questions about the capabilities of their IT resources and the means required to make changes. These questions follow shortly. However, if your technical proficiency is somewhat limited, or requires a quick refresh, you may find the following review of IT architectural concepts and historical trends useful in preparing to answer these questions with your IT colleagues.

IT Trends That Influence IT Strategy

The following represent important events that have influenced the evolution of IT. They also reveal decisive trends and shed light on how the future of IT may evolve.

Applications and APIs

A fundamental challenge to all organizations is keeping pace with the information needs of its users. Different groups need different systems for different reasons. Early IT strategy was based on departmental software applications that were either developed internally or bought as off-the-shelf software packages. In most cases, they were transaction-oriented software that automated repetitive tasks specific to a business function or department, such as early accounting software or payroll applications. Modifications or customizations of the software were done using proprietary application programming interface (API) tools that, with highly skilled effort, were able to modify the logic and user interface of the software but were limited in their ability to integrate with other departmental solutions.

Workflow and EDI

But doing business requires multiple business functions to cooperate internally and externally with suppliers and customers. Workflow technology and tools emerged and were deployed to automate interdepartmental document flow between various employees that supported a business process, such as product information management or invoice processing. But many workflow systems were based on document scanners and digitization, or optical character recognition, software used to convert document images into computer readable code. This limited their use to support only business processes with high-volume, interdepartmental document flow. Electronic data interchange (EDI) standards defined common formats for electronic documents to be exchanged among external trading partners (suppliers, customers, logistics service providers, banks), but cost and complexity limited their deployment to only high transaction volume trading partners. Gradually, demand increased for workflow-based business applications causing software vendors to develop integrated application suites and application integration toolkits.

ERP

Enterprise resource planning systems emerged that handled multiple business functions such as finance, accounting, human resources, and shortly thereafter, supply chain management, and customer relationship management. Some included flexible workflow configuration capabilities and basic application-to-application integration with trading partner systems using EDI, file transfer protocol (FTP), or other proprietary data exchange techniques. When implemented correctly, they used a common database to share information about customers, suppliers, and products. Often, they had built-in business process designs to support common processes such as order processing and accounts receivable and payable. Many were not implemented correctly or entirely. They used proprietary development languages and tools requiring specialized training. They were costly to deploy, maintain, and integrate with other applications. Multiple systems still remained in organizations making it difficult to handle cross-functional business processes that spanned the organization.

ETL

The need to integrate disparate applications continued. Extract, transform, and load (ETL) software emerged that supported data translation and transformation from one format and system to another. It helped simplify large system implementation, but it, too, was complex and expensive. The need also sparked the growth of systems integration firms that would charge lofty fees for on-site consultants who often hard-coded interfaces between various applications to support a cross-functional business process. Only larger organizations could afford such efforts.

EAI

Seeking flexibility and efficiency, a new generation of technology was needed. Enterprise application integration (EAI) emerged using preconfigured connectors and components to link more popular software applications and ERP suites. EAI also included toolkits to integrate other less common or custom applications. These, too, were costly complex tools requiring specialized talent, affordable only by larger organizations.

Business Process Modeling and Analysis

EAI linked various applications with one another within an organization. This created the need to improve how data flowed between applications. Tools emerged from EAI projects to help map data flows in complex configurations. Stand-alone process mapping tools also began to evolve to include more sophisticated modeling and simulation of manufacturing and general business processes. Business process analysis software vendors entered the market to support total quality management (TQM) initiatives and complex systems design. EAI vendors began acquiring such technology to build out their EAI suites to include business process design and development as part of their solutions.

Business Rules Management

As process modeling and analysis grew in sophistication, it exposed the need for better control of the business rules that govern execution. Business rules are often hard-coded within software applications making any change to the rule, the software, or the process difficult and costly. Business rules management engines (also called inference engines) emerged to help manage and control business rules by decoupling them from business applications. This enables applications to call relevant rules from the rules engine as required by the application logic or business process.

* * *

With each evolutionary step described above, more proprietary technology was created to enable flexibility. Making it all work together became a growing challenge.

Internet

Fortunately, the Internet emerged, based on a set of open technology and integration standards, making it efficient to capture and share data across multiple and disparate platforms. Among these technologies are HTML (hypertext mark-up language) and HTTP (hypertext transfer protocol), both of which gave rise to web browsers and web servers, forming the foundation for the World Wide Web (the web). They made it easier to access data globally and present them in virtually any type of user interface. XML (Extensible Markup Language) also emerged, providing an efficient means to translate and transform data from one format and system to another. And, AS2 (applicability statement 2) emerged as a secure, flexible, and reliable means to exchange data with external trading partners using the Internet.

Open Source

Internet technologies also sparked the growth of "open source" software that made source code for various operating environments, tools, applications, and services freely and openly available to anyone. A few prominent successes of note include the Linux operating system, the Apache web server, the Firefox web browser, and Joomla, a website content management system. Countless other unique and specialized open source code became available that provided similar capabilities found in ETL and EAI tools to integrate applications. However, for many organizations the concerns associated with reliability and support limited their use.

This evolution has led many to seek the best of all these worlds. As such, nearly all IT vendors are now evolving their technology, product line, and services based on a services-oriented architecture (SOA).

SOA

SOA is an architectural framework that provides flexible methods to develop and integrate software functionality by creating and using discrete interoperable building blocks called *services*. Services can be:

- Discretely defined functions (such as "create packing list" or "print a shipping label"), or they can be:

- Applications (a combination of discretely defined functions integrated to execute logic or perform activities such as "select least cost shipping carrier" or "ship an order," e.g.), or they can be:
- Processes (a logical sequence of discretely defined functions and applications such as "manage orders" or "replenish inventory") designed to create and deliver value.

Services communicate by passing data between them. SOA provides the definitions, rules, and techniques for designing services and making them interoperable. Solutions based on SOA require less custom development and integration, saving time and allowing faster deployment.

The flexibility and benefits of SOA are natural enablers for business process management and continuous improvement. Interoperable services can be modified, swapped, substituted, and changed more easily than application components or objects that comprise traditional transaction-oriented software. As a result, business process designs and redesigns can be deployed relatively quickly, consuming fewer resources at lower costs.

SaaS and Cloud

IT solution vendors use SOA to expand their business models and offerings. Traditionally, business software is licensed to run on "in-house" IT infrastructure (servers and networks). But the flexible service designs enabled by SOA and Internet technologies have given rise to a new software-as-a-service model. Using SaaS (may also be referred to as "Cloud" computing), an organization's workforce accesses software via the Internet, paying periodic subscription fees (monthly, quarterly, or annually) determined by the number of users. This saves considerable time and expense associated with supporting in-house IT infrastructure and software application maintenance.

SaaS/Cloud has helped create a new paradigm in computing and application development. Using SOA and Internet technologies, some IT vendors have been very effective at creating a platform to assemble preconfigured application components (services) dynamically into custom, integrated application suites. Salesforce.com has pioneered and is mastering these capabilities. It first came to market with a low-cost, flexible CRM SaaS solution targeting small and mid-size organizations. Its architecture evolved, becoming flexible and adaptable and enabling nontechnical users to configure and manage databases, workflow processes, messaging, alerts, document management, and reports with little effort. The vendor then expanded its capability, and market share, by encouraging third-party software vendors to develop preintegrated applications that would add value to its base CRM functionality. It now represents a benchmark and model against which many IT vendors are measured.

BPMS

Meanwhile, workflow technology continued to evolve, converge with business process modeling and analysis tools, and integrate with SOA-based solutions. Platforms known as business process management suites enable organizations to model, create, and manage all aspects of a process. Essentially, BPMS is a combination of process modeling and analysis tools, workflow systems, EAI concepts, and SOA technologies. Designed as an integrated framework, they can support process modeling, analysis, design, development, integration, execution, and measurement of end-to-end, cross-functional processes. A BPMS can create a visual representation of a business process that can be used to generate executable code, combining both development and run-time IT environments. Implementation of new process designs can be reduced from months to days, saving considerable IT costs while making the organization highly adaptable to change and responsive to opportunity.

BAM and BI

The advantages afforded by SOA, SaaS/Cloud, and BPMS have improved the way information is presented and reported to the workforce. Dynamic and real-time assembly of information has enabled considerable improvements in traditional business activity monitoring (BAM) and business intelligence (BI) technology. BAM evolved to support real-time evaluation of how various transactions, operations, and processes are performing against KPIs, whereas BI evolved with greater flexibility to analyze data that reveal previously unforeseen trends and patterns of behavior. Both exploit Internet technologies and sport improved "dashboard" interfaces that make creative use of graphics and visualization technology to simplify the presentation and interpretation of data.

ASSESSING IT READINESS

Armed with a new or at least refreshed perspective of IT trends you may find it easier to ask questions of your IT colleagues to determine the adaptability (or lack thereof) of your in-place IT infrastructure, systems, and business applications. To do so, for each IT system participant to the target process you must ask four questions for each of the IT capabilities that follow.

1. How is this currently done? And, if a change in each is needed what...
2. Resources are required to make a change?
3. How much effort and time would be required to make the change?
4. What are the costs (total monetary value) associated with the change?

IT Capabilities Enabling Process Change

1. User/Role
   a. Set up a new user?
   b. Set up new role?
   c. User- or role-based security?
   d. Create/modify access privileges (internal user)?
   e. Create/modify access privileges (external user)?
2. Application
   a. Add new module or component from the software vendor?
   b. Modify user interface?
   c. Modify logic?
   d. Develop new app. (on average)?
3. Process
   a. Define/create a process?
   b. Configure workflow, internal to a single system?
   c. Configure workflow, external to other systems?
   d. Change internal workflow(s)?
   e. Change external workflow(s)?
   f. Generate documentation from the process design and redesign (used for training and continuous process improvement)?
4. Data/Integration
   a. Capture data, ensure quality, and manage data continuity?
   b. Capture the data required to measure KPIs (if not available to an IT system, e.g., currently recorded on paper)?

    c. Assemble data if needed from other systems?

    d. Transform/translate data to new format?

    e. Integrate the systems necessary to support the process?

5. KPIs/Rules

    a. Define/manage KPIs?

    b. Establish thresholds for KPIs that trigger alerts?

    c. Define/manage rules?

    d. Change rules?

    e. Track rules compliance?

6. Messaging/Alerts

    a. Create system-to-system messages?

    b. Create system-to-user messages?

    c. Create/manage alerts?

    d. Establish timing thresholds?

7. Collaboration

    a. Information dissemination?

    b. Managing known or anticipated events (exception management)?

    c. Managing unknown or unanticipated events (resolution management)?

    d. Negotiate and record commitments?

8. Reports/Analysis

    a. Create a new preconfigured report?

    b. Create ad hoc reports?

    c. Create/modify dashboards?

    d. Create/modify business activity monitoring?

    e. Enable other business analytics?

    f. Track and report commitments?

9. Systems/Networks

    a. How is hardware capacity increased, if needed?

    b. How is software capacity increased, if needed?

    c. How are networks (technology or services) enabled or adapted, if necessary?

    d. How are services (SaaS or other) capacity increased, if needed?

    e. How are security measures created or modified?

    f. How are disaster recovery or business continuity capabilities created or modified?

    g. Note any fees associated with change.

    h. Note any other in-place capabilities effected.

10. Findings/Conclusions

    a. Note: Costs represent an estimate for changes to individual capabilities that may or may not need to be changed. There is no value in summing the costs. Doing so may be misleading. Rather, state general conclusions regarding the costs associated with potential change.

    b. What are your conclusions? Note specifics for each conclusion.

Overall IT Readiness

Once you are satisfied with the answers to the above questions you should draw a general conclusion about the overall readiness of your IT systems to support process change by choosing from the most appropriate responses below.

Collectively, the IT systems participating in the execution and support of the process targeted for this assessment are deemed to be (select one):

- *Very ready* (merits a rating of 9–10 on a scale from 0 to 10, 10 being highest) means that most of the in-place IT systems (or stand-alone IT system) inherently support process-centric system design. They (it) require(s) general IT skills, consume(s) little effort and can be quickly adapted at low cost. The in-place IT architecture creates competitive advantage.
- *Ready* (merits a rating of 6–7–8 on a scale from 0 to 10, 10 being highest) means that several of the in-place IT systems (or stand-alone IT system) are (is) sufficiently flexible to adapt when necessary. Specialized resources are required, but effort is moderate and can be completed within predictable timeframes and at reasonable cost.
- *Unremarkable/adequate* (merits a rating of 5 on a scale from 0 to 10, 10 being highest) means that the in-place IT systems (or stand-alone IT system) most critical to the execution and management of the process are (is) capable of change but require(s) skilled resources that must be scheduled and budgeted. Effort and costs sometimes exceed expectations, and although frustrating, change is manageable.
- *Not very ready* (merits a rating of 2–3–4 on a scale from 0 to 10, 10 being highest) means that several of the in-place IT systems (or stand-alone IT system) are (is) difficult to adapt to most types of change. Highly skilled resources are necessary but usually unavailable. Effort is considerable; cost and timeframes often exceed expectations.

- *Not at all ready* (merits a rating of 0–1 on a scale from 0 to 10, 10 being highest) means that most or all of the IT systems (or stand-alone IT system) cannot be changed or are (is) in "maintenance-mode," whereby any change will make them (it) unstable. Highly specialized resources are required and difficult to find, effort is extraordinary and unpredictable, and done so at high cost. The in-place IT architecture creates competitive disadvantage.

Depending upon the findings of your IT readiness assessment you may find that you will need to upgrade or evolve in some way your in-place IT systems. When this is the case, certain decisions need to be made about how these systems can support a process redesign. They may need to be integrated, centralized, virtualized, reconfigured, upgraded, or replaced. This may affect your organization's IT strategy in some way. You may be required to make recommendations as to how your organization's IT portfolio should be structured. If so, you will have to make a compelling argument for any IT investment necessary to support your process improvement project. Our next discussion aids you in these efforts.

CRAFTING A PROCESS-CENTRIC IT STRATEGY

As noted earlier, IT is gradually trending away from a transaction-oriented model that automates repetitive tasks, using fixed logic, running on dedicated in-house infrastructure, to a process-centric model that shares strategic information and assembles unique services dynamically to execute any logical series of activities and tasks across many disparate and distributed off-site systems. Organizations that master the use of process-centric systems create formidable customer value and competitive advantage. Organizations that do not, expose themselves to increasing risk.

This does not mean that to exploit these trends business professionals need to possess the same skills as IT professionals. It does mean that you should remain current on IT trends, discussing them with colleagues and peers to better understand the business value of IT evolution and to determine how best to "improve your value every year," as Treacy and Wiersema (1995) advise in *The Discipline of Market Leaders*.

Moreover, this also does not mean that you have to spend a lot of money to enable a process-centric approach. For some, this evolution may be inevitable. Most organizations do not currently have SOA or BPMS solutions, however, they likely will at some point, when they eventually upgrade existing software or subscribe to SaaS or cloud-based solutions. Newer systems are likely to be SOA-based and Internet-accessible, exposing process-centric capabilities and benefits as part of their solutions. This is yet another reason for you to follow IT trends, particularly those being driven by the IT vendors you currently use.

This is not to say that all IT solutions are perfect. Indeed, far from it. IT vendors will continue to move in this direction, but their results will vary. For some, support and maintenance challenges associated with legacy platforms will hinder their efforts and the quality of their solutions. Others may execute poorly. In addition, IT innovation does not stop evolving, so it is impractical to get the "best of all worlds" in an integrated framework from a single vendor when the best of all worlds keeps changing.

As a leader or manager of your organization, you need to know how your IT resources can support your business today and how they need to evolve to support your strategy over time. The IT readiness assessment discussed earlier should help you understand how your existing IT resources are equipped to handle change. You may find that they are not, requiring you to consider restructuring your IT budget allocations or petition for supplemental investment to adapt your IT systems.

In either case, you may be called upon to make educated recommendations regarding your IT strategy and investments. Learning IT trends is a good start to enhance your IT IQ. But when making IT recommendations to support process change, you will need a better understanding of the architecture and constructs of process-centric systems.

As a leader or manager, you may drive or influence the direction of your IT strategy. At some point, either as a result of an IT readiness assessment or part of periodic IT planning, you are likely to contribute information about your needs and requirements. Your input should be guided by what we learned thus far about business strategy, organizational behavior, business processes, and IT trends.

Often, managerial input to IT strategy can be either too macro or too micro with solution requests focused on "lagging" problems. Your input is too macro when you request a new CRM, billing, or order-processing system, for example, because the existing systems are too inflexible or difficult to use. Your input is too micro when you emphasize the need for a new type of report, or a better way to track sales commissions, for example. Both cases represent requests to resolve lagging needs, meaning, they are pain points that cause frustration and inefficiency. This is not to suggest that this input is trivial or of no value. On the contrary, these needs and requirements must be addressed as you see fit. But, IT planning based on lagging requirements is limited in its ability to do the following:

- Increase customer and shareholder value
- Enhance value propositions
- Enable competitive advantage
- Become more responsive to market dynamics and customer needs

Your input and advice best serve your organization when they guide IT strategy with "leading" requirements that help enable and facilitate strategic objectives. The best way to do this is to recommend improvements to the core business processes that deliver customer and shareholder value, and ones that emphasize measurement and control of desired outcome measures and performance drivers. This requires you to reconsider how you present macro and micro requests and think about IT in terms of a "process-centric" system.

Process-centric systems empower all stakeholders (individuals and groups, internal or external, as required) of a process, as opposed to automating the execution, measurement, and reporting of repetitive tasks as is the case with traditional, transaction-oriented software. Process-centric systems are designed to ensure that the desired results from a business process are achieved. For example, part of the O2C process discussed earlier includes order fulfillment whose key performance driver is "delivery performance to customer commit date."

Figure 7.1 illustrates the O2C process' fulfillment activities. Activities highlighted in black directly affect KPI achievement. Activities highlighted in dark gray have lesser impact but, nevertheless, require oversight to prevent KPI variance.

A process-centric system would track and manage all the activities and tasks associated with the end-to-end fulfillment process and report all outcome measures (common to a strategy) and performance drivers (unique to a strategy) associated with the process. To ensure achievement, process-centric systems place priority on making strategic information available, measuring KPIs and managing events as they occur to prevent or minimize process variance and its adverse effects on performance measures. In this example, emphasis is placed on managing the data and controlling the events that can affect the "delivery performance to customer commit date" KPI. To

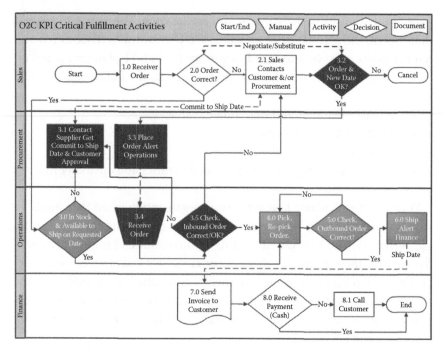

FIGURE 7.1

O2C process map demonstrating fulfillment activities.

enable such process-centric capabilities, your IT systems may require some of these architectural building blocks as illustrated in Figure 7.2.

- Application Development
    - New applications should be created using SOA methods. This means evolving from programming and maintaining application code to creating and assembling applications from a tool kit of interoperable and reusable services. User access to services and services-based applications is most flexible using web browsers or "thin" web browser–based clients found in mobile devices and other forms of personal technology.
- Process Modeling
    - Use tools to map, model, and measure business processes and control processes (exception and resolution). These tools should include simulation and analytic capabilities to measure and compare the economic impact (resources consumed and efficiencies) of alternative process models.

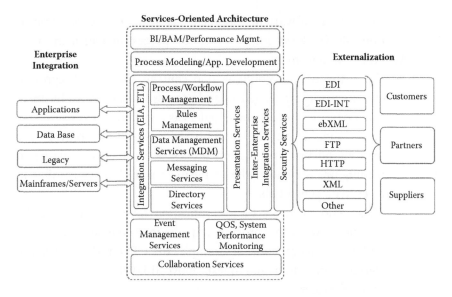

FIGURE 7.2
Process-centric architectural building blocks.

- Data Structure and Integration
  - When multiple systems are used to support a business process, methods and techniques will be needed to access and share data from across these distributed systems, and be accessible by the workforce, business processes, control processes, reporting, and analytic tools. This requires tools, techniques, or services to translate and transform data from one format or system to another, or a common data structure that can be shared by many heterogeneous systems, such as is enabled using XML, or master data management (MDM) techniques that broadly manage all aspects of data quality and use.
- Rules Management
  - These are tools or systems that decompose business rules from application logic, making it easier to add or modify the rule based on business need, for example, when procurement authorization changes from a VP-level to the CEO for all purchases above $10,000.
  - These can be in the form of a separate rules engine (also referred to as an inference engine: software specifically designed to manage business rules and execute them when called upon to be an application), or capabilities or services built into workflow

software, a software development platform, a business application suite (ERP system), or a business process management suite.

- Workflow Management
  - These are tools or configuration controls that can design and execute workflow sequences and process flows between business functions and process stakeholders as required.
  - These should include "rules-based" workflow control that separate business rules from process flow, making it easier to reconfigure workflow when a business rule changes (similar to rules management above).
  - These automated alert-and-notification tools are governed by rule-based workflow processes to ensure stakeholder awareness and acknowledgment. For example, the CEO and VP-level are alerted to procurement requests above $10,000.
- Directory Services
  - A directory is a set of objects with attributes organized logically, usually in a hierarchy as in a telephone directory. It helps organize and structure associations of resources and services, such as people, organizational units, groups of people, systems, applications, nodes, printers, documents, rules, or anything else. Your organization's domain name, www.company.com, for example, is listed in a directory (a DNS server, domain name system) that associates it with an IP (Internet protocol) address that can look something like 192.0.32.10.
  - This is used to track the IT access privileges of, and alerts assigned to, the workforce to simplify and streamline changes associated with attrition, new hire, turnover, or reassignment.
- Performance Measurement
  - This is used to design, measure, track, and manage outcome measures and performance drivers.
  - In environments where multiple systems support the execution of a business process, data may need to be aggregated using data integration techniques into a common "system-of-record" or other form of data warehouse or operational data store for reporting and analysis.
- Event Management
  - This includes policies and capabilities to define KPI performance thresholds that trigger alerts when events occur, engaging

exception control processes to known or anticipated events, or resolution control processes to unknown or unanticipated events.

- Exception Management
  - This includes prescribed control processes, organizational behavior, escalation policies/procedures, and collaborative objectives designed to solve anticipated events, facilitated by the workforce or IT system(s).
  - This has capabilities to track and manage outcomes of corrective actions taken.
- Resolution Management
  - This covers resolution control processes and rules-of-engagement to resolve unanticipated events, facilitated by event management and workforce collaboration tools that guide the workforce to interpret and make decisions about how best to act.
  - This has capabilities to track and manage commitments and accountability associated with the chosen resolution actions.
- Collaboration Tools
  - These are general-purpose tools to enable dynamic collaboration among process stakeholders, such as e-mail, instant messaging, portals, conferencing systems, Web 2.0, social web services, and various mobile solutions.
  - Tied to event management processes, these are the reports and analytic tools to ensure the desired workforce behavior (sense-and-respond) is consistently practiced.
- Reports, Analytics, and Dashboards
  - These are the periodic, ad hoc, and on-demand reports necessary to empower and motivate the workforce and track achievement of outcome measures and performance drivers tied to strategic objectives as well as performance against incentives tied to individual, group, organizational, and collaborative objectives.
  - These analytic tools help identify unforeseen trends or patterns in process execution that can affect outcome measures and performance drivers or aid in the discovery of new ways to add customer and shareholder value.
  - Dashboards enable real-time visibility into execution and transaction data, typically using a graphical interface to expose data to relevant stakeholders and monitor business activity (BAM) or intelligence (BI).

Petitioning for Process-Centric IT Strategy

There are several ways to bring the benefits of process-centric systems to the attention of decision makers. One way is to introduce process-centric concepts into planning discussions or when existing systems are evaluated for upgrade or replacement. Suggest that the selection criteria of any new IT resource include all relevant process-centric building blocks.

An analytical approach would be to begin a business process improvement project. Real-world examples make the best arguments. Presenting the conclusions drawn from a readiness assessment of in-place IT systems and the findings from a process modeling and simulation exercise can strongly influence decision makers when you demonstrate what is necessary to support strategy or business process change. Transactional systems will likely be revealed as steadfast, supporting little change, paving the way to introduce process-centric systems as a means to enable new process designs and strategy.

Absent a real world example, it is important to include discussion of process-centric IT capabilities into business and IT strategic planning. Business and IT leadership must be educated in the ways that process-centric systems can improve the adaptability and responsiveness particularly when forces demand the organization become more responsive to market dynamics and customer needs.

A strategic approach to petition for process-centric IT strategy is to conduct a derivative analysis of how well your organization's resources (people, processes, and information technology) are aligned with business strategy. Derivative analysis demonstrates the links among strategy, measurement systems, business processes, workforce behavior, and the systems used for execution. The details of derivative analysis are discussed later in Section III. There, all that was learned about using best practices to align business strategy with people, processes, and technology for execution is wrapped up. But before it is, a final critical topic must be discussed.

Enabling a process-centric IT architecture will likely require financial investment and thus approval from strategic planners and decision makers. If you are not the decision maker, or do not have strong influence among those who are, you will need to make a compelling case to justify any investment request. This may present a challenge in some organizations that view IT as an expense rather than as an asset.

INVESTING IN PROCESS-CENTRIC IT ARCHITECTURE

IT Portfolio Management

Over the years, there has been considerable debate questioning the value of IT. Some argue that it is required simply as a cost of doing business, and therefore adds little strategic value. Others agree that without IT, innovation would cease and organizations simply could not operate. The debate persists not to conclude whether organizations should divest themselves of IT—try doing business without it—but because the perception of IT value varies among leaders and managers in and across organizations. The more relevant question is, "How does management view and treat IT?" Is it a means to drive business strategy, and therefore merits careful investment, or is it a necessary evil that should be governed under strict cost controls? This question becomes important when your BPM initiative requires IT funding.

Requests for funding join a perpetual balancing act that struggles to keep aloft demanding objectives with limited resources. In the book *IT Portfolio Management Step By-Step: Unlocking the Business Value of Technology* (2005, p. 1), the coauthors, Bryan Maizlish, chief technology officer—program team at Lockheed Martin Integrated Systems and Solutions, and Robert Handler, vice president, enterprise planning and architecture group at Gartner, Inc., state the challenge this way:

> Constraints based on available funding, core capabilities, risk thresholds, labor and material resources, complexity and maturity, time, organizational priorities and requirements, compliance and standards, and value and benefits serve as important factors that must be assessed, prioritized, and balanced in a portfolio of IT investments.

Such constraints introduce the need for IT portfolio management. Maizlish and Handler continue by stating:

> IT portfolio management provides the day-to-day management and operations of IT investments, assuring IT investments are performing according to plan, scope creep, redundancies, and risk are identified early, limited resources are providing maximum benefits, and any changes to IT portfolio as a result of business redirection are efficiently and effectively executed (p. 4).

IT portfolio management views and manages IT resources as assets whose purpose is to add value. As such, an IT portfolio can be viewed in the same light as a financial asset portfolio that seeks to improve financial returns of investments. Financial returns from an IT portfolio are achieved though improved budget oversight and by managing the return-on-investment yields across various IT asset classes. IT portfolios also seek nonfinancial returns that contribute to strategic objectives, improve governance, define standards against which IT procurements are made, and control the various risk and constraints described above.

An IT portfolio can be structured in many ways. For example, assets may be classified as the following:

- *Resources*: Such as hardware, software, personnel, outsourced services, and so on
- *Domains*: Such as data center, help desk, application support, and so on
- *Operations*: Such as facilities, projects, maintenance, and so on
- *Strategic*: Such as finance, supply chain management, customer relationship management, and so on, as illustrated in Figure 7.3

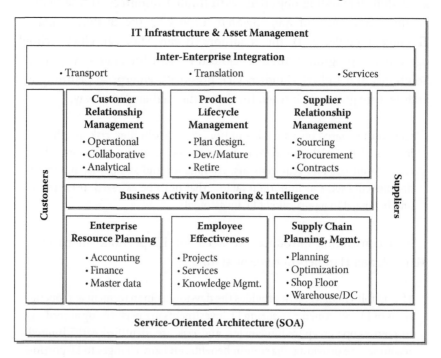

FIGURE 7.3
A sample IT portfolio classified by strategic assets.

Industry leaders use business strategy to drive the structure of their IT portfolios. To them, IT enables business strategy by managing the business issues necessary to create customer value and the processes that deliver that value. IT portfolio management helps reconcile opposing or divergent views among leaders and managers by creating a forum within which business and IT professionals can find common ground. Maizlish and Handler (2005, p. 4) concur: "IT portfolio management provides the tools, processes, and disciplines needed to translate information technology into a common taxonomy that both business and IT executives understand."

But IT portfolio management is not a common practice; as such, the perception that IT as an expense prevails, and because it does, many decision makers fail to consider, with necessary rigor, what is required to align IT to support business strategy. As mentioned earlier, many leaders and managers assume that IT software applications immediately support strategic objectives and business processes upon deployment. They fail to understand, or take the time to determine, how applications and processes must be configured to execute strategy properly. These decision makers still take a traditional approach to IT by viewing it as purely a budget allocation exercise. As such, they are unaware of the implications of their decisions regarding IT. This ignorance can lead to many poor IT funding decisions.

Similar findings are echoed in the book *Strategic IT Portfolio Management: Governing Enterprise Transformation* (2005). In it, Jeffrey Kaplan, the author and lead partner in the strategic IT management practice of global management consultancy Pittiglio, Rabin, Todd & McGrath, points out:

> To find evidence of this deficiency, map out the organization's budget process. The typical budget planning process requires the IT department to estimate the IT budget before the business units determine which initiatives they plan to pursue. How sensible is that approach? If business decisions should drive IT decisions—a fact we've known for decades—then why would a CFO ask the IT department to submit its budget without first understanding what the business plans to do and how IT plays into that strategy? Yet most organizations follow this practice. Why is it done that way? Because it is how most organizations have always done it. Business strategy does not drive IT investment decisions. In more cases than not, the IT budget is decided before the business determines IT strategy, and the two are aligned ex post by well-intentioned middle managers who, by the by, know the process is broken but are not empowered to fix it (p. 9).

Organizations that fail to value IT fall prey to such behavior. Business strategy and IT budgeting become mutually exclusive rather than dependent on each other. IT is merely an expense to be budgeted and managed as such.

It is more common, however, for organizations to be indifferent to the value of IT. In these organizations, perceptions vary among leadership and management, causing IT to be treated as both an asset and an expense. The pendulum swings with changing economic conditions and leadership priorities. In good times, IT investments are made, measured, and managed as such; in bad times, the IT budget gets cut or simply isn't funded.

Lastly, your organization may, indeed, treat IT with reverence as a portfolio of assets necessary for the creation and delivery of customer and shareholder value. This type of organization views IT more strategically, using portfolio management and investment techniques, seeking improved ways to run, grow, and transform its business.

- Investments to *run* the business enable improvements in IT portfolio assets that support day-to-day operations, such as IT infrastructure, personnel, facilities, maintenance agreements, and so on
- Investments to *grow* the business enable improvements in IT portfolio assets that support the expansion of existing business by improving IT asset utilization or migrating to more effective/efficient processes, including software upgrades, incremental capacity, and so on
- Investments to *transform* the business enable improvements in IT portfolio assets that are necessary to pursue new opportunities or business models requiring process-centric IT system designs, improved performance, greater returns on assets, and so on

Organizations that treat IT in this way will be open to investment requests, but approval will not be guaranteed. When recommending IT investments to facilitate a process-centric IT architecture, you must understand the attitude and perceptions of the various IT planners and decision makers in your organization, and then appeal to their decision criteria. Your approach for IT funding approval must be able to do the following:

1. *Justify* the investment in terms of financial returns.
2. *Demonstrate fit* with the overall business strategy and existing IT portfolio investments.

3. *Overcome objections* of skeptical or uneducated decision makers by demonstrating the business value of IT investments.

Compelling arguments for each are particularly important when the perceptions and criteria of various planners and decision makers are incongruous.

To do so effectively, use the techniques that follow to study your organization's IT portfolio structure and budget. You can best support your arguments when you understand the context in which prior IT investments were made and their impact on your organization's strategic objectives. These techniques are valuable regardless of whether the rest of your organization practices IT portfolio management. They represent common business practices that can be applied to any type of investment.

Objective Evaluation and Financial Analysis

Many works have been published that outline the benefits and practices used to create and manage an IT portfolio. We have cited two such notable works above, and we encourage further study on the topic. But to help you quickly and properly prepare an IT investment request, we need to simplify an otherwise complex framework. To do so, we focus our discussion of IT portfolio management on the techniques used to judge IT assets and allocate budget: objective evaluation and financial analysis.

When making an IT investment request, your justification should include both objective evaluation that demonstrates thoughtful improvement and financial analysis that measures returns suitable to warrant the investment (or expense, as the case may be).

Objective Evaluation

Objective evaluation means that you have analyzed a range of options and can demonstrate how your specific IT investment can improve the quality, value, and performance of the business process, and if possible, bring greater benefits to the organization at large.

For example, let's assume that you need to examine your order fulfillment process, seeking to improve the percentage of orders that are delivered to the customer commit date (the "delivery performance to customer commit date" KPI discussed in our earlier example, as illustrated in Figure 7.3). Using BPA software you model the "as-is" process and measure and simulate its execution to determine cause-and-effect relationships of the activities and tasks that comprise it. Your findings determine that fulfillment is delayed, because the process stakeholders in the shipping department (part of operations) are unaware of customer commitment dates. After exploring multiple process redesigns and options, you conclude that the best improvement is to expose these data to the shipping department by granting it access privileges to an existing order management module in the organization's ERP system. However, this requires a software license upgrade from the ERP vendor, a financial implication that we discuss next.

Your objective evaluation of this solution should include the process modeling and analysis results of two or three process redesign options. Here, you want to quantify the impact on outcome measures and performance drivers defined by the KPI set for the process, including the impact on the core "delivery performance to customer commit date" KPI. This will demonstrate the rigor with which you examined various possibilities.

You may also wish to include in your objective evaluation other potential benefits associated with the license upgrade. Learn what prior evaluation was done to justify the order management module. If applicable, include these findings in your justification along with any other benefits afforded the shipping department, because the stakeholders now have access to the strategic information managed by the order management module.

Financial Analysis

Financial analysis means that your justification is based on a return-on-investment analysis that can include the following:

- Payback/break-even timeframes that determine the time required to recoup the original investment, and when benefits can begin accruing.
- Rates of return or the amount of money gained (or lost) as compared to the original investment as a percentage. Most organizations require a certain "internal rate-of-return" (IRR), whereby an investment must be able to yield greater returns than are possible from other forms of more assured investments, such as in treasury notes or municipal bonds, for example.
- Net present value (NPV) that compares the current value of a dollar (the investment) to the value of the same dollar earned in the future (the expected cash flow from the investment), when considering inflation and rates of return. It is used in capital budgeting to

determine the profitability of an investment. NPV results must be positive, meaning the future value expected from the investment must be greater than the current value; otherwise, it is wise to leave the investment dollars where they are (negative results will likely be rejected). When comparing alternative investments, those with the greater NPV are usually, but not always, chosen. Other strategic reasons may drive the decision to select the investment with the lower NPV.

- Cash flow projections or the expected cash inflow generated by the investment over a predetermined timeframe.
- Total cost of ownership (TCO) or the sum of all costs associated with making the investment over a predetermined timeframe.

Such analysis can be done by using the findings from an IT readiness assessment to provide a baseline cost model. ROI measures can then be determined when the baseline findings are compared to the modeling and simulation findings of the alternative process redesigns discussed above. Each can be evaluated and measured to determine the best result, consistent with the decision-making criteria of leadership and management, which then can generate the ROI analysis results.

Competing for IT Budget

Objective evaluation and financial analysis help justify your investment request. But you are not alone. Various leaders and managers in your organization will compete to get more than their fair share of limited funding allocated to their projects. When competing for funds against worthy adversaries, you must also differentiate your request by showing how it "fits" within your organization's value chain and IT portfolio. "Fit," as you recall from Chapter 5, is a term used by Porter in *Competitive Advantage* (1985), describing how well an *"entire system of activities"* (or value chain) enables cost reduction or improves differentiation. In other words, the better the fit, the greater the potential for advantage. Your request must include arguments to these points.

Demonstrate fit by again using the results from the objective evaluation and financial analysis. Show how each positively affects the value chain (e.g., by enhancing differentiation through improved fulfillment process performance) and the IT portfolio (e.g., by enabling cost reduction from an IT asset class). Then demonstrate how your IT investment helps the following:

- Increases customer and shareholder value
- Enhances the organization's value propositions
- Enables competitive advantage
- Improves responsiveness to market dynamics and customer needs

These and other benefits you determine relevant then need to be positioned relative to other competing requests and reflect how your request merits priority and funding approval. You are almost there. But, just because you demonstrate value through the following:

- Objective evaluation
- Financial analysis
- Fit with the value chain
- Fit with the IT portfolio
- Positioning your request better than competing managers' requests

it still doesn't mean you get the money!

Your request may not coincide with annual budgeting cycles. This means that those leaders and managers holding the purse strings are in a position to say, "We didn't budget for that this year." However, budgeting (as we know) is fungible, meaning when you have knowledge of its structure, sources, and allocation priorities, you may be able to argue to have the rules changed. The final competitive edge you need to help secure your IT funding request is a better understanding of how your organization's IT budget is currently committed and allocated.

IT Portfolio Budget Structure

There are various ways to "slice and dice" an IT budget's structure. Whether it is managed as a pure expense, as a portfolio of assets, or both, you must learn how your organization classifies IT resources, allocates budgets, and evaluates requests. To prepare you, we discuss IT budget structure from several perspectives. We begin from a cost perspective describing various ways IT costs may be categorized and managed. Then, we gradually refine the perspectives, concluding with a description of how IT may be categorized and managed as strategic assets. Such awareness will help you understand the decision framework your organization will use to approve or deny budget for your IT investment request.

Funding Availability

First, learn how much IT budget is available. If budget levels are kept proprietary, you can estimate it based on IT industry research.

An IT budget, on average, can range from 1.5 to 7% of an organization's annual gross revenue. Of course, this varies by organization, size, and industry. It can be on the high side for smaller organizations with limited purchasing power to exploit economies of scale, or it can even exceed 15% of revenue in industries that derive their principal value from IT, such as in financial services, outsourced hosting providers or Internet-based e-commerce businesses. Or it can be on the low side for organizations and industries that rely principally on other forms of investment, such as facilities and capital equipment as compared to IT. IT budgets can also vary by as much as 50% among organizations of comparable size, meaning there can be a big spread between your organization and your closest competitor. A final point to note is that funding levels are not stable year over year. Funding can shift from one end of this spectrum to another and 1.5 to 7% represents a broad range. Organizations that invest heavily in one year may not need to in subsequent years. Do your best to get as accurate an estimate as possible so you know what you have to work with when making your IT funding request.

Funding Sources and Accounting Methods

The sources of the IT budget and accounting methods used to track expenditures can also vary greatly by organization. Potential sources can include c-level executives, such as the CEO, CFO, or CIO; various internal lines of business; or external sources such as a parent company or autonomous subsidiaries.

Some organizations fund a centralized IT budget that is unallocated by business function or group. Others account for IT costs based on services consumed using a so-called charge-back model. Here, each business function or group reserves a certain percentage of its assigned budget for IT resources and services. The organization's IT department then charges against that budget. If the IT department's resources (expertise, infrastructure, systems, etc.) are limited or otherwise constrained, then this budget may be used to procure external IT resources and services directly by the business functions or groups. You should be aware of policies or restrictions associated with bypassing your existing IT department (or consultant or outsourced services provider, as the case may be) to use other external IT service providers of your choosing. Such flexibility may simplify the effort in making an IT funding request.

We do not discuss all possible sources and accounting methods associated with IT funding. We simply want to point out that this can vary depending on the size and structure of your organization. In smaller organizations, this is not likely to be a challenge. However, if your organization is large, distributed, or complex in some way, you should learn the sources and accounting methods it uses to fund its IT operations. Your IT funding request should then include arguments that demonstrate how it, too, fits with the objectives and measures used to track the funding source's performance and complies with existing accounting methods. How this is done may depend on how IT budgets are tracked and managed. What follows represents a few perspectives on how this is done.

IT Budget Management: Resource Perspective

At a high level, an IT budget may be tracked across several IT resource categories, as illustrated in Figure 7.4.

These categories are typically used as a means broadly to track spending. For example, it is no surprise that IT personnel command the majority of

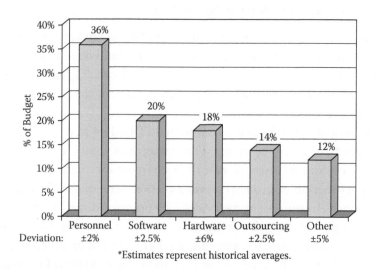

FIGURE 7.4
IT budget from a "resource" perspective.

the budget, followed by software. These two categories represent the most common high-level resources requested. They also represent the biggest targets when management seeks to cut costs. Some IT decision makers may "pigeonhole" your request into such categories. Avoid this at all costs. It conceals the potential benefits and returns from your investment, relegating it to a mere expense.

IT Budget Management: Domain Perspective

Some organizations manage their budget across various IT domains, as illustrated in Figure 7.5. Depending upon your investment need, you might be tempted to request a budget from a particular domain. For example, if your process improvement analysis concludes that a new application needs to be developed, you might request a proportion of the 20% of budget allocated to that domain. But allocation does not mean availability. Some of this budget will be earmarked to support continued development of existing applications.

Realize, too, that IT investment requests will usually incur expenses from multiple domains. Let's recall our earlier example. Upgrading the

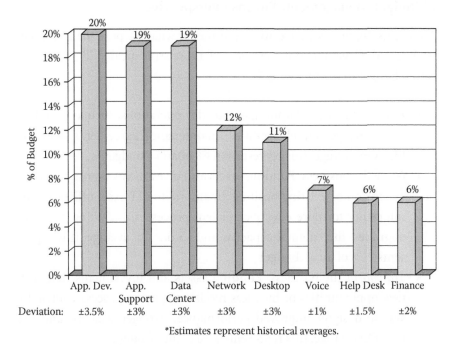

*Estimates represent historical averages.

FIGURE 7.5
IT budget from a "domain" perspective.

ERP software license to expose it to the shipping department may require budget from other domains, including the data center, network, and help desk, not just from application development or support domains. It is best practice to include in your investment request how it affects the resources and budget that comprise various domains if, indeed, your organization tracks such categories.

Domains, too, view IT largely from an expense management perspective. But they begin to shed some light on how IT budget supports business execution. On average, 39% of a typical IT budget is allocated to support existing applications or to develop new ones. Applications and application support typically serve departmental needs (as a general ledger supports accounting) or cross-organizational value-chain processes (such as inventory management supports manufacturing and order processing). Budget decisions from this perspective begin to consider how process execution may benefit, but they fall a bit short of viewing IT investments as strategic assets.

IT Budget Management: Purpose Perspective

A more useful perspective is to determine for what purpose the IT budget is allocated. Organizations that view IT more strategically do so by allocating budget to the following:*

- *Run* the business: Funding day-to-day operations, such as IT infrastructure, personnel, facilities, maintenance agreements, and the like. On average, this represents 64% of an IT budget.
- *Grow* the business: Funding assets and investments that support the expansion of existing business by improving IT asset utilization or migrating to more effective/efficient processes, including software upgrades, incremental capacity, and so on. On average, this represents 21% of an IT budget.
- *Transform* the business: Funding assets and investments that seek new opportunities or business models requiring process-centric IT system designs, improved performance, stronger security, and the like. On average, this represents 15% of an IT budget.

---

* These budget allocation percentages represent historical averages and can fluctuate plus or minus 4% depending on the business and economic cycle.

This perspective helps us understand how the IT budget begins to support strategic objectives. Nearly two-thirds (64%) is allocated to helping run the existing business and over a third (36%) is allocated to grow or transform the business and its operations. Each purpose (run, grow, and transform) plays a key role in execution depending upon the business strategy. For example, if the strategy calls for improved operating efficiency, and is measured by increased margins, then the purpose of IT will be to transform operations. If the strategy is to increase revenue, then the purpose of IT will be to grow the business. Organizations that view IT as the means to help run, grow, or transform the business will seek, and respond favorably to, IT investment requests that contribute improvements to these purposes.

Position your IT investment request by demonstrating how it either helps run, grow, or transform the business. Be prepared to focus and provide clear justification for one of these purposes. Indeed, it is possible that your investment can contribute to all purposes, but if so, make sure your reasoning and justification are clear to avoid confusing the primary purpose of your investment request.

The next step in positioning your investment request is to understand the flexibility in your organization's IT budget. Some funding, particularly that associated with running the business, will be fixed and nondiscretionary. Other funding is much less so. The greater the flexibility, the better are your chances of being funded.

IT Budget Management: Asset Class Perspective

Some organizations, particularly those that practice IT portfolio management, structure investments into asset classes based on their value or risk. Typical asset classes can include the following:

- *Operational assets:* Enable the IT operation to run the business and can include mainframes, servers, operational support systems, facilities, maintenance, power, and so on.
- *Nondiscretionary assets:* Typically forced expenditures necessary to run the business caused by regulatory compliance, equipment failure and repair, or the need to replace outmoded or unsupported assets such as older software versions, servers, memory, storage, routers, and the like.

- *Discretionary assets:* Required to upgrade or replace existing assets, such as platforms and application versions necessary to run, grow, or transform the business.
- *Strategic assets:* Typically applications and processes necessary to run, grow, or transform the business based on business strategy. Examples include upgrading CRM capabilities, implementing a product life-cycle management (PLM) system, expanding supply chain planning (SCP) capabilities, and providing mobile computing to field personnel, among others. Strategic assets can also include unique proprietary technology, such as an internally developed analytic algorithm, or intellectual property, such as the findings discovered through the use of such an algorithm.
- *Venture investments:* Allocated to research and development, or used to incubate future business opportunities or experiment with the transformation or growth of a business, business model, or product/ service lines.

In general, IT budgets allocated to core operational and nondiscretionary assets are committed with little flexibility to change. In fact, these asset classes can draw budgets away from other asset classes (discretionary, strategic, venture) when unforeseen or other forced events occur.

The availability of venture investment can vary greatly in most organizations. But if a budget is available, it is possible to make a case for its allocation. A venture budget is speculative in nature, and therefore carries greater risk. Requesting it requires additional positioning using market, customer, and competitive intelligence, as advised by Porter in *Competitive Strategy* (1980), and Treacy and Wiersema in *The Discipline of Market Leaders* (1995). Simply attempting to "take a shot" at this funding without such preparation will likely be perceived as ill-prepared and possibly jeopardize your request. IT investments that result from a business process improvement project are often funded from either discretionary or strategic asset classes. They usually are the most flexible.

IT Investment Practices of Industry Leaders

Industry leaders continually adapt technology to improve execution using best practices that do the following:

- Assess IT readiness for process change

- Track trends that influence IT strategy
- Enable process-centric capabilities and systems design
- Increase investment returns from IT resources using IT portfolio management

A particular skill that the leadership and management of these organizations master is the ability to precisely map IT portfolio investments to a chosen business strategy.

For example, an industry-leading retailer whose business strategy is based on customer intimacy would consider a product information management system as an operational asset used to run the business, whereas its customer relationship management system would be considered a strategic asset to grow the business. IT investments that "fit" (per Porter) and improve customer-oriented outcome measures and performance drivers would be the retailer's priority.

These asset classes may be reversed for an industry-leading consumer electronics manufacturer whose business strategy is product leadership. Here, the product information management system is viewed as a strategic asset to grow and transform the business, whereas its customer relationship management system would be an operational asset to run the business. Here, IT investments that "fit" and improve product-oriented outcome measures and performance drivers would be the manufacturer's priority.

These IT portfolio priorities may seem obvious at a high level, but successful execution of a well-planned strategy requires meticulous synchronization of workforce behavior, business processes, and IT assets. Industry leaders pull ahead of their market because they possess unique analytical skill and the managerial discipline necessary to consistently perform this way. Any organization can acquire these skills by pulling together the best practices discussed in this book, being aware of the obstacles, and incorporating this knowledge into a formal strategic planning process.

Making an IT Investment Request

From the perspectives provided above, study your organization's IT portfolio and budget. Observe how the portfolio is structured, the budget is allocated, and what decision criteria are used to prioritize and fund investment requests.

To secure funding, you must justify your investment request using objective evaluation and financial analysis techniques, as prescribed by IT portfolio management. Position the investment relative to competing requests by demonstrating its compatibility with strategic objectives. Emphasize how advantage is created, because the IT request best fits your organization's value chain and IT portfolio and helps to run, grow, or transform the business as called for by strategic objectives.

Carefully prepared, justified, and positioned IT investment requests that fit within an organization's business strategy, value chain, and IT portfolio are likely to be favored and awarded over others that are not.

SECTION II CONCLUSION: RESOURCES STRUCTURED FOR EXECUTION

While reading, you may have reflected upon the alignment of your organization's business strategy and resources, perhaps realizing the following:

- Strategic business planning processes are too informal.
- Parts of the current business strategy are noncompetitive.
- Aspects of workforce behavior are ineffective.
- Business processes may be too rigid or nonexistent, causing stakeholders to "wing it."
- IT resources are overburdened and technology is outdated or inflexible.

Indeed, there can be many other internal reasons for ineffective alignment. Similar shortcomings are common in many organizations. Even in well-run organizations, external influences can knock strategic alignment off balance. Mergers, acquisitions, regulatory requirements, changing customer needs, or new competitive threats force organizations to re-evaluate business objectives and how best to deploy the resources required to achieve them.

To overcome organizational shortcomings and properly respond to market dynamics, leadership and management typically institute a structured strategic planning process. Periodically, either monthly, quarterly, semi-annually, or annually (otherwise as required), they analyze the effectiveness of business strategy as determined by key performance measures and are critical of how resources are structured to support execution.

Such critical analysis should include the guidance offered in this book. To briefly recap:

- In Section I, entitled *Best Practices Used in Strategic Planning,* summary reviews of the top best-selling authors on business strategy were provided. The key messages from each were distilled to reveal the essential proven and reliable best practices used by leading organizations to create a strategic planning framework necessary to accomplish the following:
  - Command competitive knowledge.
  - Define strategy and focus investment on high-priority areas.
  - Measure performance from multiple perspectives.
  - Quickly respond to change or customer need.
- In Section II, entitled *Execution—Best Practice Use of Strategic Resources,* the discussion focused on how industry leaders prepare their resources—people, business processes, and information technology—to execute their strategy by:
  - Empowering and motivating the workforce, using workforce collaboration and collaborative objectives
  - Modeling and analyzing business processes to include workforce accountability and enable techniques to control, measure, and manage the necessary performance outcomes
  - Adapting information technology with process-centric capabilities needed for workforce collaboration, performance measurement, and outcome management, as called for by business strategy and business process designs

So far, you have learned the best practices used to structure business strategy, people, processes, and technology. Now, you must learn how to align resources with business strategy for consistent execution. To do this I introduce the derivative analysis technique for business strategy and resource alignment.

Section III

How to Align Strategy and Resources to Improve Execution, Adaptability, and Consistency

The authors discussed in Section I have inspiring approaches to strategy and resource alignment. Indeed, there are many other well-respected consultants and authors on this topic from which to choose. Common to all is that their advice to readers is transferred through carefully written books with passages punctuated with relevant case studies. Indeed, case studies are effective means of revealing and explaining best practices. However, when the reading is complete, the student is sometimes puzzled. Believing their organization to be different or unique from those discussed in the case examples they wonder, "How can I apply this to my organization?"

The published works of each author and consultant represent their unique line of reasoning. Applying their lessons to a specific organization requires that line of reasoning to be used to facilitate dialogue among its leadership and management. But translating such logic from book form to a structured and productive discussion and debate usually means calling upon the author or consultant to lead the effort. The conclusions are recorded in a formal report or presentation for the organization to act upon. As change occurs, the author or consultant might be asked for a return visit to revitalize the recommendations.

An alternative approach is to translate the line of reasoning of the book into a self-assessment guide to facilitate structured discussion and debate without the need of an outside facilitator. Of course, I realize that a fresh set of eyes is valuable to remain objective. However, when time is of the essence or resources are scarce, being able to self-assess strategy and resource alignment can be expedient and economical. Here, I offer the derivative analysis technique for business strategy and resource alignment.

8

The Derivative Analysis Technique for Business Strategy and Resource Alignment

Derivative analysis is a disciplined approach to facilitate discussion and debate among executives and managers during strategic planning sessions. Its techniques enable participants to derive and structure the resources necessary to execute a chosen strategy by calling to action the sage advice from the thought leaders discussed in Section I. These include the lessons from the following:

- Porter, on how best to structure activities to form a competitive value chain
- Treacy and Wiersema, on how best to structure an operating model to support a chosen strategic discipline
- Kaplan and Norton, on how best to structure performance measures and reveal cause-and-effect relationships between various assets using a balanced scorecard and a strategy map
- Haeckel, on how best to adapt to change and opportunity using sense-and-respond techniques, the adaptive loop behavior model, a modular organization, and the commitment management protocol

Derivative analysis uses the relevant best practices of all thought leaders discussed throughout this book, building upon each to create a more comprehensive framework within which to formulate strategy, align resources for execution, and prepare the organization to respond properly to change as it occurs. Moreover, it guides discussion and decision to derive specific and discrete details for resource alignment without which strategy and execution can become unraveled. Here, derivative analysis helps conclude how:

- Workforce behavior must be guided to overcome anticipated and unanticipated anomalies in execution
- Business processes must be designed and augmented with control processes to maintain performance consistently within predetermined thresholds
- In-place information technology must be adapted or augmented to support dynamic process-centric capabilities. Process-centric systems monitor business activity in real-time, assisting the workforce with process execution and using exception and resolution management controls to keep performance from varying outside acceptable thresholds and prevent, or minimize, adverse consequences to key performance indicators

It is necessary for executives and managers charged with strategy and execution to understand resource alignment to this level of granularity. Without such understanding, critical details necessary to manage performance may be left unaddressed or relegated downstream in the organization where they may be overlooked. As noted earlier by Bossidy and Charan (2002, p. 22), "Execution is a systematic process of rigorously discussing 'hows' and 'whats', questioning, tenaciously following through, and ensuring accountability." If you don't know the critical "hows" and "whats," and don't ask the right questions with sufficient detail, resources fail to align, hobbling a strategy from its beginning.

DERIVATIVE ANALYSIS DEFINED

Derivative analysis draws conclusions from the answers to a series of deterministic questions posed and debated in a reasoned sequence. When using derivative analysis to align strategy and resources, questions are answered in the form of a conclusion or decision about what approach or actions the organization should take. This prompts questioning about the structure and resources required to support the approach or enable the actions. Subsequent questions are derived based on prior answers forming (if guided correctly) a derivative line of reasoning. Alignment occurs successively upon analysis of specific answers or conclusions following the line of reasoning. When complete, the derivative relationships are revealed for a particular strategy, identifying specific resources, actions, and if necessary, investments.

For example, a strategy postulated for product leadership requires definition and differentiation. Product differentiation can occur in many ways. Organizations must define and choose the characteristics of differentiation that are, according to Porter, "Defendable in the industry." Selecting from durability, feature/functionality, design, or a combination of such is determined using industry, market, customer, and competitive analysis. Next, organizations must ask what actions are required to enable the chosen characteristics of product differentiation. Durability might require renewed R&D investment in materials, feature/functionality may require customer "focus group" interviews and usability tests, design may require the acquisition of new artistic talent, and so on. The decisions made here then launch a new set of questions about how best to structure resources (people, processes, and technology) to execute in support of the chosen strategy.

Derivative analysis is a structured exercise that leadership and management can use during strategic planning to be critical of how business is to be done. It engages controlled and thoughtful debate leading to actionable decisions that have been vetted and agreed upon to execute a chosen strategy. Sometimes strategic planning sessions can be unproductive, misdirected, or bogged down by endless debate. Derivative analysis avoids wasting time by using the best practices presented in this book to craft a productive line of reasoning while simultaneously debating the proper structure of the resources needed for execution. I demonstrate how this works shortly. Before I do, it is valuable to contrast derivative analysis from its progenitor: cause-and-effect analysis.

Flexible in its interpretation, cause-and-effect analysis is most frequently used as a problem-solving method to identify the sources or causes of problems for correction after they have occurred. Its techniques emanate from several schools of thought that consider the context in which it is being used. For example, popular instantiations of cause-and-effect analysis focus on finding the root causes for problems associated with some type of failure or performance degradation of structures, processes, production, safety, or other complex systems. It is based on the belief that problems are best solved when analysis reveals the originating (or root) causes and not merely the resulting symptoms of the problem.

Cause-and-effect analysis can be used as a predictive model helping to reveal risk "before the fact." Some organizations and noted consultants use it as a forward-looking tool to align strategy and resources. For instance, Kaplan and Norton in *The Balanced Scorecard* recommend its use to link performance measures to strategy. Here, they advise (Kaplan and Norton, 1996, p. 149):

> A strategy is a set of hypothesis [sic] about cause and effect. Cause-and-effect relationships can be expressed by a sequence of if-then statements. For example, a link between improved sales training of employees and higher profits can be established through the following sequence of hypotheses: If we increase employee training about products, then they will become more knowledgeable about the full range of products they can sell; if employees are more knowledgeable about products, then their sales effectiveness will improve. If their sales effectiveness improves, then the average margins of the products they sell will increase.

Later in *Strategy Maps,* the authors flesh out how best to reveal cause-and-effect relationships among the assets necessary to execute strategy using a strategy map. Indeed, cause-and-effect analysis illustrates the relationships among strategy, people, process, and technology. But for it to be truly deterministic, or forward looking, it must be guided by a slightly different line of reasoning—a derivative line of reasoning—which is best explained in the following way.

Cause-and-effect analysis usually begins with an existing effect (result or outcome). It then decomposes the various possibilities leading to it to determine the most likely root cause or causes. It is an analytic technique that is most often used after the fact to re-create what has happened to determine a solution to prevent the outcome from reoccurring.

Derivative analysis begins with a desired effect (outcome, result, or goal). It then composes various possibilities to determine how to affect or cause the result. It is an analytic technique (line of reasoning) used before the fact to create what needs to happen to derive the desired outcome.

To some, this argument will seem semantic. But I believe it is important to make these distinctions because the questions, skills, and talents required of executives and managers to engage in each type of analysis are, indeed, different.

Consider for the moment the talents of two teams. Team 1 is an architect and a structural engineer. Team 2 is a detective and a coroner. Which is likely to use cause-and-effect analysis and which is likely to use derivative analysis? The skills, talent, and questions used to examine an effect (a corpse) and determine how it came to be (heart failure caused by violent struggle) are different from postulating an objective (an earthquake-resistant bridge) and creating a means to achieve it (invent a self-anchored suspension span). Determining the cause of death is best accomplished using a cause-and-effect line of reasoning, whereas inventing the mechanics of a self-anchored suspension bridge requires a derivative line of reasoning.

Another way to explain the difference is by looking at the movement of an antique grandfather clock. Many people can examine the interactions (cause-and-effect relationships) of the various gears, levers, and weights and figure out how it keeps time. However, few people can invent such a device with no prior knowledge of its existence. Creating a mechanical clock for the first time required painstaking experimentation through trial and error to derive the cause-and-effect relationships among gears, levers, and weights necessary to accurately keep time.

Fundamentally, it's the difference between "re-creation" and "creation." Cause-and effect analysis and derivative analysis differ in the skills, talents, and questions (or line of reasoning) used by the person or team challenged with such analysis. As a leader, executive, or manager, it is important to assemble the correct analytic or creative talent available to craft a strategy and properly align resources for execution. Let's demonstrate how derivative analysis works.

Using Derivative Analysis to Align Strategy and Resources: A Self-Assessment

The following represents how derivative analysis can be used to facilitate a self-assessment discussion in a strategic planning meeting. It follows the same line of reasoning discussed in Sections I and II in this book. It begins by asking questions based on the best practices used for strategic planning and progresses to debate the best practice use of strategic resources. Derivative analysis does not need to begin with a review of the classic approach to strategic planning and analysis of competitive forces as demonstrated here, although this is always helpful to set the stage for productive discussion. Planning or review can begin at any point of the successive flow, as long as leadership and management team participants are confident of the decisions and conclusions prior to where the analysis begins.

During the analysis, participants must abide by the following rules:

- The analysis will be led and driven by an executive sponsor who will be held accountable and responsible for its outcome. The use of a facilitator is acceptable to maintain progress and control but only when the executive sponsor is present. Derivative analysis requires decisions to be made; this cannot happen without active participation of sponsoring leadership.
- Each question should be answered in the form of a conclusion or decision about what approach or action the organization should take.
- Then pose all relevant follow-up questions, either about strategy or resources as the case may be, that help to determine how best to act upon what was concluded.
- Disagreement or conflicting views must be debated to conclusion or consensus about what to do or how to do it.
- Indecision is not acceptable. If this occurs, suspend the planning session to gather the necessary data or intelligence to draw a conclusion or consensus, and then resume.
- Indifference or "groupthink" to "get it over with" is counterproductive, unacceptable, and a waste of time. Those participants who cannot, or will not, make thoughtful and valuable contributions should be excluded from participating, or be encouraged to reread this book prior to rejoining the discussion.
- Be specific. Generalities, anecdotes, uncertainty, and other forms of incomplete logic or noncommittal thoughts cause confusion and delay. If specificity is lacking throughout the discussion, suspend the planning session to gather the data or intelligence necessary to be specific or decisive, then resume.
- Engage constructive criticism, not just criticism. Criticism from participants must make a productive contribution to the analysis. It should be followed by constructive recommendations or at least create a forum to postulate such recommendations and debate to conclusion or consensus.
- Record the findings and results.
- Hold accountable and responsible named leaders and managers for execution.

When complete, the derivative relationships are revealed for a particular strategy, identifying specific resources, actions, and if necessary, investments.

A GENERIC DERIVATIVE ANALYSIS

Section I: Best Practices Used in Strategic Planning

1. *How to Compete:* Assemble the participants and begin the discussion using the classic approach to formulating competitive strategy. Refer to Chapter 1 for guidance. Establish a baseline by stating the purpose of the organization (What value is being created? Who are the customers? What are their needs?), the combination of ends (or mission, goals, objectives) for which it is striving, and the means (or policies, tactics, procedures) by which they are achieved. Discuss these factors by considering three lines of questioning:

   a. What is the business doing now, what is its current strategy, and what are the implied assumptions and data upon which the current strategy is based?

   b. What is happening in the environment as determined by analysis of the industry, competitors, societal influences, and strengths and weaknesses of the organization?

   c. What should the business be doing, meaning, how do the original assumptions hold up to a current analysis of the environment, and what are the feasible strategic alternatives given the findings of this analysis?

Answering these questions will require you to understand the four key factors that determine the context within which strategy is formulated. Be prepared to discuss the following:

   d. The organization's strengths and weaknesses as defined by its profile of assets and skills, such as financial resources, technology profile, and brand recognition among others, relative to competitors.

   e. Opportunities or threats in the industry, such as those posed by economic conditions or technical advances.

   f. Personal values or the motivations and needs of key executives and personnel responsible for implementing the strategy.

   g. Societal or governmental expectations and trends that influence directions and decisions.

Also, analyze how your competitive landscape is structured and influenced using Porter's competitive forces model.

  h. Determine the rigor and impact of rivalry from known competitors.
  i. Evaluate the probability, potential, and risk posed of new entrants.
  j. Identify the potential and sources of feasible substitutes to your products and services and assess what risk they pose.
  k. Determine the bargaining power of buyers (customers) and the sources of this power.
  l. Determine the bargaining power of suppliers and the sources of this power.

Discussion of the classic approach to competitive strategy and Porter's structural analysis provide the framework necessary to understand the factors and forces influencing strategy. However, before conclusions can be drawn, the discussion must include Treacy and Wiersema's guidance in *The Discipline of Market Leaders* (1995). Pose and debate the new rules of competition and how customers define value. Refer to Chapter 2 for guidance.

  m. What are the dimensions of value about which the customer cares?
  n. Where does the company stand relative to its competitors on each of these dimensions?
  o. Where and why does it fall short?
  p. What would customers perceive as unmatched value?
  q. Could competitors quickly better that value?
  r. For topics m through q: What are your conclusions? What needs to change? Summarize and record findings.

Based on this analysis, what strategic approach creates the best defensible position given this competitive environment?

  s. Consider Porter's offensive or defensive actions and generic strategies of cost leadership, differentiation, or focus.
  t. Consider Treacy and Wiersema's value disciplines of customer intimacy, product leadership, or operational excellence.

u. Consider other strategies as are relevant.

v. What are your conclusions? What needs to change? Summarize the conclusions and findings of this portion of the derivative analysis, 1. How to Compete.

Progress Report: How to Compete. At this point in the derivative analysis, you should have derived and documented your strategic approach to creating customer value and competitive differentiation. Depending upon the approach chosen (e.g., product leadership, operational excellence, or customer intimacy), you need to craft an operating model that begins to identify and structure the high-level resources required to support it. Your next line of questioning, therefore, must help you derive how best to structure and focus operations.

2. *How to Focus Operations:* Continue using Treacy and Wiersema's guidance in *The Discipline of Market Leaders* (1995) to define and structure one operating model. Refer to Chapter 2 for guidance.

a. What kind of operating model would deliver the value proposition at a profit? Consider its structure using the operational excellence, product leadership, and customer intimacy operating models (or derivatives of such), or use one of the other generic models posited by Porter or Kaplan and Norton as guides.

b. How would the operating model work? Define the core processes and the attributes of culture, organization, management systems, and information technology (as demonstrated in Chapter 2) that support the customer value and competitive differentiation chosen.

c. What change initiatives must the organization launch?

d. Will the organization require restructuring? If so, how?

e. How will the organization manage these changes and maintain its focus?

f. What risks will be incurred, and how will the organization manage them?

g. Determine to what degree other secondary and tertiary strategies are required to maintain customer value while keeping competitors at bay. How does this affect the operating model?

h. What are your conclusions? What needs to change? Summarize the conclusions and findings of this portion of the derivative analysis, 2. How to Focus Operations.

Progress Report: How to Focus Operations. At this point in the derivative analysis, you should have derived and diagrammed the attributes for each component of your operating model (core processes, culture, organization, management systems, and information technology) based on your chosen strategic approach to competitive differentiation. You must next generate a new line of questions necessary to derive a performance measurement system needed to track strategic execution and the structure of your operating model.

3. *How To Manage Performance:* Using Kaplan and Norton's scorecard approach pose and debate the key measures that are specific and relevant to the effectiveness and efficiency of the chosen strategy and operating model. Refer to Chapter 3 and Chapter 6, "Managing Process Execution," for guidance.

    a. The measures and drivers selected should distinguish between long- and short-term objectives, between financial and nonfinancial measures, between lagging and leading indicators, and measures affecting cost, quality, and schedule. Consider measures from each perspective.

        i. Financial perspective
        ii. Customer perspective
        iii. Internal business process perspective
        iv. Learning and growth perspective

    b. What outcome measures common to most strategies should be selected to track performance?

    c. What performance drivers are unique to your strategy and should be selected to track performance?

    d. Pose and debate what threshold levels of performance must also be maintained for other supportive (secondary and tertiary) strategies? Consider threshold measures from each of the four perspectives listed above.

    e. You may find it helpful to draft a strategy map to identify the tangible and intangible assets required of your chosen strategy. Map the core processes identified in your operating model to the four internal business process clusters called for in the strategy map. If the operating model does not identify core processes within each cluster, then review the clusters to determine what other core processes are required to execute your strategy. Remember, each process cluster of a strategy map requires a strategic theme that then must be defined and structured to state the specific objectives sought from each of the four scorecard performance measurement perspectives. Identify the theme and the specific measures to be managed and tracked for each scorecard objective. Prescribe action plans that identify specific strategic initiatives for each measure sought.

f. Use the strategy map, what constructive and destructive cause-and-effect relationships will or may exist among and between the organization's assets, process clusters, and performance measures chosen for financial, customer, business process, and learning and growth performance.

g. What cause-and-effect relationships will ultimately affect financial measures?

h. What are your conclusions? What needs to change? Summarize the conclusions and findings of this portion of the derivative analysis, 3. How to Manage Performance.

Progress Report: How to Manage Performance. At this point in the derivative analysis, you should have derived and documented all relevant performance measures (outcome measures and performance drivers) necessary to track and manage your chosen business strategy and operating model. If you chose to draft a strategy map, it should illustrate these findings along with the strategic assets, core processes within each process cluster, and strategic themes required for execution.

Consistently executing to achieve the desired performance measures and outcomes requires the means to manage events and respond to opportunities as they occur, making corrections before they adversely affect the chosen measures. This will require effective workforce behavior that holds people in key roles accountable and responsible for outcomes.

Your next line of questioning, therefore, must help you derive a means to protect your performance measures from risk and how best to make corrections when variance occurs or opportunity knocks.

4. *How to Adapt:* Using Haeckel's sense-and-respond model, determine the rules and means to best adapt when change or events occur to cause the performance measures or outcomes associated with the

core processes identified in your operating model (or strategy map) to veer off course, or when new opportunity presents itself. Refer to Chapter 4 for guidance.

a. How will you enable sense-and-respond behavior across the organization? How will adaptive loop processes be practiced and applied?

  i. How are change, events, and opportunity that have the greatest impact on strategic outcomes sensed?

  ii. What resources are needed to interpret its meaning?

  iii. What governance is required for making decisions and acting upon them?

  iv. What tools are needed to access and disseminate strategic information?

  v. Are these methods and tools in place now and are they sufficient?

  vi. What are your conclusions? What needs to change? Summarize and record findings.

b. What "modularity" will be required of your organizational structure to support sense-and-respond behavior?

  i. What organizational structure will best support your chosen strategy?

  ii. How will your operating model, particularly culture, support flexibility and structure required of a modular organization?

  iii. What "rules of engagement" and boundaries of behavior must be established and disseminated among the workforce to guide how they interpret, decide, and act when various events occur?

  iv. Who will be the named individuals of the workforce placed in key roles and how are they empowered to interpret, decide, and act within these bounds?

  v. What is your conclusion? What needs to change? Summarize and record findings.

c. How must the workforce collaborate and manage to commitment?

  i. How will you implement discipline similar to the commitment management protocol to support resolution management?

  ii. What systems or tools are needed to facilitate workforce collaboration using the commitment management protocol?

iii. What is your conclusion? What needs to change? Summarize and record findings.

    d. Summarize the conclusions and findings of this portion of the derivative analysis, 4. How to Adapt.

Progress Report: How to Adapt. At this point in the derivative analysis, you should have derived how change and opportunity are sensed, the key individuals who will be held accountable and responsible for the outcomes of performance measures, what rules of engagement and collaboration will be necessary to empower them to interpret, decide, and act when change, opportunity, or risk is sensed in support of your operating model and chosen strategic approach. Before moving on to discuss how best to derive and structure specific resources, review the progress made to derive your strategic approach.

Progress Report—Section I: Best Practices Used in Strategic Planning

At this point, your leadership and management team should have decided upon and committed to a specified strategy, operating model, performance measures, and methods to adapt to change. Collectively, these best practices represent a comprehensive summary of the knowledge required, and the decisions executives must make, to craft and execute successful business strategy. The conclusions, findings, and actions required should be documented and used as the foundation for your organization's strategic plan. Your next line of questioning, therefore, must help you derive and structure specific resources necessary to execute the conclusions derived from Section I of the analysis.

Section II: Execution—Best Practice Use of Strategic Resources

Pose and debate the type and structure of the resources (people, processes, and technology) needed to execute.

    5. *How to Structure Organizational Behavior Necessary for Strategic Execution:* Evaluate how effective and efficient the workforce is currently in achieving strategic objectives, and then determine what needs to change to support the business strategy and operating model and to achieve the selected performance measures. Pose and

debate questions considering the findings and conclusions drawn from your analysis of 4. How to Adapt from Section I of the derivative analysis. Refer to Chapters 4 and 5 for guidance.

a. How, and to what degree, must the organization disseminate business strategy to the workforce?
    i. Is dissemination of value? If not, why? If so, why?
    ii. How does this affect execution and strategic achievement?
    iii. What is your conclusion? What needs to change? Summarize and record findings.
b. What methods and practices will be required to empower and motivate the workforce?
    i. How must the workforce be empowered?
    ii. How must the workforce be motivated?
    iii. What rules of engagement are necessary and what boundaries will be defined to control risk?
    iv. What policies and rules are necessary to demark such boundaries?
    v. Is this sufficient to drive the sense-and-respond behavior necessary for the organization's strategy, operating model, and performance control?
    vi. What is your conclusion? What needs to change? Summarize and record findings.
c. Describe and discuss the quality and frequency of workforce collaboration across your organization's various business functions. Consider this with respect to the core business processes necessary to deliver customer value of your chosen strategy.
    i. Does your organization consider workforce collaboration to be a value-added process (an asset)? If not, why? If so, with what rigor is it scrutinized? Is sufficient attention paid to its effectiveness, or is it overlooked?
    ii. What type of workforce collaboration is imperative and a priority?
    iii. What processes and systems must be in place to facilitate the required workforce collaboration?
    iv. Does workforce collaboration sufficiently support the stated objectives and realize desired outcomes?
    v. What is your conclusion? What needs to change? Summarize and record findings.

d. For each core cross-functional business process identified in your operating model discuss and debate the use and value of collaborative objectives and how they might affect execution, results, and workforce collaboration.

    i. Does your organization consider collaborative objectives to be of value? If not, why? Pose and debate how collaborative objectives can affect performance.

    ii. What collaborative objectives are required for each core cross-functional process?

    iii. With what rigor do you plan to measure and scrutinize each? Is sufficient attention paid to their effectiveness, or are they overlooked?

    iv. Are they correctly tied to relevant performance measures that drive strategic achievement?

    v. What is your conclusion? What needs to change? Summarize and record findings.

e. Discuss and debate how the workforce is held responsible and accountable for outcome measures and performance drivers.

    i. Who are the named individuals who will be held accountable and responsible for performance and outcomes?

    ii. How will they be held responsible and accountable for the performance measures and outcomes necessary to track and manage strategic achievement?

    iii. Does the organization track and manage responsibility and accountably consistently using appropriate motivation and incentive systems? If so, how? If not, why?

    iv. What is your conclusion? What needs to change? Summarize and record findings.

f. Summarize the conclusions and findings of this portion of the derivative analysis, 5. How to Structure Organizational Behavior.

Progress Report: How to Structure Organizational Behavior. At this point in the derivative analysis, you should have derived the rules and processes that disseminate strategy throughout the organization; empowered and motivated the workforce to collaborate in the execution of the core processes defined in your operating model; and reinforced behavior through collaborative objectives that hold accountable and responsible the workforce and individuals to achieve the key performance measures required of your chosen business strategy.

The knowledge gained about workforce behavior and what needs to change to support strategic objectives must be used to generate your next line of questioning that will help you derive how best to manage processes as assets that support workforce collaboration, and structure the core business processes identified in your operating model (and/or strategy map).

6. *How to Structure Business Processes Necessary for Strategic Execution:* Evaluate how effective and efficient your organization's core business processes are currently in achieving strategic objectives, and then determine what needs to change to support the business strategy and operating model to achieve the selected performance measures and to facilitate proper workforce behavior and collaboration. Refer to Chapter 6 for guidance.

   a. Does your organization consider its business processes to be value-added assets? If not, why?
      i. How does your organization categorize, classify, or prioritize processes?
      ii. With what rigor and discipline are they managed as assets?
      iii. How are risks and returns identified and scrutinized?
      iv. What is your conclusion? What needs to change? Summarize and record findings.

   b. Of the core cross-organizational business processes necessary to deliver customer value identified in your operating model,
      i. How effective, or how must they be structured to support your chosen business strategy?
      ii. How effective, or how must they be structured to achieve your chosen outcome measures and performance drivers?
      iii. How effective, or how must they be structured to support event management and control processes when events occur?
      iv. How knowledgeable is the workforce about the upstream and downstream performance of the processes? Are they aware of the implications their performance, or lack thereof, has on other process stakeholders?
      v. What is your conclusion? What needs to change? Summarize and record findings.

   c. Discuss and debate the means, tools, and resources committed to business process design, analysis, and management.
      i. How knowledgeable, attentive, or indifferent are leadership and management regarding the current methods, practices,

and technology available for business process modeling, design, analysis, and execution?

    ii. Does this create a strategic advantage or disadvantage?

   iii. Are tools available to conduct process modeling, simulation, and analysis? Pose and debate their capabilities and limitations. Are they sufficient to measure and simulate KPI results, execution performance, and resources consumed?

   iv. What impact do these tools have on strategic achievement?

    v. What is your conclusion? What needs to change? Summarize and record findings.

d. Pose and debate how well performance measures are controlled by your core business processes. Consider outcome measures and performance drivers (KPIs) specific to the business strategy and measures of the time, resources, and costs consumed during process execution.

    i. For each core process are all KPIs relevant to the strategy accurately tracked? If not, why? If so, is this done consistently? What impact does this have?

    ii. For each core process are all KPIs relevant to the execution of the process performance (time, resources, and costs consumed) accurately tracked? If not, why? If so, is this done consistently? What impact does this have?

   iii. Are all measures (or the data necessary to determine such measures) always available to the workforce and systems necessary to track and manage them? If not, why? If so, is this done consistently? What impact does this have?

   iv. What is your conclusion? What needs to change? Summarize and record findings.

e. Pose and debate how effective the current event management techniques are to support and maintain threshold performance for strategic outcomes. Consider the details of both exception and resolution control processes.

    i. Does your organization consider event management to be an important effort? If not, why? If so, with what rigor is it enabled? Is sufficient attention paid to its effectiveness, or is it overlooked?

    ii. What policies, business rules, control processes, and process controls will be critical to your strategy and the core processes needed for execution?

      iii. What systems are in place to enable event management? Are they sufficient to ensure the performance thresholds are not exceeded?

      iv. Is the workforce properly prepared, empowered, and motivated to execute event management practices?

      v. What is your conclusion? What needs to change? Summarize and record findings.

  f. Summarize the conclusions and findings of this portion of the derivative analysis, 6. How to Structure Business Processes.

Progress Report: How to Structure Business Processes. At this point in the derivative analysis, you should have derived the discipline, or lack thereof, with which your organization values processes as strategic assets, designs and manages the core processes that directly enable the strategy chosen, and places value on the use of business process analysis tools to test the effectiveness and efficiency of process execution as measured by the performance measures chosen for strategy. Finally, you should have concluded whether your organization's event management practices can ensure that process execution and outcomes remain within defined thresholds.

Findings drawn from the analysis of your organization's business processes should be used to improve upon current methods and practices associated with overall business process design and management. The decisions made about how best to improve process design and redesign, and how events are to be controlled, must be used to generate a new line of questioning that will help to derive how best to structure your organization's information technology to support process execution and workforce collaboration to best achieve the performance measures sought.

  7. *How to Structure Information Technology Necessary for Strategic Execution:* Evaluate how effective your organization's existing information technology is in achieving strategic objectives and its ability to adapt to support changes in business strategy and processes. Refer to Chapter 7 for guidance.

    a. What IT applications are crucial to the execution of your chosen business strategy? Prioritize each in order of importance as determined by your business strategy and operating model.

      i. ERP (accounting, finance, HR, other administrative applications)?

      ii. Supply chain management?

     iii. Customer relationship management?

     iv. Product life-cycle management?

      v. Supplier relationship management?

     vi. Content/document management?

    vii. Electronic commerce applications?

   viii. Other(s)?

b. For each of the top three priorities identified above,

      i. What are the critical capabilities necessary to support your chosen strategy?

     ii. To support your core processes?

    iii. To support the performance measures sought?

    iv. To enable event management?

     v. To enable adaptive response?

c. Given the answer to b above,

      i. What IT services are needed?

     ii. What IT skills are needed?

    iii. What IT infrastructure is needed?

    iv. What IT methods and practices are needed?

d. What are your conclusions? What needs to change? Summarize and record findings.

e. Identify from the list below the process-centric capabilities your organization's IT infrastructure possesses to enable the core processes identified earlier, and evaluate their quality and effectiveness. State any plans to enhance these capabilities. Identify those needed or missing, and state any current or future plans to enable them. Does your IT environment . . .

      i. Provide tools to track and report KPIs for outcome measures and performance drivers?

     ii. Provide event management capabilities, define KPI performance thresholds, and set up alerts?

    iii. Control processes to manage anticipated events using prescribed activities and tasks?

    iv. Engage resolution processes guiding the workforce to interpret unanticipated events and make decisions about how best to act?

     v. Manage alerts to ensure relevant stakeholders engage timely responses?

     vi. Provide periodic, ad hoc, and on-demand reports necessary to empower and motivate the workforce and track achievement of outcome measures, performance drivers, and collaborative objectives?

    vii. What are your conclusions? What needs to change? Summarize and record findings.

  f. Given the conclusions and findings above, what process-centric building blocks are required by your IT architecture for proper execution, performance measurement, and event management? State and explain in order of priority.

     i. Application development

    ii. Process modeling

   iii. Data structure and integration

   iv. Rules management

    v. Workflow management

   vi. Directory services

  vii. Performance measurement

 viii. Event management

     1. Exception management

     2. Resolution management

   ix. Collaboration tools

    x. Reports, analytics, and dashboards

   xi. What are your conclusions? What needs to change? Summarize and record findings.

  g. Pose and debate the readiness of your organization's existing information technology to support business process redesign.

     i. Has it kept pace with emerging technology trends in recent years or has it remained stagnant?

    ii. Can it adapt quickly at low or justifiable cost, or will it require considerable investment and resources?

   iii. How does this affect strategy? Does this create competitive advantage or disadvantage?

   iv. Are process-centric capabilities considered valuable, important, misunderstood, or are leadership and management indifferent to such capabilities? What are the implications of these findings?

    v. What are your conclusions? What needs to change? Summarize and record findings.

h. Summarize the conclusions and findings of this portion of the derivative analysis, 7. How to Structure Information Technology.

Progress Report: How to Structure Information Technology. At this point in the derivative analysis, you should have analyzed the capabilities and limitations of your organization's information technology and IT strategy, drawing conclusions about how well it supports strategic achievement, business process execution, workforce collaboration, performance measurement, event management, and its ability to adapt to change. You should have derived the process-centric capabilities that are necessary to support core process execution and control the key performance measures managed by the operating model and required of the business strategy.

Progress Report: Execution—Best Practice Use of Strategic Resources

At the conclusion of Section II of the derivative analysis your leadership and management team should have crafted the collaborative behaviors and objectives required of the workforce, developed a consistent means to design/redesign the business processes required of your strategy, and crafted the necessary control processes to manage performance as part of an event management strategy. Finally, you should have identified the various process-centric building blocks and structure of your IT systems necessary to support organizational behavior, business and control processes, and the event management capabilities needed to execute your strategy. You are now ready to assemble the findings and conclusion from Sections I and II of the analysis to compose your final report.

FINAL REPORT: DERIVATIVE ANALYSIS

Collectively the findings and conclusions drawn for your derivative analysis should be compiled into a final report that reveals the derivative relationships for your chosen business strategy, identifying specific resources, actions, and if necessary, investments that will enable your organization to execute and adapt to achieve consistently the performance measures and outcomes it seeks. The final report should be as brief as possible to convey its findings and recommendation quickly without burdening the reader with excessive details. It should follow the line of reasoning used to conduct the analysis and may be organized as follows:

- Business strategy
  - Defensible position
    - Competition
    - Customer value
    - Risks
  - Value chain and operating model
  - Performance measurement system
    - KPI sets
  - Adaptability requirements
    - Sense-and-respond techniques to risks posed
- Organization behavior
  - Accountability and responsibility
  - Empowerment and motivation requirements
  - Workforce collaboration requirements
  - Collaborative objectives
- Process design
  - Process portfolio
    - Core processes
    - Noncore processes
    - Control processes
  - Process modeling and analysis techniques
  - Performance measurement and controls
    - Events, exception, commitment, and resolution management
- Information technology structure
  - Critical information requirements
    - Acquisition, assessment, dissemination, and event monitoring
  - Process-centric systems requirements
    - Building blocks needed
  - Reporting, control, and management systems
- Action plan
  - Change requirements
  - Investments required
- Change management plan

SECTION III CONCLUSION: STRATEGY AND RESOURCES ALIGNED

The generic derivative analysis we walked through was intended to help you think about how to use the guidance provided in this book to craft a defensible business strategy and then pose a series of questions to help you successfully derive the resources needed for its execution.

The initial questions you posed should have generated debate leading to conclusions or decisions about what strategic approach your organization must take. The chosen strategy then prompted incremental questioning about the actions necessary to achieve strategic objectives. You then should have analyzed workforce behavior to determine what characteristics will be required to be effective. This, in turn, should have prompted questions about how business processes should be structured to support workforce behavior and strategic objectives. Business process design and effectiveness then should have prompted questions about how the organization's information technology should be structured, or restructured, to enable the process-centric IT characteristics needed to support process execution, workforce behavior, and strategic objectives.

The output of this exercise should be a final report that includes a summary of the conclusions drawn from the derivative analysis and an action plan describing what changes or investments are needed. This becomes an indispensable contribution to your organization's operating plan.

* * *

I hope that this generic line of questioning is helpful. Indeed, you may have found it to be *too* generic. My goal was to walk you though a derivative line of reasoning, absent a specific business strategy, to help you develop a sense of how to conduct one properly. Any example I would choose is likely to be different from your strategy thus posing a risk of misinterpretation. A generic example avoids such risk.

You will find, however, that derivative reasoning gets a lot easier when you are actually basing your derivative questions on a specific strategy. For example, in the beginning of this chapter, I suggested that a strategy developed to establish product leadership through differentiation can occur in many ways. Organizations must define and choose the characteristics of differentiation that they believe to be defensible in the industry. Selecting from durability, feature/functionality, design, or a combination of such is determined using industry, market, customer, and competitive analysis as advised in Section I of the analysis. From here organizations can derive the proper questions needed to derive what actions are required to enable the chosen characteristics of product differentiation. I suggested that durability might require renewed R&D investment in materials, feature/functionality may require customer "focus group" interviews and usability tests, design may require the acquisition of new artistic talent, and so on. The decisions made here then launch a new set of questions about how best to structure resources (people, processes, and technology) to execute the strategy. So, if product durability was chosen to enable a product leadership strategy then the line of reasoning, and subsequent deterministic questions, come into focus, much more so than the generic analysis we walked through. Nevertheless, I hope you found the generic walkthrough useful. With the final derivative analysis report in hand, you now have the map you need to execute and adapt to remain on plan.

Epilogue: The Management Team Reconvenes

THE CHAIRMAN SPEAKS

I greeted each member of the management team with a hearty handshake as they entered the boardroom. It had been six months since our first tension-filled meeting. In the opposite corner of the room at the credenza the CEO was pouring a cup of coffee having a cordial chat with the chairman.

The chairman was not expected at this meeting. His presence usually coincides with really good news or really bad news. He rarely shows up to chat. As the team members approached their seats, they put on their best game faces. Not knowing what to expect, all in the room were on edge, including me.

The CEO approached the corner of the table with the chairman standing next to him at its head. He called the meeting to order.

Ladies and gentlemen. Before I introduce the topic at hand, the chairman has asked to share a few words with you.

The CEO seated himself at the corner of the conference table; he was relaxed, even smiling a bit. The chairman, expressionless as always, took his seat and began.

Thank you all for giving me a moment of your time.
Six months ago our CEO presented the board with very disappointing news. The market reacted harshly. But not because our performance faltered. Indeed, the responsibility of any management team is to prevent these circumstances from arising. However, regardless of your skills and efforts, sometimes challenges overcome even the best of us. Shareholders and investors expect performance to be impacted in tumultuous times; they understand risk and what it takes to manage it. They don't understand being caught blindsided. It is simply unacceptable. The reason our market cap

tanked was because we couldn't explain ourselves properly. Several board members called for heads to roll.

I could feel the tension mounting in the air again. What must the management team be thinking right now? What haven't we done to gain the reassurance of the board?

As you know, that didn't happen.

The chairman reached to his right and heartily patted on the CEO's shoulder as he said:

I had confidence in our CEO when he presented to me his recovery plan, and he had confidence in this team to execute it. The board approved it, after some prodding, and you proceeded to take the necessary action guided by Mr. Lehmann's good advice.

Tomorrow we have our quarterly conference call with our major shareholders and Wall Street. I want you to know that we are not out of the woods yet. But, because of you we now have a field glass and a compass to guide us back to leadership roles in our markets. Our losses are declining and our guidance looks strong. Whispers on the Street are very favorable and we expect a few top analyst firms to upgrade our stock. I even got a call from the CEO of one of our competitors hinting at being acquired.

You couldn't hear it, but all in the room breathed a sigh of relief.

Our efforts are paying off and the markets are recognizing us for it.

He continued.

Now, when you leave this room I don't want any of you buying our stock. You're all too valuable to us right now. We can't afford to have any one of you subpoenaed by the SEC for insider trading.

Everyone broke out laughing. The chairman was confused at first, but after a second or two, he also chuckled. He wasn't trying to be funny. It just came out that way. You could see by his grin that he was proud of himself. He rarely makes people smile much less laugh. Still chuckling he said,

I came here today to personally thank you. And, while the rest of the board may not say it outright, they thank you too. But, please don't let this happen again.

The entire team looked at one another nodding in concurrence.

Being a man of few words, and certainly fewer laughs, the chairman then turned the meeting over to the CEO, walked to the back of the room, and took a seat along the wall. The CEO continued the meeting.

Ladies and gentlemen, thank you for all your hard work these past six months. Now, as the chairman stated, we must use our field glass and compass to find our way back to growth and profitability, and stay there. We have worked very hard to re-evaluate our markets and reformulate business strategy. We know the strengths and weaknesses in our organization's behavior. We have taken stock of our business processes and have begun to improve measurement and control of those that are core to our businesses, and we know which ones to improve next and what it takes to do so. We will continue making the necessary modifications to our information technology to track and manage our efforts so we are prepared to respond to variance of almost any kind.

That being said, I called this meeting so we could all take a deep breath and step back for a moment to consider what we have learned and what we could have done better during these past six months of transformation. I want us to be sure that the lessons we learned are carried forward so we can continually manage the change we failed to see before. Change is something that happens and most people prefer to stay in their comfort zone by keeping things status quo. But, as we discovered the hard way, sometimes change doesn't happen, the consequences of which can destroy everyone's comfort zone.

So, considering the techniques afforded us by Mr. Lehmann these past six months I want to remind you that in the final analysis proper execution, adaptability, and consistency really all come down to our people—our leadership, management team, and workforce. These are our greatest strategic assets. Our organization doesn't exist without them.

Once again I asked Mr. Lehmann to address us. This time, not with techniques but rather with some good old-fashioned common sense. Not every challenge can be controlled by patterns of behavior or well-designed technology. During our careers as managers we all have developed our own gut feel as to how to handle things. These innate skills collectively make a powerful management team. Nevertheless, we all must be reminded from time to time of the basics—the fundamentals of getting things done the right way. I'm sure you will agree that sometimes common sense must rule the day. However, sadly, common sense isn't very common after all so we must be reminded of it periodically. To that end Mr. Lehmann will share what he believes to be the practical success factors, the common sense if you will, needed to sustain performance and improve returns from our business process manaagement and continuous improvement initiative.

The CEO then gestured for me to take his place and walked to the back of the boardroom to join the chairman. I took the seat at the head of the conference table and sat back.

* * *

What follows is my commonsense guidance to management teams when pursuing any business process management and continuous improvement initiative.

SOME PRACTICAL SUCCESS FACTORS FOR IMPROVING EXECUTION, ADAPTABILITY, AND CONSISTENCY

Business strategy and process management require a balance of things your organization should and should not do as represented in these practical success factors.

Start Where Common Sense Tells You

Selecting a process for improvement is easy when one creates a problem. Your organization may have no choice but to act to improve it. However, continuous process improvement is an initiative to increase customer and shareholder value, and create competitive advantage. This will require your organization to understand the relative effectiveness and efficiency of its core processes over time, and against industry peers and competitors. Selecting the "correct" processes for improvement depends upon business strategy and the relative health of processes used overall. Poorly performing core processes, or too many inefficient noncore processes, can create competitive disadvantage, causing customers to look elsewhere and giving your competitors a "leg up" without even trying.

Continuous process improvement and management, therefore, is just that: a continuous call to quality that does not, and should not, abate. However, this does not mean that you must begin with a "big bang" effort. On the contrary, a small focused effort to get your feet wet is the best first approach.

Admittedly, a business process inventory exercise used to build a business process portfolio (discussed in Chapter 6) can seem daunting. A cursory review of a reference model, such as that offered by the APQC with its 1,400+ processes and activities, may put you off. Do not let this diminish your enthusiasm. It is intended to alert leadership and management to the breadth and depth of what business process management can entail.

Start where your common sense tells you. Approach it as advised in Chapter 6 by first defining, prioritizing, and inventorying the "critical few" or "core" processes most valuable to your organization. Once you become comfortable with how to engage business process portfolio management, you can inventory and evaluate other process categories, groups, and processes as part of a continuous process improvement program.

Avoid Complexity at First

Confidence is built upon success. Continuous process improvement requires confidence. The best way to build it is for you to select a process from the portfolio that can lead to a quick hit, or an improvement project that can yield measurable results within 90 days.

If there are several symptomatic processes requiring immediate attention, or processes that require improvement to support a strategic initiative, select the one that is least complex and can yield the greatest returns within 90 days. To control the scope of the initiative, evaluate the candidates using the complexity assessment matrix introduced in Chapter 6. Select the one deemed most "doable." At first try not to tackle end-to-end processes that span the organization. Indeed, many of these will be core to your operating model and therefore must be candidates for continuous improvement. However, it is best to develop and hone BPM skills before taking on these more complex challenges. Instead, select a portion of one or something simpler. Poorly run improvement projects can do more harm than good.

Assign Ownership

Business processes often suffer from a bipolar disorder: they have either no ownership or too much ownership. When no one is held accountable and responsible for a process, then the outcome measures, performance drivers, collaborative objectives, and results expected of it run adrift. The probability of success for its execution and outcome can approach 0%. Conversely, too many "owners" are created when cross-functional business processes confuse the span of control. Sometimes this instigates stakeholders to protect their turf. Turf wars can also affect processes in much the same way as lack of ownership.

Industry leaders assign owners—named individuals—to process classes, subclasses, and specific processes, holding them responsible and accountable for performance and results. An example of this is highlighted in the book *Good to Great: Why Some Companies Make the Leap . . . and Others Don't*, published in 2001. In Chapter 6 of *Good to Great,* entitled "A Culture of Discipline," the author, Jim Collins, a renowned management consultant and former Stanford University Graduate School of Business faculty member, explains a technique developed by Bernard H. Semler, a financial officer of Abbot Laboratories. "He created a new framework of accounting that he called Responsibility Accounting, wherein every item of cost, income and investment would be clearly identified with a single individual responsible for that item."

Essentially, for each line item on the income statement and balance sheet, Semler assigned a named individual to be held responsible for results (or lack thereof), not departments, groups, functions, or accounting practices. So, too, must processes, process performance, and outcomes be assigned specific ownership. In cases where processes span the organization and require cross-functional collaboration, an ownership hierarchy must be established. For example, a "procure-to-pay" process spans control of the procurement and accounting departments. If the process fails, delaying supplies, the manufacturing group may be held responsible for failed product shipments. Here, leadership and management must agree on who owns the process. The owner then is responsible for developing collaborative objectives to bind all participants holding them responsible and accountable as a team, and implementing control processes within an event management system to protect against variance during process execution or failed outcomes.

Address Misconceptions

Your workforce may be fearful of any type of BPM initiative. Fear of it harkens back to the early twentieth-century technique of "time and motion" studies, emanating from the work of Fred Winslow Taylor to improve workforce productivity. Often the results led to a reduction in force. Those remaining were treated as automatons with little say about how things were done or how things could improve. Much has changed since then. Nevertheless, misconceptions persist.

Any misconceptions about the intent of a BPM initiative must be addressed early and often. Misconceptions are born of a root cause: uncertainty. Uncertainty creates fear, fear creates resistance, and resistance defeats BPM.

When an improvement effort is first announced, many members of management, and the workforce, will sense uncertainty, wondering, "Does it threaten me?" Others may respond differently, wondering, "What's in it for me?" Questions such as these arise when the announcement fails to clarify specifically the intent of the effort and the result sought of it. For example, a process improvement project devised to "control costs" may be perceived by the workforce as a "headhunting" mission. The effort may truly be intended to reveal an array of cost controls, but if headcount is among them, you will encounter resistance.

I realize that under some circumstances drastic approaches make force reduction unavoidable. Nevertheless, do not position BPM and continuous improvement initiatives as the vehicle or cause for this, certainly not your first process improvement effort. It may work the first time, but subsequent process improvement initiatives are likely to be met with suspicion, obstruction, or worse: your good people may leave.

Address these questions immediately upon announcement of the initiative, before they create misconceptions. Kick off a project citing clear and concise goals absent reduction in labor. Communication must position the initiative correctly, as indeed process improvement is intended as a way to improve customer value and experience, and empower the workforce. Its goal is to improve the financial results of the organization to enable growth that ultimately increases the pool of funds available to in-place or new incentive systems.

A technique you can use to minimize uncertainty is to involve the workforce directly, immediately upon announcement, by using a simple questionnaire to solicit their input and assess their feelings. Simple is better. Complex questionnaires can spawn misconceptions. Ask the relevant stakeholders the following about the process targeted for improvement:

1. List three things you like about the process.
2. List three things you don't like about the process.

3. How would you change the process?
4. Other comments?

Such questions instill a sense of involvement, helping to empower stakeholders by asking them for their opinions, advice, and counsel. The objective of such an exercise is to have the stakeholders directly contribute to an improvement effort that, upon conclusion, benefits the organization and the workforce.

Communicate

"Failure to communicate" equates to failure (period). Success is predicated upon consistent, reliable, and frequent communications of accurate information to all participants on a timely basis.

Check Reversion

A "tongue-in-cheek" adaptation of a popular phrase, "Nothing *recedes* like success," reminds us that making improvements causes change that many people will resist.

This is not a surprise to most people. However, what is surprising is how little is done by organizations to ensure that their workforces do not revert to old ways. You may recall from our earlier discussions that many management team members overlook or assume that newly implemented systems automatically support their business processes and that the workforce will collaborate effectively using new systems and processes.

Indeed, change requires follow-through to prevent new processes from being circumvented. The best way to do this is to eviscerate any system or tools that enabled the old process. Upgrading to a new ERP, procurement, or accounting system may accomplish this, but maybe not. For example, a common problem in many large organizations is "renegade spending." It occurs when procurement professionals (buyers), and in some cases requisitioners, directly buy supplies from unapproved suppliers or without recording the transition in a procurement system. Long-term buyer/supplier relationships, whereby orders were historically conducted personally, or via telephone, could have resulted in the failure to track the necessary information to audit the transaction. Such behavior is, of course, poor practice, but it can be worse. It can violate laws such as the Sarbanes–

Oxley Act that hold executives of the organization personally responsible for financial transaction accuracy.

You must follow through with periodic or random audits of newly implemented processes and systems to ensure they are practiced as intended, and results are meeting expectations.

Proceed Diligently

On a final note, the best practical success factor for BPM and continuous improvement is that of diligence. Diligence by an organization, its management team, and workforce is best summarized in the book *Good to Great: Why Some Companies Make the Leap . . . and Others Don't*, which we discussed earlier. Again in Chapter 6, Jim Collins excerpts another research interview, this time with George Rathmann, the cofounder of a biotechnology company, Amgen. In it, Rathmann attributes his success in creating a "Great" company to discipline and diligence:

> ... [W]hen you set your objectives for the year, you set them in concrete. You can change your plans through the year, but you never change what you measure yourself against. You are rigorous at the end of the year, adhering exactly to what you said was going to happen. You don't get a chance to editorialize. You don't get a chance to adjust and finagle, and decide that you really didn't intend to do that anyway, and readjust your objectives to make yourself look better. You never just focus on what you've accomplished for the year; you focus on what you've accomplished relative to exactly what you said you were going to accomplish—no matter how tough the measure (p. 122).

Business strategy, process management, and the techniques needed to improve execution, adaptability, and consistency demand nothing less.

Section IV

Summary Conclusion

The mission of this book was to develop your understanding of the best practices used by industry and thought leaders to help organizations execute their chosen business strategy. If I succeeded, you should now possess the planning framework, the mindset if you will, needed to craft a defensible business strategy and align resources for execution, adapt when needed, and consistently maintain performance and results when presented with challenge, change, or opportunity.

The book opened with an introduction to a CEO and management team who failed to see the changing conditions around them. Such a scenario is not uncommon, and provided a useful metaphor to highlight the pain points with which many leaders and managers can empathize. The stalwart CEO set out a campaign to transform his firm and return it to profitability by focusing on the fundamentals necessary to recraft its business strategy and properly configure its resources for execution.

I presented these fundamentals in reasoned sequence, first by offering summary reviews of the top best-selling authors on business strategy. The key messages from each were distilled to reveal the essential proven and reliable best practices used by leading Fortune 500 and Global 2000 companies to analyze and formulate highly competitive business strategy. Collectively, they created a strategic planning framework, providing organizations with the insight and techniques necessary to do the following:

- Command competitive knowledge
- Define strategy and focus investment on high-priority areas
- Measure performance from multiple perspectives
- Quickly respond to change or customer need

Next, I built upon this work, discussing how industry leaders prepare their strategic resources—people, business processes, and information technology—for execution by:

- Empowering and motivating the workforce using workforce collaboration and collaborative objectives
- Modeling and analyzing business processes to include human accountability and enabling techniques to control, measure, and manage the necessary performance outcomes
- Adapting information technology needed for workforce collaboration, performance measurement, and outcome management, as called for by business strategy and business process designs

I then described an analytic technique designed to pull together all the important lessons provided herein. Derivative analysis demonstrated how to align business strategy, people, processes, and technology by revealing the proper links among strategy, measurement systems, business processes, workforce behavior, and the systems necessary to achieve strategic objectives.

I concluded by using my metaphor once again, reconvening the CEO and management team, this time including messages from the chairman and CEO: the chairman, reminding us that vigilance in all aspects of business must be a habit, not a reaction, and the CEO, reminding us that in the final analysis people are an organization's greatest strategic assets and common sense must indeed become common and be used to help guide decisions going forward.

The knowledge presented in this book offers proven and reliable techniques of industry leaders necessary to shape the mindset needed to guide your decisions and stay focused as you pursue business process management and continuous improvement initiatives. You are now prepared to think as they do.

Carry on.

Summary of Key Guidance

Use these summary pages to recall the key guidance offered in this book.

PROLOGUE: MANAGEMENT TEAM IS SUMMONED

The difference between running a business, and running it well, lies in how well we know our customers, how well we assess our competitors, how well we deliver value, and how quickly we bring an appropriate response to change. The vehicle we use to make these assessments, strategic planning, also helps us organize people, resources, and investments to achieve revenue, profitability, expense, and market share targets. Industry leaders pay close attention to how well they run their business by continuously analyzing and practicing how best to do the following:

- Formulate business strategy by:
  - Analyzing competition
  - Focusing operations
  - Managing performance
  - Adapting to change
- Organize people, and empower and motivate them to successfully execute strategy
  - Through workforce collaboration
  - Using collaborative objectives
- Reveal performance measures and controls to help achieve strategic objectives
  - Through process modeling and analysis
  - By managing events, exceptions, commitments, and resolution efforts through control processes
- Structure information technology to ensure strategic achievement
  - Through information acquisition, assessment, dissemination, and event management
  - Using a process-centric systems approach

- By managing information technology as assets using portfolio management techniques
- Align strategy, people, processes, and technology
  - By learning how to ask and answer the right questions using derivative analysis techniques to structure a line of reasoning that derives what is necessary to support an organization's chosen strategy

SECTION I: BEST PRACTICES USED IN STRATEGIC PLANNING

Many organizations struggle with poor performance. Understanding why requires them to examine the answers to fundamental strategic planning questions.

- Are objectives realistic and achievable?
- Are the challenges misunderstood or underestimated?
- Are enough of the right resources available?
- Is the chosen strategy correct given the resources, challenges, and objectives?

Answering these questions requires analysis of visceral business concepts such as competition, execution, measurement, control, and adaptation to change. Many seminal research works have being written on these topics, but those practiced with great success by industry leaders and that stand out are:

- *Competitive Strategy: Techniques for Analyzing Industries and Competitors* and *Competitive Advantage: Creating and Sustaining Superior Performance* by Michael E. Porter
- *The Discipline of Market Leaders: Choose your Customers, Narrow Your Focus, Dominate Your Market* by Michael Treacy and Fred Wiersema
- *The Balanced Scorecard: Translating Strategy into Action* and *Strategy Maps: Converting Intangible Assets into Tangible Outcomes* by Robert S. Kaplan and David P. Norton

- *Adaptive Enterprise: Creating and Leading Sense-and-Respond Organizations* by Stephan H. Haeckel

Each represents timeless, commonsense approaches to business strategy and management. In architectural and engineering terms, they represent the "pillars and arches" upon which modern business strategy and execution are founded.

All include commonsense themes on how best to formulate strategy, measure performance, and align resources. These particular works were chosen because of the best practice concepts unique to each.

- Porter teaches organizations how best to compete by expanding upon the classic approach to formulating a competitive strategy using his Five Forces Model of Industry Competition to help define and structure the activities that comprise an organization's value chain.
- Treacy and Wiersema teach organizations how best to focus operations by carefully defining customer value and using this to craft an operating model that creates and delivers this value through focused efforts on one of three strategic disciplines: operational excellence, product leadership, or customer intimacy.
- Kaplan and Norton teach organizations how best to manage performance by crafting a performance measurement system, or balanced scorecard, that expands beyond purely financial measures to include measures from the customer perspective, an internal process perspective, and a learning and growth perspective. The cause-and-effect relationships across these perspectives can be revealed using a strategy map to determine how best to align assets to improve overall execution that ultimately influences overall financial performance.
- Haeckel teaches organizations how best to adapt when presented with change or opportunity. Sense-and-respond techniques empower the workforce using adaptive loop behavior to sense change, interpret its effects, decide what best to do, and act upon the findings, by calling upon diverse resources of a modular organization and recording and tracking negotiated commitments using a commitment management protocol.

The best practice lessons from each successively build upon the other, providing a comprehensive approach to analyze and formulate highly competitive business strategy. Collectively, these lessons create an unparalleled strategic planning framework, providing organizations with the insight and techniques necessary to command competitive knowledge, define strategy, and focus investment on high-priority areas, measure performance from multiple perspectives, and quickly respond to change or customer need.

SECTION II: EXECUTION—BEST PRACTICE USE OF STRATEGIC RESOURCES

When preparing to execute strategy, it is best to learn how highly effective organizations structure their people, business processes, and information technology (strategic resources) for execution. The best practice structure of each strategic resource was discussed in succession.

- The discussion about people addressed how to empower and motivate the workforce and introduced the concepts of workforce collaboration and collaborative objectives as a means to help successfully execute business strategy.
- The discussion on business processes involved how to include human accountability and responsibility in the process designs that support workforce collaboration, and introduced effective techniques to control, measure, and manage the performance outcomes of tasks, activities, and collaborative objectives. Emphasis was placed on the importance of control processes and the value of software tools to model and analyze process designs, testing assumptions about redesign alternatives prior to making change or investment. Critical to process design are capabilities to track performance measures continuously and expose variance to relevant stakeholders using event management capabilities to prevent adverse effects on performance and outcomes.
- The discussion on information technology outlined the process-centric capabilities that business systems need for a workforce to collaborate, have ready access to strategic information, measure

performance, and manage outcomes as called for by business strategy and business process designs. We introduced concepts that will help overcome managerial indifference to process-centric IT investment using budgeting and portfolio management techniques, helping elevate the status of both IT and business processes from "expenses" to revered strategic assets.

SECTION III: HOW TO ALIGN STRATEGY AND RESOURCES TO IMPROVE EXECUTION, ADAPTABILITY, AND CONSISTENCY

In Section III, we pulled together all that was discussed in this book using derivative analysis as an alignment technique.

Derivative analysis is a disciplined approach to facilitate discussion and debate among executives and managers during strategic planning sessions. It helps expose discontinuity, revealing the proper links among strategy, measurement systems, business processes, workforce behavior, and the information systems necessary to achieve strategic objectives.

Derivative analysis draws conclusions from the answers to a series of deterministic questions posed and debated in a reasoned sequence. When using derivative analysis to align strategy and resources, questions are answered in the form of a conclusion or decision about what approach or actions the organization should take. This prompts questioning about the structure and resources required to support the approach or enable the actions. Subsequent questions are derived based on prior answers forming a derivative line of reasoning. Alignment occurs successively upon analysis of specific answers or conclusions following the line of reasoning.

When complete, the derivative relationships are revealed for a particular strategy, identifying specific resources, actions, and if necessary, investments. A generic derivative analysis then demonstrated the successive line of reasoning using the lessons learned in Sections I and II to align resources with strategy and to show how its conclusions and findings contribute to the organization's operating plan.

EPILOGUE: MANAGEMENT TEAM RECONVENES

The book closes with a reminder that in the final analysis proper execution, adaptability, and consistency really all come down to people: your leadership, management team, and workforce. These are your greatest strategic assets. Organizations cannot exist without them.

Finally, use common sense when initiating change by abiding by a few practical success factors.

- Start where common sense tells you
- Avoid complexity at first
- Assign ownership
- Address misconceptions
- Communicate
- Check reversion
- Proceed diligently

Appendix A: Important Terminology

The definitions of the following terms and phrases will help you to understand their proper meaning within the context of this work.

A

Activity: Work performed within a business process or subprocess that requires one or more resources, initiated by input and results in output. Can be comprised of a task or multiple tasks and analyzed via "drill-down" examination. For example, "Approve invoice for payment."

B

Business Activity Monitoring (BAM): Is a means to provide real-time visibility into business activities, operations, and transactions of a departmental or cross-functional business process as they execute. It uses a process-centric IT architecture coupled with business intelligence dashboards (graphical user interface software) to expose performance measures to relevant process owners and stakeholders.

Business Policy: A declaration or statement of guidelines that govern business decisions.

Business Process: *See* Process.

Business Process Improvement Program: A structured methodology used as part of an organized strategic planning effort to manage business processes as assets. It defines a continuous effort to (1) inventory, categorize, and prioritize critical business processes; (2) analyze their efficiency and effectiveness toward achieving strategic objectives, outcome measures, and performance drivers; and (3) control and govern the effort and resources required to manage multiple business process improvement projects.

Business Process Improvement Project: An organized effort guided by a structured methodology to (1) model a specific critical business process; (2) analyze its efficiency and effectiveness toward achieving strategic objectives, outcome measures, and performance drivers; (3) simulate adjustments or redesigns to improve measurable results and test feasibility of alternatives; (4) select the best alternative and determine return on investment; (5) implement adjustment, redesign, or design; and (6) monitor to ensure performance meets desired outcomes.

Business Process Inventory: An itemized list of business processes categorized as assets and prioritized by importance and value to an organization. Used to assess the core processes necessary to create and deliver customer value and noncore processes that affect costs. Often part of a strategic planning process that precedes or otherwise initiates a continuous process improvement program.

Business Process Management (BPM): A managerial discipline that is focused on execution. It is the art and science of how organizations do things and how they can do them better. BPM attempts to optimize process performance to achieve strategic business objectives consistently while adapting, when necessary, to change or to new opportunity. As a managerial discipline, it addresses how best to structure and align multiple resources, including workforce and information technology to meet and exceed specific performance measures. BPM provides structure, methods, and tools to align resources with strategy. It helps leaders and managers consistently realize business objectives and performance measures teaching them.

- How to align and structure resources (people, processes, and information technology) to support business strategy
- How to motivate and empower the workforce for proper execution
- How to design business processes to achieve business objectives
- How to select and manage strategic and tactical performance measures
- How to select and structure information technology to efficiently and consistently perform to plan

Business Process Map: A high-level flowchart diagram illustrating the various activities, tasks, decisions, and relationships of participant functions, departments, or groups associated with the execution of a process. It is used as a starting point to be critical of the efficiency and effectiveness of business process execution.

Business Process Model: A detailed workflow diagram that expands upon a process map by including detailed descriptions of subprocesses, activities, and tasks including all input, output, decisions, and exceptions, as well as measurements of the resources consumed (such as time, FTEs, material, capital, systems, etc.) during the execution of the process. Supports analysis via drill-down examination and can provide the metrics necessary for use by software capable of process simulation and what-if scenario testing of alternative variables.

Business Process Portfolio: A classification system and common data repository used to inventory, document, and manage detailed information about business processes. Information captured and managed within a portfolio includes activities, tasks, performance measures, and resource requirements that comprise a process. It does not map or model workflow. Other tools and techniques are reserved for this purpose. Rather, the portfolio assists management teams in evaluating process quality, effectiveness, and efficiency, thus revealing the core processes that require improvement and exposing the noncore processes that require streamlining, consolidation, or decommissioning.

Business Process Portfolio Management: Focuses on how to improve the returns from diverse business processes that comprise an organization's value chain, such as those associated with

- Creating and sustaining customer and supplier relationships
- Developing and managing products and services
- Controlling administrative functions such as finance, human resources, and regulatory requirements

It provides techniques and tools used to document and evaluate business processes as assets and manage their ongoing performance improvement. It reveals business processes that yield the greatest strategic value and financial returns and exposes those that do not. It provides clarity of vision, helping organizations to pinpoint investments in ERP, supply chain management, customer relationship management, and BPM suites: the IT portfolio.

Business Process Portfolio Manager: A named individual who is accountable and responsible for inventorying business processes and creating and managing the business process portfolio. This person has authority within the organization to be able to call upon other executives, management team members, and business process owners as required to create and maintain the portfolio.

Business Rule: A measure, condition, or constraint that defines and governs execution, or the behavior of activities and tasks; it asserts control and influences further action. Business rules may result from, or be a subset of, business policy.

C

Case Management: Control processes and organizational behavior that determine how best to correct unknown, unanticipated, or otherwise unpredictable events, or properly respond to new sudden and/or unexpected opportunity. Typically requires dynamic collaboration of multiple functional groups, subject matter experts, and stakeholders accessing one or more internal and external information and management systems.

Also see Resolution Control Process.

Control Process: A series of activities and tasks performed to adjust or correct a business process (operating, support, or other management process) or its outcome, when performance measures vary, exceed acceptable thresholds, or when a new opportunity is presented. Examples of control processes include escalation procedures that accelerate responses to customer complaints, quality-control processes that make corrective actions when errors or defects are discovered, and collaborative processes that respond to something unexpected by interpreting options, deciding what needs to be done and then taking action. There are two common types of control processes: exception control processes and resolution control processes (the latter may also be referred to as case management processes). *Also see* Exception Control Process, Resolution Control Process, *and* Case Management.

D

Decision-Making Processes: Management processes that define objectives, study alternatives, analyze available data, and reflect on intuitive beliefs. They interpret findings and compare alternates to form a conclusion or make a choice upon which the organization may act.

Derivative Analysis: Draws conclusions from the answers to a series of deterministic questions posed and debated in a reasoned sequence. When using derivative analysis to align strategy and resources, questions are answered in the form of a conclusion or decision about what approach or actions the organization should take. This prompts questioning about the structure and resources required to support the approach or enable the actions. Subsequent questions are derived based on prior answers forming a derivative line of reasoning. Alignment occurs successively upon analysis of specific answers or conclusions following the line of reasoning. When complete, the derivative relationships are revealed for a particular strategy, identifying specific resources, actions, and if necessary, investments.

E

Event: Something that happens or doesn't happen during the execution of a business process that requires action, or may or may not happen because patterns of process behavior, performance, or outcome measures begin to vary, requiring proactive response.

Event Management: The coordination of organizational behavior, control processes, information technology, and escalation policies used by the organization to prevent events or correct any problems they cause before they adversely affect desired performance measures and outcomes.

Exception Control Process: A type of control process that manages and corrects known and anticipated events. They are engaged when an event triggers a predetermined measurement threshold. They alert relevant stakeholders of the event and prescribe a series of predetermined activities and tasks, usually performed sequentially, to make the necessary corrections.

I

IT Readiness Assessment: A technique developed by BPMethods to understand the ability of an organization's existing IT resources to adapt to, or otherwise support, a business process design or redesign. Used to determine the feasibility of effort and as a basis for calculating return on investment (ROI) by measuring the time, costs, and resources required to modify IT systems and train the workforce to enable a proposed process or process improvement.

K

KPI (Key Performance Indicator): A measure used to quantify performance and outcomes.

KPI Set: A mix of outcome measures and performance drivers necessary to monitor strategic achievement. The structure of the set should include KPIs that measure performance from financial, internal business process, customer, and learning and growth perspectives. For each perspective KPIs should also be defined to measure: (1) factors critical to cost, quality, and schedule; (2) short- and long-term objectives; and (3) leading and lagging indicators.

L

Leader: An executive or other representative of an organization empowered with policy and decision-making authority, who is held accountable for overall strategic outcomes.

M

Manager: A representative of an organization empowered with decision-making authority and control of specific resources, who is held responsible for execution leading to desired outcome measures and performance drivers.

Management Process: A process type that provides the means to measure and control quality and ensure the desired performance outcomes. This process helps make decisions, control variance, and resolve problems. It helps guide the organizational behavior needed for a strategy by facilitating workforce collaboration, accountability, and responsibility. *Also see* Control Process.

Map: *See* Business Process Map.

Model: *See* Business Process Model.

O

Operating Model: A model used to structure the resources of an organization to support a specific business strategy. Each operating model has common components but different attributes defining effort and focus. The common components include the core processes, culture, organization, information technology, and management systems. Attributes vary for each component depending upon the business strategy it serves.

Operating Processes: A process typically noted for creating or delivering value for which customers are willing to pay. They develop, make, sell, and deliver products and services. They are often at the heart of an organization's operating model, because they are specifically designed to execute an organization's stated business strategy.

Organization: A generic term used to describe a private or public business, business unit, subsidiary, or partnership; a government, government agency or department; or a nonprofit entity structured to execute processes to achieve desired outcomes.

Outcome Measures: Performance measures common to most business strategies, such as financial ratios, revenue goals, profit margins, and market share.

P

Participants: Internal employees or external parties organized within a team, playing a role in business process management, continuous improvement, designing, or executing business processes. *Also see* Stakeholder.

Performance Drivers: Performance measures that reflect the uniqueness of a particular business strategy, such as product durability and reliability measures, quality assurance thresholds, or economies of scale that enable cost leadership.

Portfolio Management: A technique used to control and optimize the efficiency of, and returns from, many diverse assets. Each asset is continuously evaluated. When necessary, structural adjustments are made to maximize its individual value and to the portfolio of assets as a whole.

Practitioner: A professional dedicated to managing and improving business process performance and results, whose skills may include project management, business analysis, process mapping, modeling, simulation, design, and redesign.

Process: (1) Basic definition, a logical series of related activities that converts input to results or output. (2) Value-added extension, designed to create or deliver customer value or shareholder value through efficiency. (3) Asset extension, an asset that affects the quality of a product, service, or brand to uniquely satisfy customer needs and differentiate its executor from competitors.

Process-Centric IT Architecture: Shares strategic information and assembles unique services dynamically to execute any logical series of activities and tasks across many disparate and distributed systems. It tracks and manages all the activities and tasks associated with a process and reports against all outcome measures and performance drivers (lagging and leading indicators, long- and short-term measures: as defined in KPI sets) associated with the process. To ensure such outcome measures and performance drivers are achieved, process-centric systems place priority on managing data, making strategic information available to all relevant stakeholders, measuring KPIs, and managing events. *Also see* Business Activity Monitoring (BAM).

Process Control: A business rule mandated by management that is embedded within, or called upon during, the execution of a process, activity, or task to ensure the organization achieves its performance objectives, mitigates risk, or complies with other obligations as required.

Process Improvement Team: The collection of professionals in an organization held accountable and responsible for the outcome of business process improvement projects and programs. May include a sponsor, project manager, program manager (or both), process developer, lead stakeholder, and subject matter expert or IT professional.

Process Modeling and Analysis: The tools and techniques used to (1) map a workflow diagram illustrating the activities and tasks associated with a business process; (2) add complete detail necessary to identify and measure all the resources consumed during the execution of the processes; (3) measure performance outcomes; (4) simulate changes to activities, tasks, sequences, resources, assumptions, and so on using what-if scenarios to test and recalculate performance outcomes; (5) conclude the best combination of adjustments or changes necessary to optimize performance outcome of the process.

Process Simulation: *See* Process Modeling and Analysis.

R

Resolution Control Process: A type of control process that determines how best to correct unknown and unanticipated events, or properly respond to new sudden and/or unexpected opportunity. This process typically requires dynamic collaboration of multiple functional groups, subject matter experts, and stakeholders accessing one or more internal and external information and management systems. It establishes the rules of engagement that coordinate the organization's behavior to interpret an event or opportunity and decide how best to act.

S

Sponsor: A leader, executive, or manager who initiates, drives, and is accountable for the outcome of a business process improvement project or continuous process improvement program.

Stakeholder: An individual participant or member of a business function, department, or group charged with, and responsible for, performing tasks or activities as part of a business process.

Subprocess: A compound activity, it describes a set of activities within a process hierarchy upon which a process is dependent, or from which it requires input. For example, "Authorize credit card request."

Support Processes: Do not directly create or add value but are necessary to facilitate or assist the execution of operating or management processes. Examples of processes that support operating processes are supply procurements, inventory replenishment, and machine maintenance. Examples of processes that support management processes are administrative, typically associated with finance, accounting, sales, or human resources.

Symptomatic Processes: Existing business processes whose performance measures vary unacceptably, threatening or exceeding a prescribed performance threshold. They place desired outcomes at risk. It is important to note that variance or errors are usually not a problem, but rather a symptom of a problem that requires corrective action. Symptomatic processes first require analysis to determine the root cause(s).

T

Task: A type of activity representing the lowest level of detail defined within a business process model. For example, "Flip power switch to off position."

V

Value Chain: A collection of activities performed across multiple business functions, such as manufacturing, marketing, procurement, and services, that design, produce, market, deliver, and support an organization's product or service.

Appendix B: How to Evaluate Business Process Analysis Software

Business Process Analysis (BPA) determines the effectiveness and efficiency of process execution and the quality of outcomes. Preferably it uses a set of tools and techniques to visualize and measure how things currently (or are proposed to) execute, and study how execution and outcomes can be improved. It helps you evaluate process designs before spending money and effort based on untested assumptions. BPA is most often used reactively to solve business problems. Industry leaders use BPA proactively to create competitive advantage when preparing for and executing strategic initiatives such as a new product launch, new marketing campaigns, or improved services delivery.

How does BPA accomplish this? BPA is best accomplished using software tools designed to diagram workflow and measure the economics of process designs. By economics we mean measuring the resources, costs, and time consumed or constrained during the execution of a process. Some of these tools can also enable simulation of the process as it executes demonstrating quantifiable outcomes. Simulation and comparison of various process alternatives will help you select the best process design.

BPA software can be generally categorized as either diagramming tools, or modeling and analysis tools. Diagramming tools create a process map that represents a high-level flowchart illustrating the various activities, tasks, and relationships of participant functions, departments, or groups associated with the execution of a process. It is used as a starting point for criticism of the efficiency and effectiveness of business process design.

Modeling and analysis tools expand upon a process map to create detailed workflow diagrams and can provide descriptions of subprocesses, activities, and tasks including all input, output, decisions, and exceptions as well as measurements of the resources consumed (such as time, labor, material, capital, systems, etc.) during the execution of the process.

Modeling can also enable detailed analysis via drill-down examination of subprocesses and activities, and provides the basis for process simulation. Simulation can test the outcome measures and performance drivers of various process alternatives using what-if scenarios to alter the process design. It offers an efficient means to test assumptions and choose the best process design.

When evaluating BPA software for use in your organization, do so considering two broad sets of criteria:

1. User-focused functionality: Include capabilities and features designed for end-users of the BPA software such as BPM practitioners, business analysts, project managers, program managers, and various IT professionals who are responsible for modeling and analyzing process design, execution, performance, and outcomes.

2. Enterprise-focused functionality: Include capabilities and features designed to support multiple cross-functional users, business/IT functions, and the organization at large. They enable sharing of data, models, analysis, and design; facilitate reuse; support other systems; and contribute to the cost-effective administration and management of the BPA software as part of a continuous process improvement program.

USER-FOCUSED EVALUATION CRITERIA

BPA software typically supports several diagramming models such as basic workflow, value stream, cause-and-effect, SIPOC (supplier, input, process, output, customer), and many others. Each of these includes and defines a wide variety of "notation elements" also referred to as "symbols," "diagramming shapes," or just "shapes." Shapes are organized in collections called "pallets" that are structured to describe the activities, tasks, and flow unique to a particular diagramming model.

Many BPA software vendors supplement pallets with preformatted diagramming models called "templates" that create a basic preconfigured process. For example, Microsoft Visio 2007 lets you choose from among several preformatted templates that diagram basic models for the following:

- Business processes
- Engineering designs
- Standard flowcharting
- Maps and floor planning
- Network design
- Scheduling
- Software and database design
- Others

As you research BPA software you will note that each pallet includes hundreds of elements, symbols, and shapes that enable you to design, redesign, or troubleshoot a process. It is important to remember that one of the goals of business process diagramming and modeling is to ensure that process stakeholders know what is expected of them and can understand the implications of the actions and inaction on the process, the key performance indicators measuring its execution, and the overall results to the organization at large. Overly complex process models using unfamiliar or esoteric symbols can frustrate this goal. Indeed, we understand that some IT and engineering professionals require diverse and comprehensive sets of symbols to express complex concepts among colleagues. However, for the purposes of business process management and continuous improvement, the symbols chosen should be easy to understand and explain if the overall goals of BPM are to be realized.

Therefore, what you should look for in a BPA tool is the means by which it diagrams a process using basic structures, workflow shapes, and connectors that do the following:

- Identify the functions, groups, departments, or others participant in the process using swimlanes.
- Identify activities, decisions, and tasks critical to the process using basic workflow shapes such as rectangles, diamonds, ovals, and circles.
- Diagram the logical sequential flow (workflow) linking shape-to-shape with solid lines with arrows signifying sequential flow (connectors).
- Map any information or message flows from one stakeholder group to another using dotted lines with arrows signifying sequential flow (connectors).
- Define resources required or consumed such as time, cost, and resources attributed to each shape or connector.

The initial goal of a BPA tool is to create a visual presentation of a specific business process so that it can be:

- Used to reach consensus among the stakeholders that the process is accurate and represents reality
- Scrutinized for continued improvement and efficiency
- An accurate and reliable measure of time, cost, and resource allocation
- Easily explained to new stakeholders during training

The following represent specific user-focused evaluation criteria to consider.

General Guidance and Support

1. Tutorials: Web-based video (or flash) tutorials are often helpful for a rapid start.
   a. Note the availability, type (breadth and depth), and quality of tutorials and their ability to guide you through both simple and complex concepts. Note tutorials for simple topics such as flow-charting, and complex topics such as how to capture and manage performance measurement data and conduct simulations of alternative process models and designs.
2. Help: Make note of the BPA software's:
   a. Contextual help: related to the topic at hand.
   b. Tool tips: simple instructions that display when cursor hovers over text, a field, or object.
   c. Shape explanations: as part of contextual help or tool tip.
   d. Connector explanations: as part of contextual help or tool tip.
3. Search
   a. How easy and intuitive are search capabilities? How is the search structured? Does it include table of contents, index, and favorites or most frequent search terms? Or is it structured using keywords only?
   b. Does it support autocomplete while typing?
4. Support
   a. Note the resources available from the software vendor to assist with use of their tools or perhaps aid in process diagramming and modeling.
      i. Note how they are scheduled and at what cost.

    ii. Is support available through annual maintenance fees or other form of subscription services?

Process Diagramming and Modeling

5. Intuitive user interface
   a. How quickly can the fundamental concepts be grasped by an unfamiliar user?
   b. Note the flexibility of toolbox/toolbar design and presentation options.
   c. Can it save user preferences as to look and feel, templates, toolbars, other?
6. Mapping, diagramming, formatting feature set: note the capabilities of the following:
   a. Pallets (shapes: notation standards)
      i. Note the number, type, and relevance of the available notation standards (shapes). Are pallets available and suitable for the diagramming and modeling tasks you pursue? Examples include:
         BPMN
         IDEF0
         ITIL
         TQM
         Value stream
         Fishbone (cause-and-effect problem analysis)
         Others
   b. Templates
      i. Note the number, type, and relevance of the available templates. Templates are simple predesigned diagrams that can be modified. They help quick-start diagrams and designs.
      ii. Are templates available and suitable for the diagramming and modeling tasks you pursue? Examples include:
         BPMN
         IDEF0
         ITIL
         TQM
         Value stream
         Fishbone (Cause-and-effect problem analysis)
         Others

    c. Model structure, swimlane creation, and management (used to represent departments, groups, functions)

       i. Note the effort required to create and modify.

      ii. Note whether automatic or manual adjustment is required when modified.

    d. Connectors: Note the various types of connectors and how they behave. Smart connectors save time; dumb connectors require manipulation when changes are made.

       i. Auto line drawing and smoothing?

      ii. Auto connect and adjustment when changes are made?

    e. Labeling: Note if auto labeling is available and how it works; also note if it can be customized and turned off.

       i. Auto numbering for shapes?

      ii. Auto labeling for decision shapes (Yes–No decision paths)?

    f. Larger and more complex diagrams may require off-page connections.

       i. How are they created, managed, and changed?

      ii. Automatic or manual adjustment required?

    g. Does the tool offer multiple synchronized work surfaces?

       i. How do they work? Are they simple and intuitive or cumbersome to manipulate and adjust?

    h. How easily can the software diagram, and make changes to, process flow without having to readjust swimlanes, shapes, and connectors?

    i. Note how the software enables resizing and zooming.

       i. How are large diagrams managed?

    j. Diagramming validation

       i. Note capabilities that check for inconsistencies or errors in diagram structure and quality as they pertain to the notation elements being used. For example, are BPMN rules validated?

    k. Note other time-saving features.

7. Modeling

    a. Resources: are used, constrained, or consumed during the execution or the process.

       i. What predefined resource libraries are available and how extensible are their structures? Resources can include, but are not limited to, workers, machines, assets, schedules, time, and so on.

> For example, workers can be individuals, belong to a department, or be allocated from a pool.

    ii. Does the BPA software help define and structure resources and help to avoid contention?

   iii. How are resources defined and what level of detail is available in the software to describe the properties of the various resources.

> For example, scheduling has multiple definitions including, hours, holidays, shifts (swing, night), and so on. Evaluate the predefined properties available to be assigned to resources, comparing them to the resources used in your organization.
>
> What flexibility exists to customize properties as required?

  b. Data capture features for resources (labor, equipment, other), time (schedule), costs consumed or constrained.

    i. How does it capture data about a process and measure its performance in terms of the cycle time taken to execute, the resources used, and the costs associated with execution?

  c. Note capabilities that enable decision or branching rule capture that help define or govern process flow given various rules (conditions).

  d. Note capabilities that enable drill-down on shapes to create or view subprocesses, activities, or tasks and capture performance measures and attributes.

  e. How are attributes created, defined, and used?

    i. Attributes communicate data or information and manage the flow of transactions through a process (e.g., an attribute can define the duration of an activity or control the flow of transactions through a decision output).

  f. Note capabilities to include (or link to) other data or reference documents, graphics, images, or other related content.

  g. Note capabilities that validate diagrams and models that check for completion, or inconsistency in design or flow.

8. Note how modeling data are displayed (a common means is to right click on a shape to view its properties).

  a. How are shape data presented and visualized in the process diagram?

  b. Is it comprehensive, complete, or partial?

9. How are data output to other tools, software, or systems (such as spreadsheets or other applications)?
   a. Note available functions or utilities and the relative ease or complexity of their use.

Documentation and Publishing

10. Documenting the process
    a. What capabilities exist to produce documentation about the process?
       i. How easily can it create (or output data for) documentation for use by IT professionals for system implementation, training professionals, and process stakeholders?
    b. How are document links created and maintained?
       i. Make note of how documents are managed without the use of a centralized repository.
11. Publishing
    a. What tools or utilities are available to make it easy to expose to various publishing modes such as content management systems, document management systems, printed output, portals, and the web?
    b. Note import/export capabilities, output to report generators or business intelligence tools, enterprise architecture tools, or other IT systems.
12. Print preview and printing
    a. How are large or multipage diagrams formatted, resized, previewed, and printed?
    b. What devices are supported? For example, large plotters?

Simulation, Analysis, and Reporting

13. Behavior: The properties of the resources defined within the process model define its behavior during simulation.
    a. Note the means by which resource properties are modified to create alternative execution scenarios for purposes of comparison.
       i. How are resource limitations or constraints handled?
    b. Note the means by which events are defined and structured such that they capture accurate data relative to the KPI set chosen to measure and analyze process performance.

        i. Events indicate that something happened, or did not happen, is delayed, or describe some other intermediate behavior or trigger during the execution of the process.

        ii. Can the BPA software accurately capture, model, and simulate the data required of the chosen KPI set?

    c. How "smart" is it at structuring behavior?

        i. For example, can it find errors and flaws in measures, sequential flow, naming conventions, or other such inconsistencies?

14. Scenarios: Describe the simulation environment or the alternative conditions under which the process executes.

    a. How accurately can it simulate the execution of the process under different conditions showing you what has changed?

    b. How easily can what-if scenarios be configured to test alternative assumptions and designs?

    c. Is side-by-side analysis of multiple scenarios available?

        i. Make note of other such visualization capabilities.

15. Statistics

    a. How are statistics about the transactions that pass through the process (such as cycle times, queue lengths, resource in use, total counts, etc.) defined?

    b. What standard statistics exist?

    c. How can custom statistics or expressions be created and managed?

        i. Expressions set initial attribute values and task durations, change attribute values, and define transaction queueing and output options.

    d. How are categories of various statistics defined and structured? Can monitors be established at certain points in the process to collect certain types of analytic data (e.g., specific to resource utilization or cycle times)?

16. Statistical analysis integration

    a. Note the capabilities of the software to support integration with popular statistical analysis tools, for example (if applicable), from:

        IBM (SPSS)

        Minitab

        Oracle

        SAP

SAS

Software AG

Others

17. Simulation

    a. How can functions (a mathematical or statistical relationship that returns a value, such as "task duration") be defined to simulate conditions for a varied range of distributed values.

        i. For example, handling "peak" times, or describing assumptions under extreme conditions.

    b. Can the process flow be traced when a simulation runs showing the execution of the process?

        i. Can you interact with it in such a way as to evaluate or perform other analysis?

    c. Report elements: are collections of related simulation statistics that create a simulation report. Can they be changed to generate a new report without having to run another simulation?

    d. How are simulations controlled such as start, pause, stop, trace, step-through, others?

        i. Are such controls intuitive and easy to use?

    e. Can random simulations be structured to generate results similar to the random factors occurring in real-world scenarios?

        i. Are such capabilities intuitive and easy to use?

18. Analysis

    a. How are simulation results displayed?

        i. Note the completeness and quality of data presentations.

        ii. Note data visualization quality and capabilities such as charting, graphing, other.

    b. How can what-if comparison be made?

        i. Note the effort required to do so and the quality of presentation of the what-if comparison data.

        ii. Note drill-down evaluation capabilities. For example, can analytic results or statistics be revealed of subprocess and activities by clicking on various shapes or results?

    c. How smart are its analytics?

        i. For example, can it find errors and flaws in measures, sequential flow, naming conventions, or other such inconsistencies?

    d. Note other analytics capabilities such as:

        i. Financial analysis

        ii. Risk analysis

   iii. Critical-path analysis

   iv. Resource analysis

   v. Others

19. Reports
 a. How does it report findings?
  i. How are reports generated and modified?
  ii. Are they sufficiently helpful for analysis and presentation to others in your organization?
 b. Are standardized reports available, and if so, how relevant are they for your purposes?
 c. How, and with what effort, are custom reports created?
 d. Can reports be generated illustrating side-by-side comparisons of the measured results, simulations, or portions of simulations?
 e. Note any advantages and disadvantages associated with the quality of the appearance and content of the reports.

ENTERPRISE-FOCUSED EVALUATION CRITERIA

Another goal of a BPA tool is to facilitate the analysis of all the processes an organization uses to run its operations, and support a continuous process improvement program that does the following:

- Focuses performance improvement on the core business processes most directly responsible for creating and delivering customer and shareholder value.
- Maximize returns from workforce and IT investments to ensure they support the strategic initiatives and outcomes measures sought by an organization.
- Assess feasibility and importance of process change before committing resources.

The following represent specific enterprise-focused evaluation criteria to consider.

Repository

1. Repository, storage, and access control
   a. Note how process diagrams and models are stored, managed, maintained, and shared in a central repository.
   b. How are data (diagram, models, reports, etc.) secured and made accessible?
   c. Can a business process portfolio be created and maintained using its repository?
   d. Can the repository also capture and manage business policies and rules?
   e. Note hardware and system requirements.
2. Versioning and audit trail
   a. Does the software support version control, check-in/check-out, lock-out?
      i. How easy is this to use or administer?
   b. How is document history managed?
      i. How is document history accessed and presented?
   c. What "roll-back" capabilities exist?
      i. How easy is this to use or administer?
3. What capabilities exist to create libraries of common elements (resources, processes, subprocesses, rules, etc.) that can be used and reused across multiple process models (such functionality helps multiple distributed users build consistent models and speeds development).
4. Note life-cycle management capabilities.
   a. How are process models and simulation analyses tracked through various stages of maturity from review to sign-off?
5. Note how other documents, not generated from the BPA tool but associated with process diagrams and models, can be accessed, stored, and managed.
6. Note search and query capabilities.
   a. How are search and custom queries enabled?
   b. How accurate and relevant are the results returned?
7. Note database technology and structure.
   a. Are support resources necessary? If so, are resources available internally for support, or will external expertise be required?

Multiuser Capabilities and Collaboration

8. How are users managed, access privileges administered, and security enabled?
   a. Note how process modeling teams and workgroups are supported.
   b. How are members invited or restricted.
   c. What privileges can be assigned to members?
      i. How are privileges created or revoked?
9. Note web browser access and capabilities for publishing, updates, reviewing, commenting, and approving.
   a. How is this enabled and administered?
10. Note workflow capabilities. If available:
    a. How is workflow defined and managed?
    b. Is a graphical user interface available? If so, how intuitive is its design?
    c. Can it also manage access controls, privileges, alerts, and notifications?
11. Alerts and notifications
    a. Note how "work in progress" is monitored and collaborators are notified of modifications and changes.
12. Multiple language support
    a. Does the tool support the languages your organization requires?

Integration

13. Note its integration capabilities and tools.
    a. Can it integrate with other software, systems, or infrastructure to:
       i. Import/export data?
       ii. Help implement the chosen process model?
14. Note its support and integration with Microsoft Office (Word, Excel, PowerPoint, Visio, Access) or other similar software used by your organization.
    a. Note whether, or the degree to which, it integrates or enables import/export with Visio. Visio is used by many organizations as a starting point for process diagramming.
       i. Note how Visio files can be imported into the repository and collaboratively shared.

      ii. Note how data can be output to Visio and distributed to workgroups or various process improvement team members.

15. What data standards are supported? For example:
    a. Extensible Markup Language (XML)
    b. Open database connectivity (ODBC)
    c. Others

16. Note if live data feeds from in-place IT systems can be integrated to support modeling and simulation.

17. Systems integration
    a. Note how finalized process models can be exposed to:
       i. Applications development environments
       ii. Business activity monitoring (BAM) systems
       iii. Business intelligence (BI) systems
       iv. Business process management suites (BPMS)
       v. Business rules engines
       vi. Enterprise architecture (EA) systems
       vii. Run-time execution systems: enterprise resource planning (ERP), supply-chain management (SCM), customer relationship management (CRM) systems, document/content management systems, others
    b. What capabilities exist to support integration with legacy/proprietary systems and applications?
    c. What integration standards are supported?
    d. What skills are required for such integration?

18. Statistical analysis integration
    a. Note the capabilities of the systems to support integration with popular statistical analysis tools. For example (if applicable) from:
       i. IBM (SPSS)
       ii. Minitab
       iii. Oracle
       iv. SAP
       v. SAS
       vi. Software AG
       vii. Others

Support for Standards, Reference Frameworks, and Methodologies

19. Note support for standardized process classifications frameworks. Examples include:
    a. AQPC's process classification framework
    b. Supply Chain Council's Supply Chain Operations Reference (SCOR) model
    c. Value-Chain Group's Value Reference Model (VRM)
    d. Others
20. Note support for models, methodologies, and standards. That is, how the tool may define and scope projects and identify progress toward goals. Examples include:
    a. Business process modeling notation (BPMN)
    b. Capability maturity model integration (CMMI)
    c. Information technology infrastructure library (ITIL)
    d. Integration definition (IDEF)
    e. International Organization of Standardization (ISO)
    f. Lean
    g. Lean/Six Sigma
    h. Object Management Group's model-driven architecture
    i. Six Sigma
    j. The Open Group Architecture Framework (TOGAF)
    k. Unified Modeling Language (UML)
    l. Zachman Framework for Enterprise Architecture
    m. Others

Administration, Management, and Maintenance

21. Note breadth, depth, and quality of various administrative functions including:
    a. Security
    b. Access privileges and management
    c. User management
    d. Updates and upgrades
    e. Patches
    f. Database/file administration and management
    g. Others as your IT organization may see fit

22. What support resources are available from the vendor?
    a. How well staffed?
    b. How relevant and current is their expertise?
    c. What online self-help resources are available?
    d. What service level agreements (SLAs) are viable?
    e. What are troubleshooting, escalation procedures, and expected response times?
    f. Note all costs.
23. Are dedicated support staff required from your organization?
    a. If so, how much staff and what skills do they require?
24. How does the software's total cost of ownership (TCO) compare with other candidates?
    a. TCO measures total cost over time; cost constructs to consider include:
        i. One-time upfront fees
        ii. Implementation fees
        iii. Licenses fees
        iv. Subscription fees
        v. Per user fees
        vi. Annual maintenance fees
        vii. Hosting fees
        viii. Infrastructure costs, upfront and recurring
        ix. Support personnel
        x. Contract work
        xi. Other
25. What is the vendor's vision and ability to execute?
    a. Is it consistent with the long-term vision, strategy, and goals of your organization?
    b. Assess the importance and relevance of the vendor's long-term viability.

CHOOSING RELEVANT CRITERIA

BPA software is used in many ways and for many purposes, thus the priority of these evaluation categories will vary by skill level and intended use.

- Novices or newcomers to process improvement may seek simple diagramming tools to map and qualitatively assess workflow. Your selection criteria then should focus on:
  - General guidance and support
  - Process diagramming and modeling
  - Documentation and publishing
- Managers or practitioners who seek quantitative analysis of process performance, resource utilization, and business performance measurement should focus on:
  - Simulation, analysis, and reporting
- Distributed process improvement teams requiring collaboration should focus on:
  - Repository
  - Multiuser capabilities and collaboration
- Skilled BPA practitioners and IT professionals who seek capabilities to convert process designs into software applications and manage the overall environment should focus on:
  - Integration
  - Support for standards, reference frameworks, and methodologies
  - Administration, management, and maintenance

Works Cited

Bossidy, Larry and Ram Charan. *Execution. The Discipline of Getting Things Done.* New York: Crown Business, 2002.

Collins, Jim. *Good to Great: Why Some Companies Make the Leap ... and Others Don't.* New York: Harper Collins, 2001.

Haeckel, Stephan H. *Adaptive Enterprise: Creating and Leading Sense-and-Respond Organizations.* Boston: Harvard Business School Press, 1999.

Hill, Peter. *Generating & Selecting KPI Sets.* Melbourne, Australia: Modulus, 2008.

Kaplan, Jeffrey D. *Strategic IT Portfolio Management: Governing Enterprise Transformation.* New York: Jeffrey Kaplan, PRTM, 2005.

Kaplan, Robert S. and David P. Norton. *The Balanced Scorecard: Translating Strategy into Action.* Boston: Harvard Business School Press, 1996.

Kaplan, Robert S. and David P. Norton. *Strategy Maps: Converting Intangible Assets into Tangible Outcomes.* Boston: Harvard Business School Press, 2004.

Kaplan, Robert S. and David P. Norton. *Building Strategy Maps.* Boston: Harvard Business School Press, 2006.

Maizlish, Bryan and Robert Handler. *IT Portfolio Management Step-by-Step: Unlocking the Business Value of Technology.* Hoboken, NJ: John Wiley & Sons, 2005.

Miloševic, Dragan Z., Martinelli, Russ J., and James M. Waddell. *Program Management for Improved Business Results.* Hoboken, NJ: John Wiley & Sons, 2007.

Porter, Michael E. *Competitive Strategy: Techniques for Analyzing Industries and Competitors: With a New Introduction.* New York: The Free Press, 1980, 1998.

Porter, Michael E. *Competitive Advantage: Creating and Sustaining Superior Performance: With a New Introduction.* New York: The Free Press, 1985, 1998.

Porter, Michael E. What Is Strategy? *Harvard Business Review*, November–December 1996, pp. 61–78.

Treacy, Michael and Fred Wiersema. *Discipline of Market Leaders: Choose Your Customers, Narrow Your Focus, Dominate Your Market.* Cambridge, MA: Perseus Books, 1995.

Index

*9 7 8 1 4 3 9 8 9 0 2 3 3 *

An environmentally friendly book printed and bound in England by www.printondemand-worldwide.com

PEFC Certified

This product is
from sustainably
managed forests
and controlled
sources

www.pefc.org

PEFC/16-33-415

This book is made of chain-of-custody materials; FSC materials for the cover and PEFC materials for the text pages.

#0221 - 211215 - C0 - 234/156/16 [18] - CB - 9781439890233